# Bloomsbury to Barkerville

I0801316

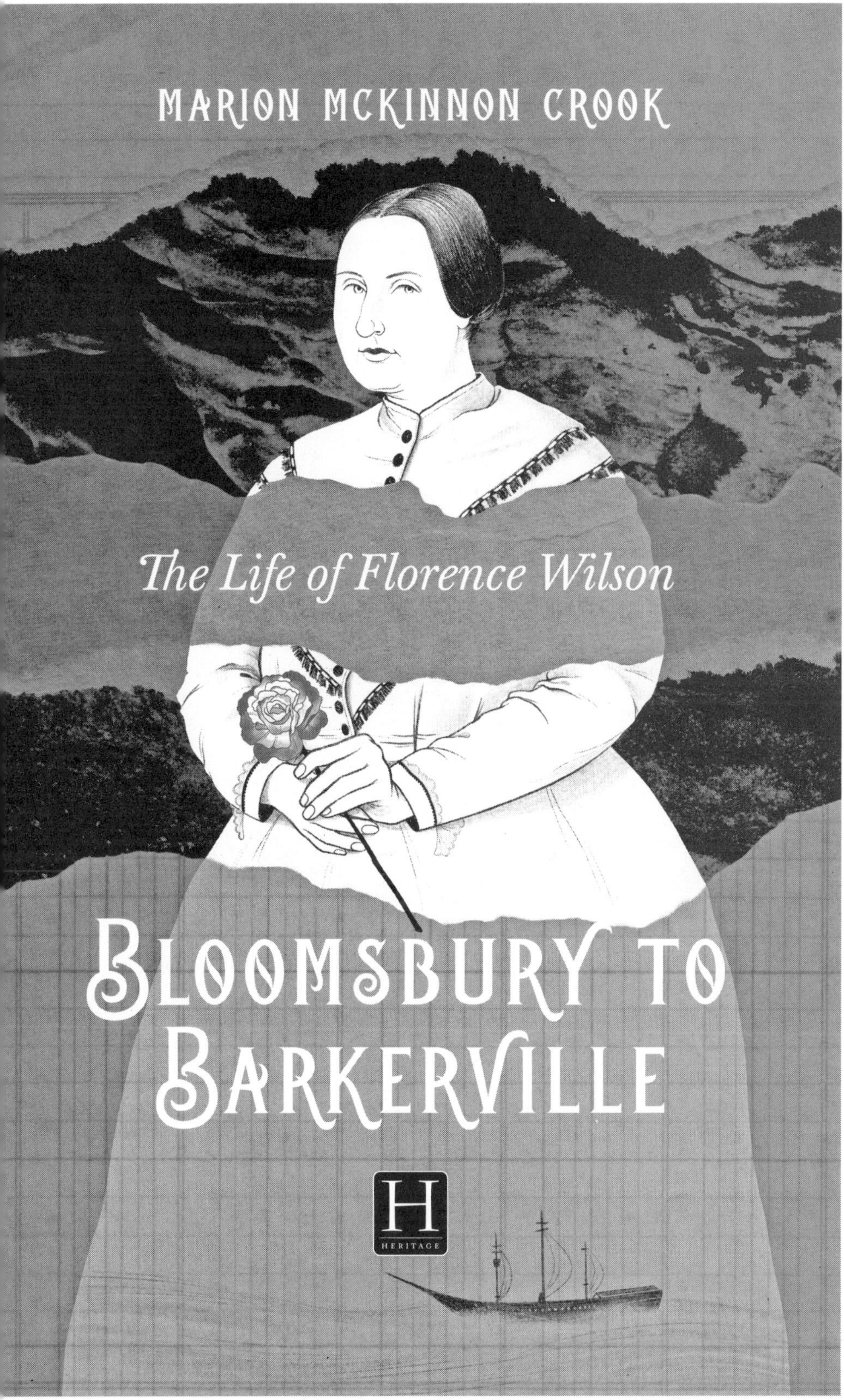
MARION MCKINNON CROOK
The Life of Florence Wilson
BLOOMSBURY TO
BARKERVILLE
H
HERITAGE

Copyright © 2026 Marion McKinnon Crook

All rights reserved. No part of this publication may be reproduced, stored in a retrieval system, or transmitted in any form or by any means—electronic, mechanical, audio recording, or otherwise—without the written permission of the publisher or a licence from Access Copyright, Toronto, Canada. No part of this book may be used or reproduced in any manner for the purpose of training artificial intelligence technologies or systems.

Heritage House Publishing Company Ltd.
heritagehouse.ca

Cataloguing information available from Library and Archives Canada

978-1-77203-564-3 (*paperback*)
978-1-77203-565-0 (*e-book*)

Edited by Kate Kennedy
Proofread by Nandini Thaker
Interior design and typesetting by Jacqui Thomas
Cover design by Setareh Ashrafologhalai
Cover image by Taryn Garrett
Maps by Eric Leinberger

The interior of this book was produced on 100% post-consumer recycled paper, processed chlorine free, and printed with vegetable-based inks.

Heritage House gratefully acknowledges that the land on which we live, work, and learn is within traditional and unceded Indigenous territories. In Victoria, BC, we acknowledge the traditional territories of the lək̓ʷəŋən (Esquimalt and Songhees), Malahat, Pacheedaht, Scia'new, T'Sou-ke, and W̱SÁNEĆ (Pauquachin, Tsartlip, Tsawout, Tseycum) Peoples. On BC's Lower Mainland, we acknowledge the traditional territories of the q̓ic̓əy̓ (Katzie), q̓ʷɑ:n̓ƛ̓ən̓ (Kwantlen), kʷikʷəƛ̓əm (Kwikwetlem), máthxwi (Matsqui), xʷməθkʷəy̓əm (Musqueam), qiqéyt (Qayqayt), Semiahmoo, Stó:lō, Sḵwx̱wú7mesh Úxwumixw (Squamish), scəw̓aθən məsteyəxʷ (Tsawwassen), and səlilwətaɬ (Tsleil-Waututh) Peoples.

We acknowledge the financial support of the Government of Canada through the Canada Book Fund (CBF) and the Canada Council for the Arts, and the Province of British Columbia through the British Columbia Arts Council and the Book Publishing Tax Credit.

30 29 28 27 26  1 2 3 4 5

Printed in Canada

*To the memory of Nancy and her long-time support of my writing. She would have loved this book.*

# Contents

# Preface

My first interest in Miss Florence Wilson came when I read that she had arrived in Victoria, BC, in 1862 on the first bride ship. What was she doing on a bride ship at the age of thirty-nine? Surely, she was old for a bride in those days. It turned out she wasn't looking for a husband, but a new beginning. The more I researched her life, the more fascinating she became, as I realized she was intelligent, well-educated, adventurous, and independent—qualities that made her stand out in Victorian society, qualities that she needed as she had to provide for herself.

I wanted to write Florence's life story from her point of view, which meant doing it in the first person. To do that, I had to carefully study her actions and any literary works she'd left in order to understand her character. In some areas of her life, such as her days in Barkerville, I had records of what she did, where she lived, with whom she lived, and what businesses she owned. In some areas, such as the years between her life in Russia and her life in the Colony of British Columbia, I had little information.

I travelled to England and did research in the Charles Dickens Museum, where they had records of articles Florence had written for Dickens's paper; in Russell Square and 3 Woburn Place, where she had lived as a young girl; and in Shropshire, where her mother and her grandparents had lived. The Museum Archives in Shrewsbury, Shropshire, were particularly helpful in sorting out her family history. I read books on the Victoria of 1862–64, spending days in the Royal British Columbia Museum and Archives in Victoria, searching through newspapers, personal letters, diaries, and accounts of that time with the help of the librarians and archivists there. I collected a shelfful of books written about Victoria and the gold rush to the Cariboo and read them looking for mentions of Florence and descriptions of the country and towns of those days. Not all historical records agree. Some accounts were written sixty years after the observations were made; some were based on articles that contained errors. When I encountered contradictory information, I went with what seemed like the most likely facts. I also went with what I thought Florence would have done.

I can't know what she would have said, so all the dialogue in the book comes from my imagination. I had no records of how she felt, so that also was supplied by my imagination.

I also had no information of the way in which Florence interacted with the Indigenous Peoples of the area, but, since she had been part of the Charles Dickens community and educated in the notions of equality of all, she would likely have been more advanced her interactions than most of her time. She gives us some insight into her approach to people in her own writings. Her vocabulary would have been of her times, though, so she would have referred to Indigenous Peoples as "Indians" as did most people of those days. I am more comfortable with the more respectful vocabulary of today. I leaned heavily on the work of Mica Amy Royer Jorgenson for a view of the world of Indigenous Peoples during the gold rush days.

At the end of the book, I have supplied references for each chapter. There, I also list which characters I invented in order to move the story on smoothly. All other characters are based on real people.

I have a deep appreciation of Florence Wilson's courage and intrepid enthusiasm for living her best life. After I finished writing the book, I imagined Florence sitting comfortably on a chair in her Victorian gown with her trusty Perry fountain pen in hand, reading this manuscript and writing comments on the pages. I hope she'd find I portrayed her as she was.

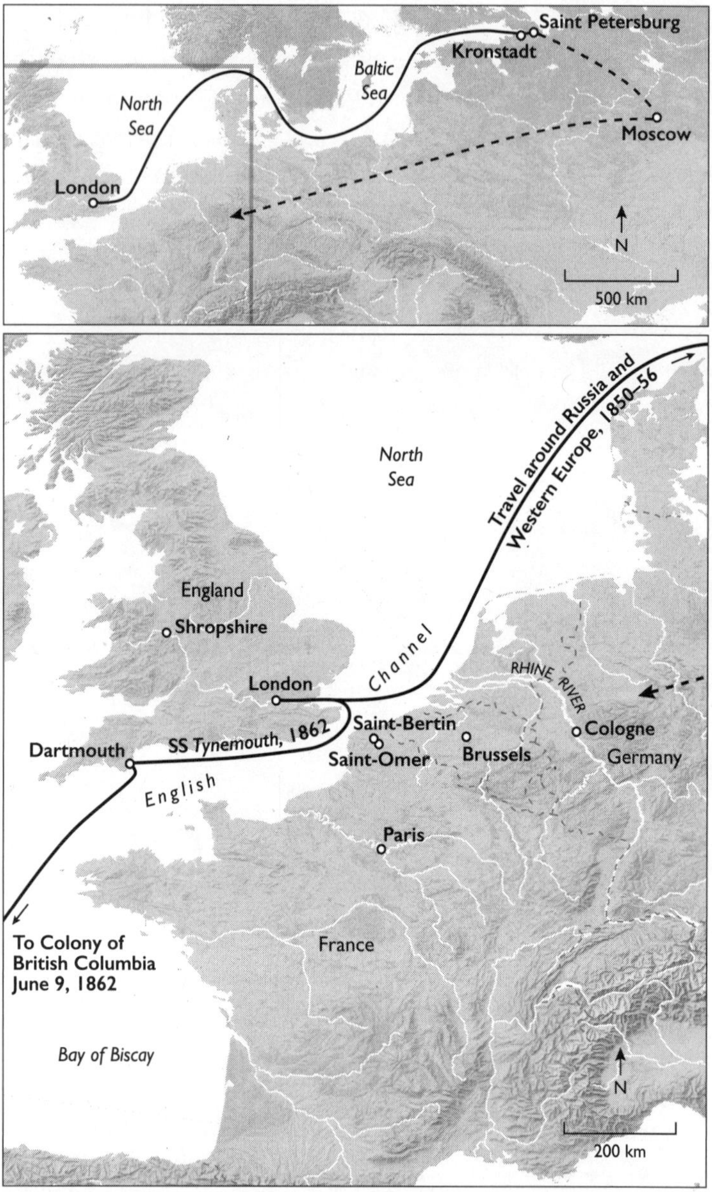


Florence Wilson had travelled more than the average young woman in the 1850s, visiting Russia and other parts of Europe while working as a governess. In 1862, she boarded the SS *Tynemouth*, sailing to the New World.

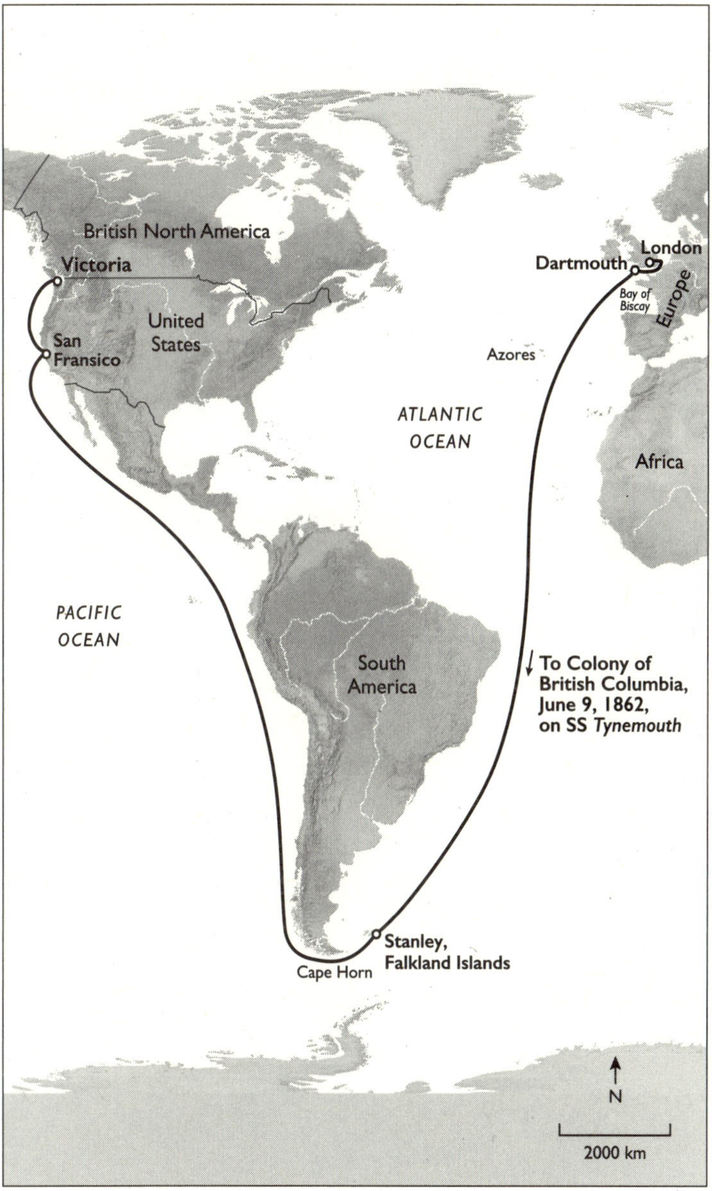


Florence Wilson's voyage aboard the SS *Tynemouth*, a brideship, to the British colony of British Columbia in June 1862.

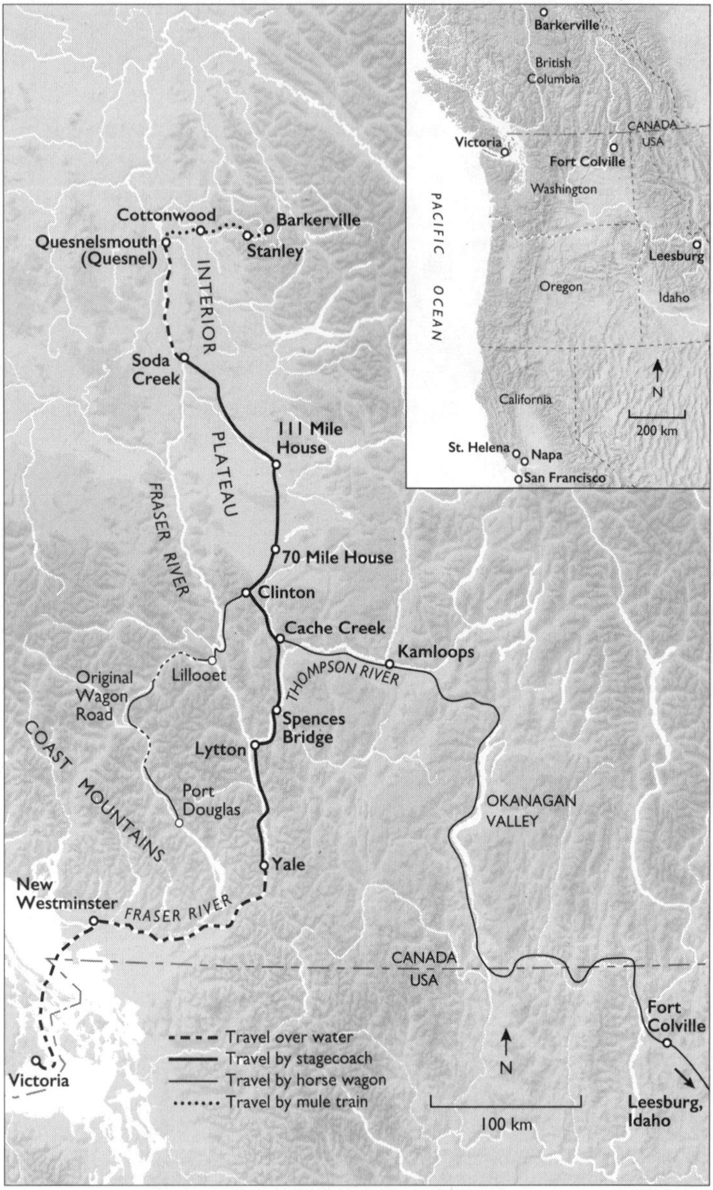


Journeying north on the Cariboo Wagon Road in the 1860s was an arduous multi-leg trip that involved travel by paddlewheeler, stagecoach, horse-pulled wagon, and mule train and overnight stops at roadhouses along the way. Later in her life, Florence also travelled south to Leesburg, Idaho, and finally to California, where she eventually resettled and remained until her death.

*one*

# A New Life

I WATCHED FROM MY mother's bedroom window as the doctor left. He hunched his shoulders against the rain, a black-shrouded shadow in the dark evening. The roof of his buggy reflected the pale light from our one street lamp, polishing it like shining ebony. He climbed in; the buggy lurched from his weight. I saw a slight movement, which must have been the reins flicking as his horse stumbled on the shiny cobblestones then moved off toward Russell Square. The steady rain would grab the coal dust that had been hanging heavily in the air and anchor it to the ground. Tomorrow we would breathe more easily without the acid air searing our lungs. My mother would not breathe more easily, if at all. The doctor had been honest.

"I'm sorry, Miss Wilson. She will not last long." He placed a bottle of cordial on Mother's bedside table. "Only a teaspoon, mind," he said. He was older than my mother and looked tired. His dark suit hung loosely from his rounded shoulders. His spectacles slid down his nose. He looked a bit like an owl, hunched over as if supporting wings.

I nodded. I didn't think the cordial helped Mother much, just made her drowsy. Her heart, so passionate and enthusiastic, was faltering.

"It's the cancer," he said, as if that was sufficient explanation and, indeed, it was. I didn't want to know more. I was losing my mother. She was forty-nine. I could barely absorb that fact. I didn't want to think of her as a patient, a body, a detached entity. I swallowed and thanked him again.

"I'll see your brother on my way out." I assumed Thomas would pay him. My brother had travelled every day over the last week from his home in Soho. He had not yet left this evening.

Mrs. Blackly saw the doctor out but returned. "You should get some rest, Miss Florence." She gave me a sharp sideways glance. She looked tired as well. She was older than Mother and must have been worn down by all she had done for her this week in addition to the usual housekeeping duties.

"I'm fine, Mrs. Blackly. It's you who should rest. Just leave the bell and go to bed. I will call you if I need you."

She hovered at the doorway for a moment, but gave a quick nod and left me.

I sank into the chair positioned beside Mother's bed and watched her sleep. Her familiar bedroom—the oak-panelled walls, the worn cognac-coloured carpet, and the flickering lamps—was comfortable. It was one of the few rooms in the house that had a coal fire burning and so was warm. Thomas had managed that, as Mother and I were getting low in coal and had little money to buy more. It had been cold when Mother first took to her bed. The first week of January 1846 had a record cold snap and the fire was necessary; now, a week later, it was warmer outside, and the fire was mainly for comfort.

Mother woke and called for me. I helped her sit up, gave her some cordial, and sat beside her, holding her hand. She seemed brighter, more lucid than she had been.

"I am worried about you, Florence."

I smiled. "You needn't worry, Mother."

"You are almost twenty-three, and you are a spinster. You need to be married or you will be poor." She coughed and gulped a little for air, but straightened.

I gave her a sip of water and she subsided back against the pillow.

"Have a little faith in me," I said. "I have your gift for writing, and I will manage to feed and clothe myself." Besides, I didn't *feel* old. There was plenty of time to find a husband—if I wanted one.

She sighed. "The literary life is not an easy one."

"But interesting," I reminded her.

"Vastly interesting," she said with a smile, and her eyes lit with mischief. My heart jumped in my chest. She was so alive. How could she be dying? I swallowed and tried to encourage her. She was probably remembering the many ways in which she had made her own life interesting.

I held her hand and sat silently for a while, appreciating her, loving her. Finally, I questioned what she had hinted at. "Is there no money then, Mother?" We had not discussed finances yet. Her worry about my single state was likely connected to money and position.

"Very little. You and Thomas will have the house, but Thomas and Laura have their own house, and you can't live here alone." She rested for a few moments.

I hadn't thought much about living alone. It wasn't done in English society. Unless I was elderly or widowed and could afford a companion, I would have to leave this comfortable house in the centre of London simply because I was a spinster—not that I could afford to keep it, in any case. When Mother died, I would be alone here. My brother Thomas was independent and had recently married and moved to Soho. He worked in theatre production and management. Society would not accept me, at age twenty-three, living alone.

She persisted. "Is there no one you have any feelings for at all? Try not to be so particular, Florence."

I laughed. That was my mother, a woman of direct discourse. I mentally reviewed the men of my acquaintance. I was past the age when I was dazzled by a handsome face and charming manners. I now wanted someone with a sense of humour and intelligence. Intelligence, I found, had become quite seductive. Handsome would be a bonus.

"Not a one," I said cheerfully. "Not to worry, Mother. I will be fine." I tried to reassure her, and I believe I succeeded. I felt optimistic myself. I would manage.

She died the next morning.

Her funeral service was crowded with theatrical characters: actors, managers, fellow playwrights, women's rights proponents, judges, architects, professionals of all sorts, as well as some flamboyantly dressed individuals I couldn't place. Mr. Charles Dickens, her publisher, was there, as was her friend the Duchess of St. Albans. I even saw Miss Barrett there. It was rumoured she had an understanding with Mr. Robert Browning and that her father did not approve. She lived near us at Russell Square in the heart of London. Other neighbours were there and our small household staff. Mother's brothers and sister were prevented from attending by a huge snowstorm in Shropshire, so it was just Thomas, Laura, and I who were exhausted when everyone dispersed. We had not hosted a reception at the house as we did not yet have access to Mother's bank accounts and could not afford to feed so many.

Thomas and I were the last of our family living in London. My mother's family was gentry from Shropshire; my father's was middle class here in London. I hadn't realized there was a difference until several years ago, when I overheard an argument in the library. My mother raised her voice often in argument or song, but my father rarely did, so I was stopped in my tracks outside the library door when I heard their loud voices.

"Why did I marry you? Why, you ask? Because you were gentry, which was good for my business, and you were damaged goods with a good dowry. Your father knew you couldn't do any better."

"Damaged goods, poof! You'd think I was a cow with a bad leg."

"Not a bad leg. Just an unexplained child."

I was rivetted to the floor outside the door.

"My son was not unexplained. He was a love child from my affair with Gus."

"A married man and an architect, and a good twenty-five years older than you at that!"

"True, and a far better lover than you, I might say."

"You're not even ashamed."

"No, I'm not." Her voice softened. "I agree society was not accepting of our behaviour and adopting Fredrick out to the Thomases was the best option, but I am not ashamed of the affair with Augustus, nor of Frederick."

"I won't have that young man here."

"I can understand that."

"Do you see him?"

"No." She was quiet for a moment, then said, "He was transported to Tasmania last month."

"Tasmania! For what?"

"For trying to pawn a stolen hat."

"For that he was transported?" Papa sounded incredulous.

"He might have done it deliberately to get his passage to Australia. I didn't know about it until he'd gone."

My father's voice was soft and kind now. "I'm sorry, Margaret. Come."

There was silence. I walked silently up the stairs and to my room. I seemed to have acquired a half-brother, Frederick Thomas, and lost him to Tasmania in the space of five minutes. I pondered the information. My mother had had a liaison with a married architect, Augustus. The only Augustus I could think of was Augustus Pugin, an architect of some renown, who had died a few years earlier. He was much older than Mother. How could she have been so foolish? But my mother was a surprising woman.

My parents seemed reconciled, and life continued as before. I did not ask my mother about her past. She was someone who threw herself into the present. She made the house chaotic and stimulating. Mother wrote several plays and was a member of the dramatic society. I was part of the excitement of rehearsals and observed the arguments and laughter that surrounded a production. My father hied off to Lincoln's Inn Fields, where he had his solicitor offices, but came home for tea about five and usually joined us for dinner at nine. He enjoyed all the activity in the house, but I don't remember him acting or reading poetry aloud. Mother had managed us all.

We sat in the drawing room after the funeral, Thomas, Laura, and I, surrounded by furniture, pictures, and the familiar contents of our home, and reminisced about our lives.

"I wish Papa were here," Thomas said.

"Have you seen him?" I was curious about our absent father. He had been an affectionate father, but I could see as I got older that he and Mother were poorly matched. I didn't miss the quarrels that raged through the house when he'd lived here.

"Not since he left," Thomas said. "Foolish to want him here, I know. He wouldn't help."

I thought about it. "He might be a comfort. He was always loving. I miss that." I could almost smell the sharp tobacco smell of his jacket when, as a child, I cuddled on his lap. I could almost hear his pocket watch ticking in my ear.

"Didn't he go to the Isle of Jersey?" Laura asked. "That's a distance away and over the channel."

We both nodded. She reminded us that Papa was far away and not to be depended upon. He might not even know about Mother's death yet.

"He was a good father when he was here," Thomas said. He, too, had sat on Papa's lap and listened to his watch.

I missed my father, but I'd miss my mother much more. Losing Mother was like losing the core of my heart. She'd been my refuge, my solace, my friend. And she'd been reliable. Nothing dreadful would happen to me because Mother wouldn't allow it.

She had been important to me since my birth. While Thomas and I had a governess, Mother had been part of our day. She'd come to the nursery, taken us for walks, and praised us for our small accomplishments. Besides the governess, Miss Parsons, we had a nursery maid, Bessie. As well, my Grandmama and Grandpa Harries lived with us. My mother's family was a complicated one. She had six sisters and two brothers, all much older than her, from

Grandpa's first wife, which meant many aunts and uncles visited us. Their mother had eight children in ten years; she must have died of exhaustion. My Grandmama, Grandpa's second wife, had only one child, my mother.

I remembered Grandpa, as I was twelve when he died. He had lived most of his life in Shropshire where he had his family and extensive property. When he married Grandmama and after Mother was born, they moved to the centre of London. I expected it was Grandmama's idea. Grandpa had enjoyed being important in the smaller world of Shropshire. Grandmama wanted the lively, cosmopolitan world of London. He left his older children under Aunt Martha's care in Shrewsbury. I remembered Thomas and I accompanying Grandpa on trips to Shropshire and visiting with our aunts and uncles there. Grandpa drove a wagon to visit his tenants, and Thomas and I learned to drive a team. We were always fed something at each small farm. It was a pleasure to remember those days.

After his death, his Shropshire properties went to his first family, but the London house came to my Grandmama. Grandmama lived with us until her death just a year before Mother's. Aunt Martha, who was nineteen years older than Mother, visited many times. She arrived at our house, bustling in with the efficiency of a successful châtelaine used to managing a large household, and tried to curb Mother's wilder ideas.

"Now, now, Margaret. You really can't introduce a donkey into the dining room at this party. It's impractical. Who will scoop up the manure? The maids will leave."

I regretted the success of that intervention. No donkey invaded our dining room.

My mother managed the day-to-day running of our London household and the elaborate preparations for the many parties with the efficient help of Mrs. Blackly, but she found time to pay attention to Thomas, Richard, and me. I only vaguely remember my brother Richard as we lost him when he was six and I was five. Thomas doesn't remember him at all. Richard died at the same time a baby sister died. She was just tiny, not yet one year. Diphtheria? I don't remember. I remembered enough about Richard to realize I had lost part of myself when he died. We'd done everything together and suddenly he was gone. I was left with a vast emptiness where there used to be warmth and love. I'd felt as if my skin was peeling off my body, as if I were disappearing. Bessie, our nursery maid, climbed into my cot with me for several nights and hugged me while we both cried for Richard.

"They've gone to join their brothers and sisters," Mother told me when I asked about Richard and the baby. "They were too good for this world."

I vowed then with fierce determination that I'd be naughty—not often, but just enough to remind the Almighty that I was not one of the good ones. In my child's mind, it was insurance for longevity.

There were several other infant deaths that my mother never talked about. After I was about eight or nine years old, there were no more babies and my mother's career as a writer blossomed. Mother became a prolific writer and wrote for *The Literary Magnet, Forget Me Not, The Keepsake,* and for her own magazine, *The New Monthly Belle Assembleé.*

She'd made sure I had a stimulating and interesting life here at 3 Woburn Place. This was Bloomsbury with Russell Square Gardens at its centre. Bloomsbury was the hub, according to my mother, of intellectual life.

When I was a young lady of about sixteen, I read my own poetry to my mother's friends. It was a small group that day, but an intelligent audience. Elizabeth Barrett, a much-admired poet, was in the group.

"Lovely," she said when I finished. I cherished that kind word.

I had friends of my own who lived nearby and who were the literarily inclined sons and daughters of judges and solicitors, artists, and actors. It was great fun. I loved it all. After I had a book of poetry published by Leonard Huxley, I earned a small reputation for literary excellence.

Life at Woburn Place continued to be almost magical until I was about twenty.

I knew my father had filed for bankruptcy in 1833, but we didn't reduce our spending immediately, and it was a few years before I noticed a great difference in our lifestyle. Mother's writing brought in some money. She won a prize for a poem to Princess Victoria—first choice over two hundred entries, but that didn't come with a purse. She was always writing: music, poems, articles, and plays. I was paid for my few contributions to periodicals, but could not earn much. We struggled along, finding employment for some of our household servants elsewhere and keeping only our cook and downstairs maid. There were many arguments behind closed doors. My mother and father divorced in 1845, when I was twenty-two. No doubt my mother sent him away. She was usually the one in charge. I wondered how Mother managed a divorce. She didn't get an Act of Parliament, something even Charles Dickens couldn't afford. It must have been a Diocese Consistory Court decision; Mother could manage almost anything. Papa disappeared soon after to the Isle of Jersey, where he was out of reach of the family.

Mother inherited the house when Grandmama died, so we remained at 3 Woburn Place.

"I will get money from my writings," Mother declared and managed to get a pension from the Literary Society. So, we struggled on. Our friends remained loyal and visited. Mother wrote a biography of her friend Harriet, Duchess of St. Albans. They were true friends, as both of them treated society's rules lightly and encouraged each other. Mother admired the duchess's belief in her worth as she rose from an actress on Drury Lane to the wife of a banker and then the wife of a duke.

"A woman can do anything these days," my mother told me. "You can aspire to great heights, Florence. Just look at Harriet."

My mother could hold contradictory thoughts concurrently: that I could do anything I wanted and that I must find a husband. I was inclined toward the first.

Mother published a second book in two volumes on notable women. It was eagerly bought for a time. She did believe in opportunities for women outside of the home. I did as well; I just couldn't see many open for me. She continued to write and produce biographies and poetry until her death.

The huge loss I felt evoked memories of my brother Richard's death, when my world seemed to disintegrate. Mother had been a source of comfort and joy to me, but I felt some relief too. My mother had not enjoyed living at the edge of poverty—and poverty seemed to loom.

The life I had known would drastically change. The week after my mother died, Thomas dismissed Mrs. Blackly and the two servants with glowing recommendations.

"It's the least I can do," Thomas said. "I'll ask around the theatre district and see if anyone needs more staff. They'll have to put up with some eccentricities, theatre people being what they are, but at least it will be employment."

"They lived in Mother's house," I said. "They're used to eccentricities."

He grinned. "True."

Thomas and I packed up Mother's house, getting it ready for sale. Neither of us could afford to live in such a big house. Society would condemn me if I tried.

Thomas's wife, Laura, was happy to take Mother's dishes and crystal. I kept one set of dishes and all Mother's books with the exception of the books of theatre and her plays, which Thomas wanted. I donated many to the library, but I still had copies of Mother's published books, articles she'd written, and poetry. Mr. Dickens had gifted Mother a copy of each of his books from *Nicholas Nickleby,* the first one, to *The Cricket on the Hearth,* his latest. She also had the complete works of

Shakespeare. I caressed their leather bindings and thought of the many hours we'd spent acting out the plays. I packed them all and stored some in trunks in Thomas's house and some on the bookshelves in my room.

"I must pay my way here," I'd told Thomas when I first arrived at his house on Noel Street after Mother's death.

"With what?" Thomas was more puzzled than sarcastic. He knew I hadn't managed to earn much.

"I have Mother's will, and it looks as though there will be something left after we sell the house and settle the debts. Grandpa left the house to Grandmama, and she left it to Mother. The Shropshire estate goes to our aunts and uncles." Mother had not talked to us about her will. She was so young and the cancer came on so quickly we never discussed it, but she had provided for us.

"That's proper," Thomas agreed.

It was a comfort to know my share of the proceeds would give me enough money to set up on my own. A small house would be agreeable. With one maidservant and a cook, I could manage. I would write critical articles on social issues, perhaps even become a drama critic. That was my modest dream.

"What does Mr. Holmes say?" Thomas had Laura to care for now and, if I wasn't mistaken, a child on the way. An inheritance would help him. Mr. Holmes had been my mother's solicitor and a former colleague of my father's. He was a meticulously tailored gentleman with a shiny bald head and, as if to compensate, a luxurious moustache in the style of a walrus. He had informed us just after the funeral that Mother had left a small bequest to our father and to Mrs. Blackly, and the house to Thomas and me, but we hadn't had a discussion about it until weeks later. He had been avuncular and reassuring.

"Your mother was very good with money," he told me. "Surprising in a female. She did manage to leave some money for you and your brother and, of course, the house will fetch a tidy sum. I'll take care of it for you."

I had gone to see Mr. Holmes on my own. Thomas was not yet so important in his theatre world as to be able to take leave from his work. I listened carefully, then explained his advice to Thomas. "Mr. Holmes will take the money, pay the debts, and give us the balance."

It did not turn out that way. After he sold the house, Mr. Holmes absconded with our funds and likely those of several others. He and our money disappeared like a magician's coin. Gone. Likely to the Continent. Mr. Holmes's associate, Mr. Best, singularly ill-named, sent us a letter. There would be no redress, no compensation, no payment of any kind. He sent his regrets.

I stormed into the solicitor's office and demanded they do something, but Mr. Best explained that there was nothing they could, or would, do. I marched home and slammed the door of my bedroom. I was so angry I blistered the air with words our coal delivery boy had taught me.

I chastised myself. *You should have known Holmes was duplicitous. You should have overseen every aspect of the transactions. You lost not only your inheritance but Thomas's as well.* I vowed from that moment I would never leave my affairs in anyone's hands but my own. Then I cried for an hour. I cried for my mother. I cried for the horror of looming poverty. I even cried for my absent father, although there was anger mixed up in those tears. Finally, I splashed water on my face, took some deep breaths, and considered what I could possibly do.

*two*

# After Bloomsbury

I NEEDED MONEY. WHERE could I find money? I remembered Mother had received a pension from the Literary Society, but that had died with her. Perhaps they would give me one. I was being paid for journalistic articles from several papers and had another book of poetry published, so I had literary credentials. My work as a journalist did not pay enough to support me. Besides, Mr. Dickens always paid late, and the others did not pay well.

Thankfully, the Literary Society granted me forty pounds. The ghost of my mother probably nagged them. It was not a pension but an outright payment. That was enough to recompense Thomas for my room and board for two years. With that relief, I stayed with Thomas, continued to write and help with the children as they arrived. I did Thomas's accounts for him, as now we didn't trust solicitors. As his business got bigger and he had more accounts, he would need a more qualified professional, but for now I was his bookkeeper. It was an active life—I saw all the new plays Thomas produced, but it was not the joyous and stimulating life I'd lived in my mother's house.

After two years, the money was gone in spite of my careful consideration of each farthing spent. I was twenty-five. I hired out as a governess and for the next two years took various positions in London, staying with Thomas between employment. I was never fired, but some of the positions didn't last long, as the children grew past my teaching or the family moved. It was a difficult existence, always being on the alert for a new position and always disappointed in those positions. There was nothing to keep me in London. Thomas did not need me to be a drag on his finances. I looked farther afield for work. I was thrilled to find a position as a teacher-governess in a diplomat's household and moved with Mr. Caloon's family to the exotic, fascinating, and rigidly cold Russian city of Saint Petersburg. I had no idea what Mr. Caloon did for the British Crown. He probably gathered information about wars and rumours of wars. There was always money to be made when there was war. The British likely wanted to secure contracts.

I had my keep and a generous salary. Someone else worried about how to feed us and keep the house warm. I was free to teach the children and enjoy the city. In Saint Petersburg, I was back in the social milieu, not of the upper middle class from which I had come, but the aristocracy. I could certainly get used to it. That didn't mean I was *of* the aristocracy. I had a maidservant to look after me, but I was not equal to the family. A governess was a convenient pawn who could be moved across social classes when needed. I found my position amusing at times, and always entertaining. I hoped it would last for years. The Caloons brought me into their pool of friends as I joined in the cosmopolitan world of a diplomat's household. The conversations around the dinner table were interesting. Mr. Caloon spoke of a group of Quaker men from England who had come to try to avert the looming Crimean War. I didn't meet them, but Mr. Cahoon told us about them, and I applauded their attempts at peace-making.

The children were well-mannered and eager to learn, so the teaching was agreeable if a little boring at times. Still, I had free time to explore the city. It had beautiful areas where the golden onion-style domes on the churches sparkled in the sunlight like illustrations in a fairy tale.

My first winter there was a revelation. I hadn't realized the air could become so cold. Even Shropshire hadn't been this cold.

People still went out in the weather and hurried through the streets, but dressed in furs and heavy woollen clothes. I made myself a woollen cloak and lined it with sable—it was marvellously warm—and joined them when I could.

Saint Petersburg was an intriguing city, full of history, old churches of the Russian Orthodox variety with their distinctive, almost Moorish, architecture. It was a romantic city full of promise and a magical sense of history and culture, but I was only an observer. Romance was not possible for the governess of a British diplomat. Now that I was approaching my thirtieth birthday, I was no longer eligible as anyone's sweetheart. It was strange how society pegged me as unsuitable as a bride when I still felt the eagerness and longing of my younger self, as if my attitudes or sense of anticipation had never changed. I was disciplined, though, and no one knew how I felt.

Nicholas I was the emperor of Russia until 1855. I saw him once. He was a handsome man, even then, but aloof as if he was constantly on military parade. He came to a few balls, where I observed him. He had a reputation for meticulous attention to detail and seemed to have a firm hold over his government. His son, the Grand Duke Nicholas, was more approachable, and I'd heard he was interested in abolishing serfdom in Russia—so obviously much more open-minded than his father. He became Alexander II in 1855 and immediately began to improve the daily life of the populace with his notions of improved sanitation. He was much more popular than his father. Not that I expressed my opinions *of* Russia *in* Russia. That would have embarrassed my employer—if it didn't get me shot. There were murmurings of war with Germany and an ongoing war in the Balkans. There was always war somewhere in Europe. The countries were quarrelsome, which was odd as many of the kings and queens seemed to be related to one another.

I scuttled about the city taking in the sights with my maid, Hilda, who flapped behind me like a lost duckling.

"But ma'am, we shouldn't go down that street." She never had a good reason for her prohibitions, so I ignored her. Such was her loyalty to me, she never reported to my employers that I haunted bookshops in search of English novels and poetry, frequented tea rooms that also served the working class, and stood alone in the cold and studied Peter the Great's statue high above me on his stone charger. I attended balls as a chaperone for the young ladies of the house, where I observed but didn't dance. It reminded me of the world of Jane Austen fifty years ago, where the social classes conducted their lives in much the same way. There was no Mr. Darcy for me; I didn't expect one. I had no opportunity to form an attachment with a man as I was outside of the social sphere of most of them and, truthfully, they didn't interest me. I was not unattractive, with dark hair, dark eyes, and a pale complexion. I was tall for a woman at five-foot-six, with a trim figure, but my most obvious detriment was my age. I was decidedly a spinster. It didn't worry me. I wasn't part of this society. Everyone spoke in careful sentences. It seemed artificial. I saved my salary. I studied Russian, as I found languages intriguing, and I enjoyed the city. Living in Russia was a marvellous opportunity to learn.

In 1854, I travelled home to England for a holiday. I was a month with Thomas, Laura, and the family and was able to bring gifts and contribute to the household. Thomas was doing well now, managing two music halls and a theatre.

On my return to Russia, I booked on the SS *Victoria* out of Hull on November 8, bound for Saint Petersburg. I sent most of my luggage ahead to await my arrival. The voyage was rough with a wicked wind, huge waves, and biting cold. On November 9 the gale was so strong and the waves so high, we gathered on the deck afraid to go below to our cabins or bunks. I thought of the Greek mythology I'd read about angry gods who punished mere mortals. I could almost believe in them. I felt abandoned by humanity in this wild sea and in the hands of those spiteful gods. We huddled together, first , second, and steerage classes, awaiting our our fate.

The *Victoria* hit the rocks near Wingo Breacon, on Wingo Island off Sweden. She shuddered and rocked sideways, then righted. We were on land, but treacherous land, surrounded by sea and precariously wedged on the rocks. The waves were monstrous and pounded the boat. I thought it would break apart at any moment and fling us into the deep. We were all thoroughly wet and cold, shivering on the deck and praying for rescue. I knew none of the passengers. I'd not had time to even learn their names. I was going to die alone. I felt a shudder start low in my body and travel up until I was shaking. I took several deep breaths. I wasn't dead yet. I needed control myself. We'd grabbed our coats and life preservers. I doubted they would help us in that cold sea. The women, and there were about ten of us, would drown quickly, as our yards of dress material would drag us to our deaths. I expected that dire fate with every pounding wave that battered us. I concentrated on what I could do to help myself. I had a choice: I could tear off my skirts and enter the sea in my bloomers, which would give me a better chance of surviving. However, on deck, the skirts kept me from freezing; I might have died of cold without them. I opted for keeping my skirts around me. A collective wail rose involuntarily from our group when a particularly monstrous wave broke over us. We endured the night with prayers. As the sky lightened, we could see the way the ship was wedged with rocks on either side of the hull. I patted the deck and mentally sent directions. *Just stick fast to the rocks, my fine boat.* The wind still howled, but with less ferocity. With the increasing light came rescue—small boats, plunging up and down in the giant waves, but coming closer. Angels disguised as boats. We managed to transfer from the wrecked *Victoria* to those rescue boats by awkwardly climbing down a webbed rope panel. The rescue boats took us to Hono Island and thence to Gothenburg, Sweden. I had no maid and no clothes.

I had never been so cold. My fingers had turned blue sometime in the night; my feet felt like wooden cubes. On the rescue boat, someone handed me a heavy man's coat, for which I was grateful.

At Gothenburg, with the very last of the money I had thought to stuff into my pockets, I bought my fare to Saint Petersburg. I heard later that thirty-one people had died in that wreck.

The Caloons were appalled by what I had endured. They bustled about.

"Hilda, tend to her, she needs hot food, warm clothes, and her bed for a day." Mrs. Caloon was kind. Hilda was crying.

"I'm fine," I said. But I wasn't. Physically, I'd recovered on the train, but my trunk was not waiting for me in Saint Petersburg.

I had first gone to the luggage office at the train station. I spoke some Russian, but in my anxiety, I struggled to make myself understood. I had my luggage tickets. I'd stowed them in my pocket when we abandoned the ship.

"*Nyet. Nyet.*" The official repeated. I did understand "No."

Mr. Caloon, who had come to meet me and accompanied me to the luggage office, said a few words in Russian, then turned to me.

"I will return tomorrow, Miss Wilson. That will give them time to sort this out."

I agreed and left without my trunk. I soon learned it had disappeared with all my goods—and all my money. I'd saved two hundred pounds in gold, enough to start a new life when I finished my duties as a governess. It was gone. Mr. Caloon inquired of the shipping company on my behalf several times and finally gave me the bad news.

"There is no trace of your trunk, Miss Wilson. I am sorry. I imagine word travelled about the wreck and looters made off with all the luggage left at the docks." He was sympathetic, but he was under no obligation to make up my loss. I was his employee, not his relative.

Now I had no future but servitude. No independence. No little house back in England. I needed that day in bed to mourn my loss. I stared at the walls of my room allowing the feeling of dread to invade my whole being. Between poverty and me lay only my brother Thomas, and I couldn't be his burden. I cursed a malevolent god and the treacherous Baltic Sea, raging at fate's particular spite. Then I sat up and took stock.

I had left some clothes at the Caloons', as I knew I would be returning, so made do with them until I accrued enough salary to buy fabric. I was an excellent seamstress and could make new gowns and revamp old ones from Mrs. Caloon. They would have to suffice. I bought pens, paper, and more books, although most of my books were on my shelves as I'd not taken them to England.

The war in the Crimea concluded in 1856 with Britain forcing humiliating terms on Russia. Nicholas I had been an incompetent leader who wouldn't leave the direction of the war to his generals. That was advantageous for Britain but difficult for Russia. His son was no better as leader. When our social life had become uncomfortable in Russia, Mr. Caloon took the family and me on a tour of Europe. By 1856, when it was obvious we could not return to Russia, Mr. Caloon gathered his family and servants, including me, and returned us to England. The children were able to do without a governess now. Mrs. Caloon gave me a lovely pearl pendant as a farewell present and Mr. Caloon gave me ten pounds. That would be enough to feed me for several months. I was redundant.

I bade the Caloons goodbye and visited Thomas and family for a week. It was lovely to be back in England, as it felt I belonged here, but I needed to be independent. I moved to lodgings at 3 Castle Terrace, New Hampstead, and at first relied on my savings. They wouldn't last long. I needed employment.

I worked as a journalist, but only sold articles, not poetry. Poetry was a decidedly financially unrewarding occupation. I sought life stories that would be acceptable to newspapers and journals, like stories of fires, weddings—anything that would capture the interest of readers and publishers. Stories about Russia were deemed exotic and usually sold, so I tried to write as many as I could. I wrote one article about a slave in Russia. I wrote another on the life of a governess, which Mr. Dickens published. I didn't work for a salary and got paid—meagrely, I have to say—only for what I produced. I lived on the edge of poverty.

I was determined to endure. *Have some fortitude, Florence,* I told myself. *You've survived the Russian winters, the cold sea in November, the loss of all your money, and you're still here. You can do something.*

I had always written letters to my mother's friends and my own friends from my youth, so I still knew people of influence. I attempted to get a pension from the Literary Society, but they rejected my plea. They must have talked among themselves, though, because I got a letter from an old acquaintance who recommended I contact a Mrs. Henry Newbury on Putnam Street. She was in need of help with her ailing husband and the position was a live-in one.

Nursing didn't appeal to me, but having three meals a day and a bed certainly did.

I started with the Newburys and found both Elizabeth and Henry delightful. They were obviously affectionate with each other, something I hadn't seen outside of Thomas and Laura's marriage, and they were considerate of their staff. The work was not arduous. Elizabeth didn't want to leave a dying Henry alone in his weak state and yet wanted to get out of the house to visit and shop. I had time to write and managed some articles for the *London News*.

Henry and Elizabeth took an interest in my writing and often asked me to read my work and the newspapers to them. Henry was not able to get out of bed by then, so we gathered around him with Margaret and Ellen, the maids who found my reading a source of entertainment—and a respite from work.

"Read me the financial pages, Florence," Henry asked. He'd been a goldsmith and was interested in the stories of gold discoveries in the New World. "What are they saying about the strikes in California?"

"Still some producing mines," I said.

"What about the Colony of British Columbia? They were getting high quality gold from placer mining."

By now I knew enough from our discussions to understand that placer mining was above-ground sluicing. I read him the news of the Colony of British Columbia.

"A man could make a million there," he said.

*So could a woman.* The thought came like a blade through my head.

"What's the cost of the passage?" he asked.

Elizabeth shot me a quick glance. Henry was going nowhere.

I rustled the paper and found the information. "Thirty pounds, steerage."

"How much for first class?"

"I'm not sure there is a first class."

"Bound to be. They'll make more money off first class."

I did find one ship that had a second-class cabin for forty pounds and first class for eighty.

From then on, I entertained Henry with stories about the goldfields of the New World as we studied the paper. I learned to tell the different between gold and "fool's" gold, which was pyrite. Henry taught me how to weigh gold. I suspect he thought I could get employment in the future as an assistant in a goldsmith's shop. If I could educate myself on all aspects of gold, then I would be of use to a goldsmith. I wasn't sure I wanted to be at the beck and call of a goldsmith—they wouldn't all be as kind as Henry. Nor did I want to exist on the paltry wage of an assistant. But I was definitely interested in the riches of British North America. Henry was interested in all aspects of gold. When we read about the rich strikes by the miners of the colony in British North America, he talked about the best ground to look for gold. Elizabeth was pleased to see him take an interest in something.

Henry died on April 10, 1861. Elizabeth had just come in from shopping, gone to see if he wanted tea, and found him dead. I left her holding his hand and crying while I informed Margaret and Ellen and sent for the doctor. I stayed a few days, helping Elizabeth with the funeral arrangements and through the service and reception at the house. Elizabeth gave me Henry's book on the business of gold and his scale for weighing gold, a delicate brass apparatus with dishes suspended on chains. I would cherish them. Then I packed my bags and returned to Thomas's house. I was no longer employed.

I managed the next year writing for Mr. Dickens and for newspapers, but I couldn't contribute much to the household. I liked Mr. Dickens. He was older than me by some ten or so years, and I admired how much he had accomplished, but he was a complex man. He had firm ideas about the need for justice for the poor, having grown up respectable but poor and experienced deprivation and the fear of starvation. Occasionally, he told me of his life at twelve, working in the boot-blacking factory while his father was in debtor's prison. It must have been overwhelming. He'd been hard-working and respectable most of his life, but now he was in a mess. His personal life was fractious.

He had fallen in love with the actress Ellen Ternan when she acted in his play *The Frozen Deep*. She was then eighteen to his forty-five. Poor Catherine, his wife, was relocated to a separate household with only one of their children, and Mr. Dickens had to balance his affair with Ellen, his obligations to his children, his obligations to Catherine, his reading tours around Britain, his writing and publication of *Household Words*, and his novel writing. I admired that writing, his socialist politics, and his energy, but I wished he'd pay a better remuneration and on time. Mr. Dickens did well by his writing, but I found it a financially precarious business.

A year later, I told Thomas I was going to emigrate.

My brother initially objected. "You'll die of pestilence out in the colonies, Florence. Stay with us. We will manage somehow."

"I'm quite looking forward to the adventure." I ignored my doubts, my fears of shipwreck, loneliness, and impoverishment in a foreign land. At times, when alone, I shook with apprehension. Was this emigration madness? Was I so desperate to make a living I'd turn my back on all I knew? Well, yes. That was the case. I was desperate. Poverty was in my future if I didn't make some drastic change. Therefore, I would manage. In any event, I couldn't stay with Thomas, although it was good of him to offer. He had a wife and family; the house was crowded already. There were three bedrooms: one for Thomas and Laura, one for me, and one for all four children. Thomas was a theatre producer, not a banker or a mining magnate. He couldn't afford to keep me and, frankly, I didn't wish to spend the rest of my life as the penniless spinster in the house. The Colony of British Columbia, with its promise of adventure and gold, looked like a much better prospect. There was a fortune to be had in that colony. I was convinced of it—if I survived the trip. Ship deaths occurred often enough to be a threat. Poor food, lack of medical care, accidents, and storms could accompany the three-month journey.

"I can't afford your passage, my girl," Thomas had said. "I'm sorry."

"My darling Thomas, there is no need for you to bother. My passage is paid by the Female Middle Class Emigration Society."

"Ah, yes. I read about them. They're joining up with the Columbia Emigration Society to help distressed gentlewomen. That's you, I guess."

"I suppose so. The organizer, Miss Maria Rye, is a friend from our years at Russell Square, remember her?"

He looked blank. Thomas had had his own friends when we were young.

"I'm surprised she joined up with the Columbia Emigration Society," I said, "as they are interested in helping 'fallen' women and girls from the workhouses and certainly don't support independence in women. Too Church-of-England for that. I wonder why Maria's group aligned with them."

"She probably needed to use their ship."

"Perhaps. Maria and I wrote to each other while I was in Russia. When I returned here, we kept in touch. She's an interesting woman."

My effort to divert Thomas failed. He was used to directing actors and employees in his theatre. He managed them all and tried to manage me on occasion.

He continued to argue. "It's dangerous. There'll be thousands of miners out there looking for a woman, any woman, and neither of the emigration societies will protect you."

I laughed. He evoked visions of sexually and socially starved men fighting over me. Unlikely. I was far to old to be a *femme fatale*. Thomas had the Harries imagination passed to us by our mother. We can imagine almost anything. "Both emigration societies are boringly respectable. Maria has given me, and other women of my class, passage money and money to start a business." It was a pitiably small amount, but I had some savings and could give myself a modest start, a new beginning. I did admire the work that Maria's society was doing.

"What kind of business?" Thomas asked sharply.

"Oh, Thomas. For heaven's sake! You don't suspect me of starting up a brothel, do you? I've reached the old age of thirty-nine without even considering it. And I've been in poverty before."

"I know. I know. You suffered more than I did when Papa went bankrupt," he said "Teaching, at least, gave you some income."

"And my poetry."

"Well . . ." He looked dubious.

He was right. Poetry, while personally fulfilling and engendering warm feelings when it was published, was financially unrewarding.

"Face it, Thomas, it's the colonies or the workhouse."

He looked at me.

"Really, Thomas, a brothel is not an option."

He laughed. "You will write."

"I will write." But we both knew it was unlikely we would see each other again.

IT TOOK ONLY A MONTH to secure my passage and venture money from the Female Middle Class Emigration Society, a much faster time than I had anticipated. They moved quickly as they were responding the all the newspaper articles on the superfluous women in England who were destitute. There were thousands of us, desperately trying to find enough to eat without selling ourselves. Maria Rye was determined to help those of us who could be independent and productive if given a chance, and, since she managed the society, she assured me she would see that I was given the financial support I needed. Her society was doing its best to keep the many women like me of good education but minimal prospects from the poor house. Quickly, in the spring of 1862, every arrangement was finalized, and I was booked on the SS *Tynemouth*.

"Do you have a first-class cabin?" Thomas asked me.

I stared at him. "The Emigration Society doesn't provide first class."

"But you're gentry," Thomas protested. "You can't go steerage." He thought for a moment. I hoped he wasn't going to put obstacles in my way. "You don't know how to do your laundry. You can't cook! How could you look after yourself for three months on the voyage in steerage?"

It was true: I didn't cook or do laundry. "I can learn."

"There will be rats!"

I imagined steerage with rats. It gave me pause.

"What's the price of a first-class cabin?" he asked.

I fetched the poster advertising the sailing. He took it from me. "First class is eighty pounds. That's beyond me, but second class is forty pounds, only ten pounds more than steerage. Do you have ten pounds?"

I had ten pounds, but I was going to need that in Victoria. I hesitated.

"I can find five pounds, Florence, if you can find the other five." He looked at me. "It's hard enough to part with you, but I couldn't sleep, imagining your travails in steerage."

I was not going to take Thomas's five pounds. He'd done enough for me. I could manage three months of discomfort if that's what it turned out to be.

"I am not going to be below decks, Thomas. Maria promised she'd put all her emigrants near the second-class passengers above decks, so there will be no rats. Don't worry."

ONE MORNING, JUST BEFORE I was due to leave, I walked from Thomas's house in Noel Street in the vibrant Soho area to the gardens in Russell Square. I couldn't face the sorrow of our forthcoming parting at his house, where he was keeping such a dismal demeanour I wanted to hit him. He walked around the house agitated like a lid on a boiling pot of worry, pacing up and down the drawing room, waving his hands. Theatre people. There was always drama. "Do you have enough money? Is the boat safe?" he bellowed at me. Both legitimate concerns. He loved me, after all, and as there were few people in the world who did, I tried to be patient and answer in a cheerful manner.

But my own anxiety and irritation with Thomas threatened to disrupt the household, so I'd taken myself off to Russell Square to worry myself into depression if I so chose. Russell Square was still a tranquil oasis in central London. Francis Russell, the fifth Duke of Bedford, who remained here in stone, commissioned this park to be built about sixty years ago and surrounded it with lovely modern Victorian houses, some stone but most a warm, red brick.

I mulled over my past as I strolled around gardens, gathering memories. The day we brought a treasure-hunting party to the park—organized around a literary theme, of course—for which my mother and I hid clues. The poetry competitions at the foot of the old duke's statue. The serious discussions Mr. Dickens and I had on that bench just there, about poverty, the oppression of the workers, and the need for social justice. What an orator that man was when he cared about a cause. I had been as awed by him then as if he'd been a prophet or an important political giant.

*I'll cherish these memories as if they are jewels. I'll take them out and polish them when I'm in the new land. I'll try to remember all of this: the green of the grass, the sharp black of the iron fences, and the smell of the roses rising from a carpet of colour near the pavement.* I particularly loved the Rose du Roi, a deep red rose that was just starting to bloom. I sniffed the spicy scent. I would miss these roses. I was struck by a thought. *Why not take them with me?*

I glanced around the square. There was only a family group on the far side who were not paying any attention to me. I reached into my reticule and extracted my nail scissors. It was the work of a moment to clip a cutting just below the node, cut the top off, and drop the cutting into my bag. I did that three times. Visions of the penalties for stealing flitted through my mind. Jail or transport to Tasmania. I shivered. I was not caught. Rose du Roi was going with me.

I HAD SPENT THE WEEK before my departure helping my sister-in-law with the children, supervising the maid as she washed, ironed, and prepared my trunk with what I imagined would be necessities. I discussed the safeguarding of my meagre savings with the clerk at the Bank of England. I took some of my money in gold and the clerk gave me letters of credit. I was not risking my gold on this voyage. It could disappear into the hands of porters and freighters. I could arrive in Victoria with no gold and little money. I wasn't having that.

"When you get to the colony," Mr. Hutchins said, "present these letters and they will credit your account."

I smiled. "Thank you." There wouldn't be much in that account to start, but I had every intention of watching that amount grow.

"Of course, you are going out on the bride ship, are you not?" The Columbia Emigration Society was the affiliated organization with the Female Middle Class Emigration Society. Their goal was to provide wives for the miners in the colonies. It was true, I was going on a bride ship.

I nodded.

"When you are married, you will have to bring your husband to the bank in Victoria to sign over the account. Bring your marriage lines, and it should all go smoothly."

I stared at him. *Sign over the account?* "Why would I do that?"

"Married women can not do business legally. Their husbands are in charge of the accounts. They have our same British law in the colonies."

I knew married women did not have property rights in England. My mother had complained about that, but I had thought the colonies would be more willing to recognize women's abilities. Of course, the colonies had the same law. It was a strong inducement to stay single. No wonder my mother had divorced my father. He was a spendthrift and a bankrupt. Divorce had given her control of her finances. I didn't inform Mr. Hutchins that I had no intention of marrying.

THE DAYS BEFORE I LEFT Thomas's house, I was decidedly cheerful. I refused to discuss with Thomas or Laura the disasters that had accompanied my life so far: the loss of my parents, the loss of my inheritance, the shipwreck on the way to Russia, the loss of my savings. I thought about them, though. I needed to remind myself I had weathered many difficulties in life; I could manage more.

I persuaded Thomas that the voyage would be one of comfort and adventure. I didn't tell him I was packing tea, lemons, cod liver oil, salt, spices,. laudanum, bandages, powdered willow bark, and as many medicaments and emergency supplies as I could think of in case the voyage turned out to be more difficult than I anticipated. My purloined rose, Rose du Roi, was safely ensconced in a sawdust-filled glass jar with a perforated lid. It had some roots and could develop more on the way to Victoria. Finally, I was ready.

"Your luggage weighs like it's full of coal. Books?" Thomas said as he struggled to load my trunks onto his carriage.

"True." The bottom third of each trunk held books. I considered life without books not worth living, and I did not want to risk being deprived in the new land. This was the biggest concern of my move—if I discounted my fears of drowning in the Atlantic or starving in the wilds of the colony. They had Indians there. Were they friendly? Could I communicate with them? Would I find food and shelter immediately? Would my savings run out before I found a way to sustain myself? I imagined myself on the shores of this new land, poor, hungry, alone, and cold. I shrugged. Whatever happened, books would make life more tolerable. I could not survive without books.

Thomas drove me to the docks in his carriage, supervised the loading of my trunks, and kissed me goodbye.

"I *will* write," I promised.

"See that you do."

It would be all we *could* do.

*three*

# The *Tynemouth*

THE *TYNEMOUTH* WAS an impressive sight with its long hull and three masts.

"She's a three-masted barque with a steam propelling screw," Thomas said as he waited by the gangplank. "I asked around. If you have wind, you can sail; if you are becalmed, you can use the steam engine."

That was reassuring. Being stranded in the middle of the ocean was not a pleasant thought.

"If the new engines give way, you can still make your way across the Atlantic. Sail has been reliable for centuries."

I nodded agreement. He was reassuring himself as much as me.

I told myself it was an adventure, and adventure held some risks. I found that a bit of physical danger added spice to life. Not all voyages ended in shipwreck, although a distressing number did. I ignored that statistic. It was summer. Sea voyages were safer in the northern hemisphere in the summer. *Do not dwell on the risks. You are committed to this voyage.*

I'd travelled to many countries in Europe with the Caloons. In those many months before we were forced to leave Russia, we kept out of the way of the authorities by travelling. It was a good chance for the children to practice their French under my direction, as the language was spoken in many countries. The teaching justified the travel in Mr. Caloon's eyes. I was enchanted by the countries of Belgium, Switzerland, and France. Our travels didn't always go smoothly, and although no disaster occurred, I knew very well that one could. I had personal experience of a shipwreck. However, I ignored my fears, hugged Thomas, then walked up the gangplank to the mid-deck. I was met by a grim-faced woman holding a list.

"Your name?"

"Miss Florence Wilson."

"Miss Wilson. I am Mrs. Robb. I am your chaperone."

I smiled. I was older than she was. She didn't return my smile. She gave me the number of my cabin and handed me over to a sailor who looked to be about twelve years old.

"This way, ma'am." He seemed cheerful enough. He didn't offer to take my heavy suitcase until we had arrived on the upper deck. Then he smiled and took it from me.

"That old besom don't want me to help the ladies. A right cow, she is. Here's your room."

He flung open the door to a cabin which, although small, contained four beds, two stacked one over another on opposite walls, and a small desk in the centre. There was a porthole above the desk, so light shone in. The porthole, I noticed, had rust around its edge. This was not a new boat, although I'd read it had new engines. I was the first one to arrive so took a lower bunk. Without adequate storage, I'd need that space beneath the bunk to store my books.

"What is your name?" I asked the sailor.

"George, ma'am."

"I am Miss Wilson. Can you show me where I hang my clothes?"

George pointed to the four small lockers behind the door.

"They said I'd have ten cubic feet?" I protested.

"Down in the 'old," George said. "For your trunk."

How was I going to fit all I needed for a three-month voyage into such a tiny space? I mentally assessed my clothes, personal necessities, writing and reading material.

"You will bring my trunk with the blue label here?" I had marked one trunk for the voyage.

"Sam will bring it. You snatch what you want, and he'll put it in the 'old. You'll get it back when we dock in Victoria."

"You're telling me I can't access it during the voyage?" That could be a problem. What if I ran out of rags for my menses? What if I ran out of something to read?

"That's right. You can't."

He turned to leave.

"Oh, George. Can you tell me if there will be four of us in here?"

He turned back and cocked his head. "Think there's just three."

"Thank you."

He left me to contemplate how much of the room I could fairly appropriate.

Sam, who turned out to be big, muscular, and silent, brought my trunk. I considered how I could reduce my belongings to fit the space allotted to me. All my careful calculations beforehand were useless now.

I got busy. I would need enough clothes for at least five days: a jumper, a coat to protect me from rain or spray, two pairs of gloves, a light wool shawl, two nightdresses, three pairs of cotton stockings, one pair of light woollen stockings, a pair of quilted slippers, two petticoats, two chemises, three pairs of drawers, two lace collars and cuffs, hair brush, comb, combs to keep my hair in place, a cloth laundry hamper, my monthly supplies, a hat for style and to protect me from the sun, a hat pin, lotion for my hands which tended to be dry, my medicines, my lemons, sewing kit, and writing materials, including notebooks, pencils, my Perry fountain pen, five nibs, and a large bottle of ink, carefully stowed in a protective box. I debated for a few minutes on my mother's books and my own books of poetry, but decided I wouldn't need them on the voyage. I would need the book on the gold business, the latest novel by Mr. Dickens, a book on mathematics as I was going to have a business and would need to understand figures, and several books of science, which would challenge my thinking, particularly the recent book by Mr. Darwin. I stacked as many books as possible under the bunk and the clothes and other sundries on top. I worked with some speed, expecting any moment a new emigrant would arrive, needing space to unpack. I didn't put anything but my coat in the first locker, then dragged my trunk out into the passage, put my suitcase in it, locked it, and put my keys in my reticule. I was just in time.

A young girl, about twenty, bounced into the cabin.

"Good afternoon, my lady." She bobbed a curtsy.

I shook her hand. "I'm Florence. Florence Wilson."

"I'm Jane Saunders. I was a housemaid back home, but I'm not going to be one in Victoria."

"No." I smiled at her. "What are you going to do? Get married?"

"At some time, but I'm going to make me fortune and get me brothers and sisters out to join me."

Her Irish accent made her speech musical. It was going to a pleasure to listen to her. "Then you'd better stop with 'my lady' and call me Florence."

She grinned. "I'll have to practice."

Immediately behind her was another woman. Taller, much quieter.

"How do you do?" she said and offered her hand. "I'm Minnie Gillan. I am going out to the colony to be a governess."

"I also was a governess some years ago in Russia."

"How interesting." Minnie removed her gloves. "You must tell me how to go on." She glanced sideways at me.

I laughed. "You'll just have to muddle through," I said. "You're young. You can do anything." She looked to be about seventeen.

"I can read and write and that is the criteria the Press-Wrights asked for."

Those were certainly the bare minimum requirements.

I considered how we would manage our lives together for three months. I turned toward the room. "George, the sailor who guided me here, tells me there will be just the three of us. I have taken a bottom bunk and one locker. How do you suggest we accommodate ourselves?"

Jane put her hands on her hips and surveyed the room. She looked at Minnie then me.

"I'm the shortest. Suppose I take the top bunk."

We both nodded.

"And," she said. "I'll take the top bunk on the other side to store my clothes and such."

"What does that leave me?" Minnie asked with curiosity and civility.

"You get storage under your lower bunk. We can use the spare locker for common things like cutlery and crockery," Jane said. She had an instant grasp of practicalities.

"Oh, my heavens. I'd forgotten I'd need that." I dashed out to the passageway and saw my trunk still there. I found my mother's china and took out four plates, four bowls, four cups and saucers, and four of forks, spoons, and knives in the silver set—one for each of us with one spare.

Jane peered over my shoulder. "Got any towels, dishcloths, bed linen in there?"

"Oh my." I had not thought of all my needs. I rooted around until I found sheets, a wool blanket, two towels, and some linen cloths. I threw everything onto my bunk and sat there watching as Minnie and Jane unpacked their belongings. While I remembered my writing materials and books, linens had always been supplied by someone else. I was almost twenty years older than Jane, but I bowed to her greater knowledge of household affairs.

"What else should we get before Sam comes to get our trunks?" I asked her.

"Sam?" Minnie asked.

"The sailor who hauls heavy trunks."

Jane surveyed the goods on our bunks and considered. "Does anyone have candles and matches? I have five, but they may not last three months. Well, they won't, but that's all I could bring."

"I have several." Minnie went into the passageway and came back with five candles.

I shook my head. "I'm sorry, I didn't think of it."

"Does anyone have a clock?"

"I have." I pulled it from my pocket. I'd bought it in Russia, gold with inlaid porcelain in beautiful red and green colours.

"Oooh. Lovely thing," Jane said.

I found I was pleased she approved of me. I laughed at myself. This slip of a girl had a lot to teach me. I'd never had to do my own washing, feed myself, or attend to household chores such as husbanding candles so they'd last longer, or preparing and cooking food. I *had* learned to sew because I needed to keep my own wardrobe tidy, and sewing my own clothes was economical. I planned to earn enough money in the colony so I could have someone do the chores of a household, but it might be several years before that happened. I needed to learn how to cope in the meantime. Jane might be a good instructor.

"Now. Does anyone have a jug for water? They've given us one and a basin, but we may need another," Jane said.

I nodded and fetched a Ridgway earthenware pitcher.

"That's the ticket," Jane said.

"Jane," I said. "I am so very glad you were assigned to this cabin. You are going to be a wonderful cabinmate."

Her smile lit her dark eyes. "You aren't so top-lofty I'll be uncomfortable. So, I guess we'll be right."

"I can sew," I said, wanting to establish my worth for this voyage. "I can repair and create garments. So I'd be happy to take that position."

"I will have to see what I can do to be useful," Minne said.

"If you had a teapot in that big trunk of yours," Jane addressed Minnie. "Then we'd be crackin'."

"I do. And even some tea." She returned with a Brown Betty. "The kitchen staff gave it to me when I left."

"Perfect," Jane said. "We'll bless you every time we use it."

Minne smiled, genuinely pleased to be helpful.

We bustled about stowing everything as securely as we could, bumping into each other, but managing. We put our crockery and cutlery, dishes, and teapot in the spare locker.

"We'll keep it all away from the prying eyes of that warden," Jane said.

"Warden?" Minnie asked.

"Mrs. Robb," I supplied. "She does look like a prison warden."

"She's going to be like a serpent in the garden," Jane said. "Hissing and spitting every chance she gets. I know her lot."

Servants, like governesses, were good at noticing errant behaviour. Our jobs often depended on our ability to avoid trouble.

We discussed the problem of hoops.

"My crinoline cage adds about eighteen inches all around my body. As you can tell, we will be crashing into each other in this small space with these crinolines." I gestured toward my skirts.

"If we take them off, Warden Robb will surely think we're fallen women," Jane said.

I reached under my skirts, untied my cage, and stepped out of it. I picked it up and studied it. "Look, I can take twelve inches out of it if I just cut it here—" I pointed. "—and slide it along and reattach it here."

They studied my cage. "I can do mine, then each of yours. When we get to Victoria, I can reconstruct them," I offered.

Minnie nodded. "I agree. It seems very unfashionable but necessary."

I slipped into my cage again. I would make those adjustments that very evening.

SAM CAME FOR OUR TRUNKS, and we set sail. The three of us hustled to the railings to watch the dock slip past. We could still see the land on either side of the river, reassuringly close. The *Tynemouth* was on a course down the Thames and around into the English Channel to stop at Dartmouth in four days. We used that time to reorganize ourselves in our small cabin and around Mrs. Robb's dictatorial commands about when to eat and how to prepare our meals. She was an annoying woman, unused to management, I assumed, and felt the need to enforce her power whenever she could. She wanted to control where we were at all times and how we conducted ourselves. She might relax and be more amenable once we were well underway. Jane went to the central kitchen below decks to prepare and obtain our food, such as it was. She brought it back to our cabin, where we ate, Minnie and I sitting on our beds and Jane on our only chair.

"Such an old cat," Jane said of Mrs. Robb. "I pity those poor women below decks. She's treating them like slaves."

"Does she give you grief?" I asked.

"Aye, she does at that. Says I don't belong up with the toffs—that's you two. Says it was an error, and I should be below. She's probably right. Do you suppose there is some poor nob down there named Jane Saunders who wonders what happened?"

"Possibly," Minnie said. "But I'd not inquire."

"Who sponsored you?" I asked.

"The Columbia Emigration Society."

Those sponsored by that organization were housed in steerage. Only Maria Rye's group were on this deck. I expected Maria made that a condition of paying for the fares. The Columbia groups likely needed her money to make it possible to book the ship.

"I agree with Minnie. Don't tell anyone that," I said. "Next time you go down, I'll go with you." We were not going to exchange someone as cheerful and helpful as Jane for an unknown.

"I have to take the dishes back. Want to help me wash them?" Jane suggested.

"I can do that." I could wash a dish. I just had never *had* to wash them.

I followed Jane forward to the communal kitchen. Mrs. Robb was sitting near the door watching everyone come.

"So, you deigned to come yourself then," she said to me. "You have nothing better to do?"

I understood her to be a minor despot put in charge of sixty women, most of them young girls who were used to doing as they were told. I had no intention of doing what I was told. I needed some kind of threat over her.

"Good evening, Mrs. Robb." I stopped and nodded to her. "I spend quite a bit of time writing," I continued in a pleasant tone. "I have a report to write for Mr. Charles Dickens. Have you heard of him? He owns and edits *All the Year Round*, the magazine that replaced *Household Words*. Do you know it?"

She nodded a little warily. Good. She was listening.

"You may have read my articles, then. I have written for him for years, and he's a family friend. I promised I'd report on the voyage. Perhaps you'll give me an interview later on. The readers might be interested in your work."

She blinked but didn't answer. I breezed past her and joined the other women at the long trough that took our dishes. Jane showed me where the soap was and how to rinse the dishes.

"Let me know if she gives you any more trouble," I said as we returned to the cabin.

Apparently, the threat was enough to keep Mrs. Robb from harassing Jane, for Jane reported she only got nasty looks but no comments.

The other chaperone from the Columbia Mission Society was the Reverend William Scott. He was travelling with his wife, Harriet, and two daughters. We attended his Sunday service, which revealed his morals and personality. He was of the "all women must obey a man" variety and best avoided. He irritated me when he prayed loudly and often from his cabin and when he went out on deck and prostrated himself in a parade of his version of Christianity.

By the time we arrived in Dartmouth, I understood more about who was on the ship and where they were. Most of my information came from fellow passengers Charles Redfern and Edward Coleman. They told me there were one hundred crew members under the command of Captain Alfred Hellyer, formerly of Her Majesty's Navy, and two hundred and seventy passengers. Most of the passengers were crammed in steerage, the dark and damp deck below ours. I shuddered, thinking of rats. Included down there were forty of the women from the Columbia Mission Society, under the chaperonage (or rather the dictatorship) of Rev. Scott and Warden Robb. Maria Rye had told me they would be on board and had explained that she had put her protégées, the Female Middle Class Emigration women, under Mrs. Robb's authority. She couldn't have known much about the woman's character.

The Female Middle Class Emigration women, of which there were twenty, occupied cabins midship on the upper deck alongside the first- and second-class travellers as well as, of course, Mrs. Robb and her family, and Rev. Scott. They were certainly not going to share the deprivations of their charges. Mr. Scott and Mrs. Robb were fanatically determined to keep all sixty women, including me and my cabinmates, under firm control. I was just as determined they would not.

My morning walk on deck was hampered by a driving rain. I was soaked in minutes and had to give up my exercise.

"All the angels are pissing on us," Jane said.

I laughed as I shook my coat free of rain. "Put a word in then, Jane, and get them to stop."

"I'd not want to draw attention to myself," Jane answered.

We started a constant battle with the damp. Jane had persuaded George to find us a rope and had strung it from the pipes that ran under the ceiling to act as our drying rack. There was always something drying.

Mrs. Robb told one of the sailors to cordon off an area on the deck outside our cabins and informed us that it was our perambulation area. In other words, except to go to the kitchens, we were not allowed to walk around the ship. I expected

Mrs. Robb thought we would surely be overcome with emotion and fall to the licentious attention of the many men on the ship. Why we would be tempted, I'm not sure. I'd noticed before that particularly fervent Christians seemed preoccupied by sexual activity. It certainly made me suspect her own inclinations—however unfair that might be. Perhaps she wanted to avoid having us catch sight of the sailors using the piss-ales, the funnels attached to the sides of the ship which were the convenient and public latrines for men. After a few days, I got used to seeing them efficiently relieve themselves. If I ignored them, they ignored me.

During the earlier days, I'd made the acquaintance of some of the women housed near us. We had no common meeting room, and our cabins were too small to invite guests. The only communal space we had was the small deck space devised by Mrs. Robb. We perambulated around our designated pen like cows at some kind of livestock sale, hooped skirts swaying and periodically jumping or stumbling as a wave rocked the ship. I needed much more exercise than this as I was used to walking all over London—and at a brisk pace. I decided to bide my time, working out what I could do.

We talked about how to negotiate our small cabin space and decided that not only hoops but wide skirts would have to be modified.

"I'll cut down one of my own skirts to a more comfortable size," I offered. "And, if you approve, I'll do the same for each of you, starting with Jane's, as she has to mix with many more people and a wide skirt will be hazardous in the kitchen." I could imagine the women crowding around the stove, stepping on each other's gowns and shoving crinoline against crinoline.

"Agreed," Jane said quickly.

Minnie took more time to think about it. "Just one skirt?" she queried.

"If you want more, I can alter more, but one to start."

She finally agreed, and I had an occupation for several weeks. The smaller skirts would reduce our girth by about four inches all around. It would be a relief not to be carrying so much weight.

During our brief stop at Dartmouth, we enjoyed the cessation of motion and spent time cleaning and reorganizing our cabin. I considered nipping into the Dartmouth shops to get some additional sugar and tea, but decided there wasn't time. Leaving Dartmouth was bittersweet. We were happy to start our adventure, but sad to be leaving our homeland. The three of us stood at the rail and watched the land drift away as we sailed toward the Atlantic Ocean. It was unlikely we would see it again.

I applied my mind to the problem of the enforced restriction of our movements. I hadn't worked out how to subvert Mrs. Robb yet. I needed to ingratiate myself with someone who was her superior. On this ship, that would be the captain. Captain Hellyer was too busy while we were in port, but I would approach him for an interview for a news article once we were underway. I would ask for the interview to take place in the first- and second-class dining room, which was close to our cabin but off-limits to us. I planned to make it on-limits.

I disclosed my plan to my cabinmates while sipping tea the morning we left Dartmouth. Jane had access to an unlimited supply of hot water. We had each offered a tin cannister of tea leaves which Jane had assessed would last about ninety days.

"If we're longer than ninety days, we'll have to use that sawdust they have for tea in the galley," she'd said.

"I'm going to get us into the dining room—not to eat," I said, "because Warden Robb would cut up about that, but to talk and to visit with other passengers."

"You'd better leave me out," Jane said. "I'd stand out like a sore thumb in there, and I wouldn't know what to talk about."

I started to protest, then reconsidered. She was right.

"I'll find my way to the kitchens below," Jane continued. "Always good to get in with the kitchen staff, and probably the crew as well. George has been helpful, and he's a cheerful body. I'll enjoy nattering away down there much better."

"What if the warden finds you down there?"

"I'll make myself useful to that Dr. Chipp, so I can go anywhere with him. He drops into the kitchen for tea when he's tired."

Jane had met Dr. Chipp in the galley as he was kept busy attending to all the passengers, including those in steerage. He required hot water and Jane said she was happy to keep a kettle boiling for him when he was below decks. Dr. Chipp occasionally asked Jane to help him with his patients. I asked George to convey a note to Captain Hellyer requesting an interview for *All the Year Round* in the dining room at his convenience. Captain Hellyer granted me an interview the night we left Dartmouth.

The dining room was a pleasant wood-panelled room. The captain had tea in front of him and beckoned to a steward to supply me with a cup. It was as good as ours. I pulled my notebook and pencil from my reticule.

"First of all, thank you for your time," I said.

"We'd better do it tonight as we are heading into a storm, and I will be too busy for you." He took a large sip of tea and sat back awaiting for my questions.

I remembered there were one hundred men who were crew or officers. If there was a storm, Captain Hellyer would, indeed, be busy managing them.

I took him through a list of questions about his prior experience: British Navy, a ship's master, but he had not held command before taking on the helm of this private company ship. He was a little older than me, about forty-five or -six, I'd say, bearded, hair receding from his forehead, and bright, intelligent eyes. He seemed to be a methodical thinker, precise and accurate in his answers. I did get the impression he was concerned about the competency of his crew, although he carefully didn't say so. That worried me, but I didn't pursue it.

Mrs. Robb came in about nine o'clock to fetch a pot of hot water. Her eyebrows rose as she saw me. I nodded. Captain Hellyer turned and nodded to her then brought his attention back to me. That was wonderful. Mrs. Robb had now seen me with Captain Hellyer. I didn't need to say anything to her.

After she left, I closed my notebook. "Thank you so much, Captain. I'm sure Mr. Dickens will be delighted to run this piece. Although it will be months before he gets it."

He smiled. "I met him once. He's quite the crusader."

I nodded. "For the rights of the poor, yes."

"He and that wonderfully wealthy woman are trying to do something for the poor women of London."

"Her Grace, Angela Burdett-Coutts. They started Urania Cottage and several other philanthropic ventures. She *is* remarkable and provided clean drinking water for the poor, which suggests a thorough understanding of their basic needs. Some philanthropists want to preach, not help with practical problems."

"Yes, a good woman."

We parted on amiable terms. "I hope to see you here occasionally," he said.

"I'll look forward to that."

I watched him leave and was well satisfied with our rapport.

*Four*

# Troubles on the Sea

CAPTAIN HELLYER'S PREDICTION was accurate. The storm began that evening in a light smattering of showers, but by the next morning was accompanied by strong winds and lashings of rain that seemed to come at us sideways. We'd hit the storm on our sixth day as we left the English Channel and entered the great Atlantic. Huge waves washed the livestock that had been tethered on the deck overboard. It seemed a cruel sea. The storm forced us to stay in our cabin. The masts moaned and creaked. We heard the screams of the remaining livestock as they were thrown about, and the bumps and rattles as loose objects careened around the deck. The ship tossed about unpredictably and, while not impossible, it was difficult to stand upright. We watched each other carefully, but the three of us were not subjected to seasickness.

Jane's meetings with Dr. Chipp in the galley over tea resulted in his request to her to help with basic nursing as Louisa Townsend, one of the first-class passengers, was violently affected by seasickness. She was very ill. Louisa's sister Charlotte was with her but needed her sleep. The ship had a doctor, but no nurses. Dr. Chipp requested Jane take the night shift at Miss Townsend's bedside. I hadn't realized seasickness could be so dangerous. Jane nursed her for a week. Minnie and I tried to keep quiet during the day to allow Jane some sleep.

After two days, when the storm blew itself out, we traipsed around the deck noting the damage. The pigs that had been kept under the forecastle were gone, and there were far fewer passengers promenading—no doubt recovering from nausea.

ON THE MAP HANGING IN the dining room, one of the crew marked our progress with pins. I traced our route south toward the Bay of Biscay and the Azores then across the Atlantic. It looked a long distance.

The days moved slowly as we seemed to be alone in a new universe. It was like a floating city-state with Captain Hellyer the king directing the lives of all inhabitants. His word was law, and I was thankful we were on friendly terms. British law seemed to consider women to be some kind of quasi-humans who didn't require or even want the rights enjoyed by men. That attitude, which had seemed so irksome when I lived under it, looked like a safe haven when I considered the lack of recourse I had to *any* law but the captain's here on the ship.

We entertained ourselves in our cabin, reading aloud to each other, although Jane only listened.

"I don't read so good," she said.

She was a wonderful singer, though, and sang the songs I created, while Minnie played the harmonica. I wrote words to Offenbach's *Galop Infernal* to immortalize Mrs. Robb. We got quite giddy over this and even devised harmony.

*Rattling on this leaky ship*
*Battling all the pesky drips*
*Who are we, few are we*
*Trying hard to kip.*

*Running round the warden who*
*Wants to squash the favoured few*
*Hide from her, slide from her*
*Give the bag the slip.*

We changed the rhythm and belted out the chorus.

*There—we will find riches, despite all the hitches*
*We will then become the great Victoria gentry*
*When we all have gold and riches*
*We will never, never invite her home to tea.*
*Ha!*

It was doggerel, I know, but it was cathartic. Jane taught it to the ladies in steerage and, since Mrs. Robb's name was never mentioned, she didn't realize they were all mocking her. Such petty revenge was satisfying.

We needed to distract ourselves from the monotony and scarcity of the food. Jane did her best, but Mrs. Robb controlled the supplies and gave out only enough for us to subsist on, not enough to create anything tasty. We got salt cod and potatoes so often we hated the sight of it.

I continued to share the occasional cup of tea with the captain in the evenings. He let slip that he was unhappy with the crew.

"There aren't enough of them, Miss Wilson," he'd said. "The men can't be expected to do the work of two, and the company saved money by not hiring the number I asked for. The men are not happy."

How unhappy they were became obvious.

One Sunday morning, we were dressing for our daily walk before breakfast. We'd heard Rev. Scott's loud lamenting to the Almighty and decided to let him importune the Deity without us. I had donned my petticoat, crinoline cage, another petticoat, skirt, chemise, corset, and bodice and was just stepping out the door to leave room for Minnie to dress—three crinoline cages wouldn't fit in our small space—when there was a sudden silence. We looked at each other.

"The engine's stopped. Glory be," Jane said. She glanced out the porthole. There was only the infinite sea.

I hurried out the door and stood near the funnels looking back at the deck. Nothing looked different except there was no smoke drifting into the air. I moved closer to Charles Redfern and Charlotte Townsend, fellow passengers who were speaking quietly near the railing. They included me and told me the coal stokers had mutinied, and the captain had confined them to the brig.

"Manacled," Charles said with, it seemed, some satisfaction.

Who was going to stoke the engines? We were near the equator, where there was no wind for the sails. I joined the ladies now crowding the deck. The crew stood by the rails. The captain came from the wheelhouse and stood above us, resplendent in his navy uniform and ready to address those assembled. When he had our attention and the crowd had quieted, he shouted in his plainly audible baritone.

"You have heard the stokers refuse to work. They have been jailed to consider their position. Without stokers we can't progress." There was a murmur among the crowd, which quickly abated. The captain continued. "We are going to need hands from the passengers if we want to continue on. I will need volunteers."

I was struck by how ingenious the plan was. Here were many able young men, particularly in the steerage class, who might help. They wouldn't need special skills, simply the ability to shovel coal. Many did volunteer. A cheer went up, and we clapped for the willing. I was surprised to see Fredrick Whymper, the artist, and Edward Coleman, the naturalist, also volunteer. I had thought them both decorative rather than practical. I might have had to adjust my opinion of them.

FOR THE NEXT MONTH, THE coal loaded by crew and volunteers kept us on our course to the Falkland Islands. I knew we were passing by the exotic islands of Jamaica and Haiti, but there was nothing to see but the constant waves. I pestered the other passengers to tell me about the British West Indies, but we were a sadly uneducated lot.

"The merchants are still buying and selling slaves there," Mr. Coleman told me. "I hear Jamaica is a beautiful country, but the slave trade is ugly."

I agreed and stared at the horizon as if I could somehow see the land so far from us. I imagined palm trees, sandy beaches, warm water. I'd read Captain Cook's reports from the Sandwich Islands. Perhaps I was confusing his descriptions of those islands with the ones in this ocean.

I retired to my cabin to read and dream. I was lulled from my ennui one day by the sound of many feet running past. We quickly opened our door and saw Charlotte and Louisa Townsend running toward the funnel followed in quick order by Charles and Edward. I followed with Jane and Minnie behind me. It was a terrifying sight. Several crew members, dirty and covered in coal dust, held Captain Hellyer and three officers trapped against the railing. The sailors were bending them back, forcing them toward the sea below. Another mutiny!

I could not think what to do. If they succeeded, we would all be subjected to the whims of the ignorant men who, while they could raise masts and repair decks, likely couldn't navigate. And there would be no one to safeguard the passengers. Mrs. Robb and Rev. Scott were adding to the confusion by insisting all their "girls" return to their cabins. We ignored them. They provided a clucking drone behind us while the mutinous sailors yelled and screamed at the captain in front of us. I wondered if the captain could exert his authority, but things got worse as a huge sailor ran up from the other side of the ship and smashed his fist into Captain Hellyer's face. That was a signal for the others to rip the uniforms from the officers and pummel them. It looked as though the huge sailor was going to throw the captain into the sea.

"I say, mates," one of the passengers said. "Lend a hand here!"

Galvanized, a group of passengers threw themselves into the fray. The remaining officers joined them. A woman screamed. Men yelled. The scene was one of entangled male bodies wrestling and rolling on the deck. I heard the thud and thump of fists on flesh. The fighting passengers and crew beat back the mutinous sailors.

Rev. Scott had abandoned his onlooker position and run back to his cabin, but Mrs. Robb had stayed to watch the insurrection. In a few minutes, the rescue team had overcome the sailors and had them manacled, leaving them lying on the deck.

The captain, bloodied but furious, commanded the sixteen mutinous sailors be confined to the brig next to the engines, where they could suffer the heat in that confined space until he handed them over to the authorities in the Falklands.

I was so relieved the captain had regained control of the ship that I failed to consider the effect of sixteen fewer sailors on the crew.

Charles Redfern was a traveller to Victoria in third class, although his cabin was on the upper deck, so I saw him regularly walking on the deck. He told me a few days after the fight that those who had been jailed were expert sailors, and there were not enough men to operate the sails.

"Not only that," he'd said, "we don't have enough coal to reach the Falklands."

We stared at one another.

"The captain will look for sailors among the passengers," he advised me. I doubted he would be successful. There would be few sailors among the passengers unless they were amateurs and few in steerage because if they had that skill, they would most likely have worked their way across the ocean rather than pay for passage.

But I was wrong. Captain Hellyer found enough experienced sailors and enough who were willing to learn that we soon were sailing smartly with the favourable winds.

We were happy for a week, then we were hit by a storm—a terrifying, wild, vicious storm.

Jane crawled into my bunk with me to decrease the possibility of her flying off the top bunk when a huge swell tipped the ship. We had put everything in boxes and stored them tightly—or so we thought. But what we neglected—a mug, the tin kettle, a pair of shoes—flew through the air and slammed against the walls. We didn't dare open the door to see how the ship was faring.

We could hear water sluicing over the decks with increasing fury, then pouring off the sides. The ship dove down into deep troughs then climbed up to great heights, only to plunge again. My stomach dropped with the ship, and I fought nausea. With the darkness, it got worse. Jane clung to me and I to her.

"Minnie," I called. "Are you all right?"

"Are we going to die?" her brave voice responded.

"Not at the moment," I reassured her. That was true, but I couldn't promise what the next hour would bring. I worked hard to ignore the memories of my night in the Baltic Sea. *Don't think of it, Florence,* I told myself over and over.

I did remember the poem I'd had published when I was nineteen. It was called "Night at Sea" and, when I compared my imaginings then with an actual storm, I judged my former self a foolish romantic. "A pall-like canopy o'er the ocean flings" indeed! This storm was more like a furious, malevolent monster bent on destruction.

With the dawn, the wind abated and gradually the ship returned to its usual slow, undulating progress.

We staggered out on the deck. The three masts were still there, as were the railings. A lifeboat had disappeared, but no one had been washed overboard, which seemed a miracle. We were all quiet. Even Rev. Scott's annoyingly loud prayers had ceased. It took days for the passengers to resume a more normal demeanour.

About two days before we were due to land at the Falkland Islands, Elizbeth Buchanan became ill and died. Dr. Chipp had

"They'll never take a sailing ship if they hear about it from us," Jane informed him. "Bad food and a crew so angry they'd fight the wind to spite themselves. Those poor people in steerage live like rats." It was dark, damp, and depressing. It could have been much better if Mrs. Robb had allowed them to go off ship to wash and pick up supplies.

"Perhaps the government can create standards," I suggested, remembering Mr. Dickens's recommendations for the workhouses.

"I will bear that in mind, but I won't have much influence. I'm junior, don't you know. I am so pleased you ladies came ashore."

"We are happy to leave the ship for a time," I said. "I may be back, as I probably will have more dispatches."

"I have to visit Captain Hellyer with some papers." He seemed struck by an idea. "Perhaps I could save you a trip."

"Don't suggest it," Jane said in some alarm. "You're our excuse for having shore leave."

His eyebrows rose. "I see. In that case, I'll look forward to seeing you here another time."

Jane and I bought eggs on the way back to the ship. We would find some way to cook them. I was anxious to buy a newspaper, but realized the news from England would not have reached here before us. Any newspaper available here would contain news I'd already read before I left home.

Minnie was relieved to see us when we returned and grateful for the meagre fare we had with us and particularly so for the soap we'd brought.

She screwed up her courage and vowed to accompany me the next day.

If I was going to demand another shore excursion, I needed another excuse. While Jane and Minnie stored our purchases in various spots in our cabin, I moved to the dining room with my pen, ink, and paper, and composed an article on the harrowing nature of our voyage for *All the Year Round*. Mr. Dickens would likely publish it. He might even eventually pay me for it.

Captain Hellyer dropped in to pick up a cup of hot tea while I was musing on my writing. He had officers who would get his tea for him and sometimes they did, but he made the best use of his officers, he had told me, and that didn't mean they had to be at his side constantly.

"Sir," I called to him.

"Miss Wilson. You're writing?"

"Yes, an article for *All the Year Round* about the storm and how well the ship came through it."

"Not about the problems we've had?" His tone indicated his worry.

I shook my head. "I believe there may be legal implications around mutinies, and by writing about them I could get the paper in hot water, so no. I'm not writing about that."

"Good."

"But I am curious. What happened to those men?"

"If the Royal Navy agrees, for they have jurisdiction here, the worst of them will serve a sentence here in Port Stanley and be available as crew when their sentences are over. They're skilled. We need skilled sailors. The rest will come back as crew with a promise to behave."

"Do you trust them?"

He looked at me seriously for a moment. Finally, he said, "I need the crew."

I stared at him. That was not reassuring.

*five*

# The Falkland Islands and Up the Pacific Coast of North America

MINNIE DID ACCOMPANY me the next day as I bustled busily to the waiting tender with another missive for Mr. Dickens. We couldn't do that every day, but I managed to wave a letter to my brother and another to Maria Rye at Mrs. Robb as if they were newspaper articles along with the Dickens article, and she let us pass. The letter to Maria contained a scathing report on Mrs. Robb, Rev. Scott, and the lack of amenities for the women in steerage.

We walked for miles along the shore to view the ships from China, California, Australia, and some we couldn't identify. We saw penguins, those amazing creatures with their tuxedo feathers and curious stare. Minnie had her sketch book and made credible pictures of the town and the harbour. I jotted notes about the country and the people. I have always kept a journal—not a daily journal, but sporadic notes of what interested me or what I experienced.

We paused for tea and fruit. We craved fruit. The choice was limited to raspberries.

"Tell me about this governess position you're going to, Minnie. Is this your first position?" She was not yet eighteen. She might be heading into a difficult situation.

She looked out over the harbour, then brought her gaze back to me. "Papa arranged it. There is no work for me in London, and he can't afford to have me on his hands much longer."

"Who are the people you are going to?" Perhaps I could keep an eye on her when we arrived in Victoria.

"The family of Archdeacon Henry Press-Wright in New Westminster. Is that far from Victoria?"

I thought about the map I had tucked away in my mind. "A day's travel by steamship."

"Oh." Her voice sounded small.

"You might quite like it, as New Westminster has an active garrison, so there will be parties and events you can attend. I enjoyed my life as a governess in Russia. I was part of an interesting family and had many opportunities."

I encouraged her. I didn't tell her about the many, many interviews in London when I was trying to find work during which the women of the house thought I would be a servant at their beck and call and would be happy to be paid a pittance. It had been irritating, insulting, and discouraging. I never wanted to be in that position again.

We were thirteen days in the harbour at Port Stanley. The weather was warm and calm as it was spring here. Jane, Minnie, and I managed to get clean and dry, but the women in the lower decks were not allowed on shore, and they remained in the damp, miserable quarters enforced by the fervent Christians in charge of them. There was no real danger for the women in that sleepy town. The danger existed in the minds of Mrs. Robb and Rev. Scott who saw sexual predation everywhere and constantly guarded against it. The women themselves had no voice in the decision; I wondered that they accepted it.

We left Port Stanley on a cool day, sailing past the Strait of Magellan to go around Cape Horn. I'd read about the storms around the cape, so we were careful to store everything in our cabin as securely as possible.

In spite of our anticipation, the ocean was calm and the sailing smooth. There was a celebratory atmosphere on deck as the men had hunted geese when we were in the Falklands and brought many on board. Women from steerage who had the skill plucked and eviscerated the fowl so that we ate roast goose for a week. After that, Captain Hellyer, on the advice of Dr. Chipp, threw the remaining geese overboard for fear they would putrefy and make the passengers sick. I understood his reasoning, but I was sorry to see such tasty food disappear.

The captain told me he expected the winds to pick up after we left the strait, but they did not. The weather stayed calm, the waters flat, and we steamed toward San Francisco under coal power. While the ship was making good time, I heard Charles Redfern tell Edward Coleman we were running out of coal. Two weeks under constant steam and one week from San Francisco, we were in a difficult position.

I was near the funnel, trying to get some fresh air and give my cabinmates some relief from my company, when I heard the captain bellow at his first officer.

"We're out of coal. Get anything that will burn and take it to the engine room. Deck chairs, boxes, tables."

I heard an indistinct murmur from the first officer.

"Yes, even the spare spars. There's no wind. The spars are useless right now. Anything, man. Use your noggin."

No wind and no fuel. We had a limited amount of food and water on board. The Pacific Ocean was a vast and lonely graveyard for the unprepared and the unwary, even close to the coast as we were. I preferred not to starve to death, floating on a powerless ship. I looked around me for flammable objects. Certainly, the deck chairs, the boxes where the life jackets were stored, possibly. I eyed the rope Mrs. Robb had caused to be strung around the deck to contain her female passengers. Would that burn? I'd be happy to see the last of it. Apparently it did burn, as it disappeared that night.

I wondered if the captain would require our extra bunk or even our own beds as fuel. He may have considered it, but stripping the ship of all extraneous wood was enough. On September 10, we sailed to the docks in San Francisco Bay. There was no need of a tender to convey us to shore as we docked adjacent to the wharf.

"What is it this time?" Mrs. Robb asked as she guarded the gangplank.

I waved my envelope at her. "Another missive for Mr. Dickens."

"You can't mail it here."

"There is a post office."

"You don't have their money."

"That's why I first have to go to the bank."

"Women don't deal with banks."

She was trying my patience. "This one does." I pushed past her, and Minnie slipped into my wake.

We hurried down the dock toward the trams that plied the streets in front of us. We stopped for a moment at the side of the street to gaze at the city. It was much bigger than I had expected. I knew the population was about ninety thousand. I hadn't realized that would translate to tall buildings near the bay, and smaller buildings climbing up the many hills. There were people, mostly men, in dark suits hurrying along the streets. Horses and carriages stirred up the dirt and tram bells clanged as the horses pulled the heavy tram cars.

"Are we going to the bank first?" Minnie asked. "I've never been to a bank."

"No. First, we are going to a wash house. We need to be clean and presentable when we go to the bank." We looked down at our dresses, spotted with unidentified food and dirt. It was impossible to stay clean on the boat. "No laundry, though. We will only have time to wash ourselves and sponge off our clothes."

I knew from George the sailor that most people in San Francisco used the bath at the barber's on the main street. That wouldn't do for us, but the barber would know where there was a respectable wash house for women.

We caused a sensation when we stopped at the barber shop. The men froze and stared at us, but the barber was respectful and directed us to a hotel a street away.

"They have two rooms for passengers who come off ships," he said. "It will be safe there."

I thanked him, and we walked up the plank boardwalk to the hotel. The streets of San Francisco were wide and the boardwalk running parallel was wide enough to accommodate two women with hooped skirts walking side by side. We sailed into the hotel, paid the proprietor our sixpence—he was happy to take British money—and spent the next hour bathing, washing our hair, and cleaning our clothes. Much refreshed, we proceeded to the bank.

I changed two British pounds for the new American national currency. The exchange rate was $5.56 for one British pound. Minnie changed one pound. Proprietors apparently still took almost any money as they used to do before the national currency was implemented that year, but there was a charge. For us, the charge was waived.

"We get so few ladies here," the clerk said as he passed us our new money.

"Do you have any hints about investing?" I asked. I didn't have any money to invest, but I was eager to learn.

"The new railway is coming next year. That's where I'd put my money."

I thanked him and thought about the reasons for investing in a railway. Goods could be brought in much more quickly and easily than the present method by ship or across the country by wagons. That would result in more shipping and more profit for railroads.

We proceeded to the post office where I parted with fifteen cents to send my letter to Mr. Dickens.

Then, we were free to explore the city and have a sustaining meal. We rode the streetcar pulled by heavy draft horses, marvelling at the grid pattern of the streets, unlike in England where they tended to follow the topography as they had for centuries. It was confusing to find so many streets that looked straight and similar.

On the advice of the hotel clerk, we found the new Ross House Hotel and joined the diners. For two dollars each we had a substantial meal. I ordered three different vegetables with my beef: cauliflower, turnips, and Lyonnaise potatoes. Minnie had the lamb with mashed potatoes, spinach, and sweet potatoes. We both had apples, raisins, walnuts, and almonds. It was a luxury, and we enjoyed every mouthful. We finished the meal with hot coffee, and I paid an extra fifty cents to get a bag of the fruits and a pumpkin pastry to take to Jane.

On the way back to the ship, we stopped at the market near the docks and each bought a basket into which we stuffed apples, lemons, luscious oranges, some sweets, and biscuits. For all it was September, there was plenty of produce as the growing season here would last several more months.

Jane fell on the baskets when we returned. With a mouthful of apple, she thanked us profusely.

We were gay that night, toasting our coming release from the imprisonment of the ship. I didn't try to leave the ship the next day. I'd seen Captain Hellyer scowling and bustling around the decks, urging the men to get the ship ready for departure. While I wasn't fond of the ship, I needed to be on it when it left. Several passengers who were late returning on September 12 when we hoisted sail were left on the dock. I imagined there would be a legal response to that.

IT WASN'T UNTIL WE WERE well underway and sailing up the coast of California that I discovered from Charlotte Townsend and Charles Redfern that many of the crew had jumped ship in San Francisco and we were even more short-handed than we had been. The extra work that fell on the remaining crew caused much discontent, and one evening when I was strolling along the main deck trying to get some exercise, I saw the captain addressing a group of about eight men.

"So, you refuse to work! Fine!" he yelled. "You are charged with mutiny and confined to the brig. Set on them," he instructed his officers, who did so immediately. The men were hauled off. I doubted they would receive the clemency the others had in the Falklands. The captain was furious.

We sailed into Victoria on September 17. I viewed the shores with their miles of evergreen forests behind them, the low hills, the sparkling blue sea as the answer to my need for a new, independent, profitable life. I breathed the fresh, humid air, smelling the pitch from the conifers near the shore. It was beautiful. I fervently hoped for a delivery from poverty.

*six*

# Arriving in Victoria

THE *TYNEMOUTH* ANCHORED off the shores of Esquimalt, the harbour close to Victoria. We would not be allowed ashore until the following day. I stood at the rail appreciating the way the twilight settled into the woods beyond the beach. The mountains beyond the trees, rising with the grandeur of the Alps, caught the last of the sunlight. I watched as a tender approached and a military man, perhaps a policeman, came aboard. Captain Hellyer took him below. I expected he was to guard the mutineers in the brig.

We spent the night cleaning our clothes and ourselves as well as we could, packing the trunks that Sam had brought to our cabin, and preparing for departure in the morning. However, it was not to be immediate. First, we had to meet the many dignitaries who arrived by small boats. We shook hands with the officers of the Royal Marines who had come to escort us to the newly prepared barracks and with a newspaperman with the outrageous name of Amor De Cosmos, Lover of the World. I wondered what name his parents had given him because I doubt it was that one. Finally, about three in the afternoon, a Royal Navy gunboat, the HMS *Forward,* arrived to begin ferrying us from Esquimalt to James Bay and the city of Victoria.

Minnie was not disembarking with us, but transferring to the paddlewheeler *Enterprise* for a trip across the Gulf of Georgia to her new position in the archdeacon's house in New Westminster. We all cried a little and promised to write. Jane and I boarded the gunboat for Victoria.

I had expected a sense of freedom, exhilaration, and relief at finally coming to the colony. Instead I felt fear. It wasn't a regulated and civilized welcome committee I saw as our boat approached the dock. It was a mob. We walked down the gangplank to a small cleared path between what seemed acres of men, jostling, calling, hovering, as if they'd tear us apart. I gathered Jane close, claiming her as a daughter. I felt thoroughly frightened. The crowd of men seemed to be animals with us their prey. Several police officers and navy officers were supposed to keep order, but the chants, hoots, and calls from the crowd of men could turn ugly quickly, and I doubted the efforts of so few constables could stop them. We hurried along the cleared path up the hill. Thankfully, I saw more blue jackets, more police, arriving. Still, we rushed, the wave of sound from those undisciplined men propelling us forward. When we reached the tall government buildings at the top of the hill, we saw tubs of hot water sitting on the cleared meadow. Some girls were washing their clothes and even their hair. While I longed to do that, I couldn't perform for an audience of hundreds of men. Both Jane and I gazed for a moment on the temptation of that hot water, then followed the others to the marine barracks beside the government buildings, where we would stay until we could find accommodation.

A sailor, a Mr. Marshall, showed us around the recently cleaned barracks.

"Will it do ye', missus?" he asked me. I suppose I was the oldest one there and he expected I was in charge.

In the absence of Mrs. Robb, who had stayed back to speak with a delegation of women, I did take charge. "It will do, but where is the food? Is there not a committee to welcome us, provide at least tea?"

"Strewth! There is. The Victoria Female Immigration Committee." He gestured to the women hovering around Mrs. Robb. "A useless lot to be sure. You'll be needing food. Me and me mates'll see to it."

With that, he disappeared. Jane and I threw our suitcases onto our narrow beds. We explored the kitchen and bathroom facilities. There was hot water. We were thrilled.

Mr. Marshall returned shortly with an abundance of tea, biscuits, and cakes, as well as pots, pans, a kettle, and a teapot. We were, at least, able to alleviate our immediate hunger. Jane and I and several other women began preparing the tea. I worked under Jane's instruction as I was quite useless in organizing food. I trusted that between the Victoria ladies' committee, Mrs. Robb, and the attentions of the navy, we would be provided with our next meals.

Our trunks were delivered and placed at the ends of our beds. Being reunited with my possessions made me feel as if I had reconnected to myself and gave me heart.

We were willing to stay in the barracks for a few days while we washed our clothes and recovered from the long journey, but Jane and I were itching to walk into the city and see the sights. From this we were prevented by Mrs. Robb, who, having sorted out her relations with the ladies on the Victoria committee, was still enacting her warden-like authority over those of us in the barracks. She had caused a fence to be erected around the barracks, and we were not allowed beyond it. Some young women had accepted proposals from the men who had lined our barracks' entrance and gone off with them. One bearded man had stopped Sophia, a young woman from the mission delegation, and proposed. She was taken aback and even more so when he shoved two thousand dollars at her and told her to buy herself some wedding clothes. She looked at the money, then at the man, and accepted. The rest, both Maria Rye's group and the mission group, remained confined to the barracks, awaiting employment or marriage. Once a day, we were allowed to walk around the barracks guarded by constables. Men crowded the fence on the other side and attempted to communicate with individual girls. They were often successful. On Sunday, we were to be herded to Christ Church Cathedral to hear Rev. Scott preach. I couldn't stomach it.

"I'm sick," I told Jane. "And you have to stay and tend me."

Jane sat on my bed and put compresses on my forehead while we enacted a pathetic scene from a play of our own making. We were both reasonably competent actors. Mrs. Robb left us.

As soon as the crocodile procession of reluctant women and girls left for the cathedral, Jane and I put on our finest gowns and bonnets and sashayed out the gate, smiling at the guard.

"Better hurry, ma'am. They've got a head start on you," the guard advised.

"We will make it, I'm sure." Out of sight of the guard, we turned off into the streets of Victoria to explore.

"The way Reverend Scott drones on, we should have two hours before we're missed," I told Jane.

"Only two hours! I'd like to walk and walk until my legs were jelly." She stomped her boots in the dusty path. "Lovely and firm, in't it?"

I agreed. Solid ground was wonderful.

There were few men on the streets this early Sunday morning, and I assumed we looked like a respectable mother and daughter. I'd reconstructed our crinoline cages to a fashionable width, and we glided down the streets regaining our sense of control and purpose with each step. Jane garnered a few compliments from the early risers, which made her eyes sparkle.

"Oh, I do hope you get a position where there'll be parties and gaiety," I said, remembering my own lively youth.

"I'm sure I'll find fun somewhere," she said.

It was wonderful to be walking on solid ground in an area we didn't know to see sights we had never seen before. It wasn't a street of solid stone buildings like I was used to in London. It was a street of wooden buildings constructed without, it seemed, much planning for symmetry or aesthetics. There were a few substantial brick buildings. We walked quickly to Government Street, the only commercial street in this new city, where a newly laid plank sidewalk allowed us to keep our skirts out of the dust. I spotted the bank, a large brick house that looked to have living quarters above it. It was closed, of course. Nothing was open on the Sabbath. I peered into the low window. It looked small, but as long as it was operating, I would be happy. A man came out of a door adjacent. I could see stairs behind him, so I assumed he lived above the bank.

"Good morning, ladies. My name is MacAdam. May I welcome to you to Victoria?"

He was young man in his early twenties. Jane glanced at him with appreciation.

"Good morning," I said. "I am Miss Wilson, and this is Miss Saunders. Can you tell us when the bank will open? I have some business to transact."

"Well now, I can help you there. It so happens I have the keys to the bank. We could conduct that business today."

I was surprised. On Sunday? I suspected he was less interested in my business transactions than he was in prolonging his time with Jane.

He opened the door and ushered us into the small space. The walls were panelled with a light-coloured wood and gave off a smell of pitch. There were three desks and a solid safe about eight feet high and four feet wide. Sunlight fell through the large front window, giving us light to see the comfortable chairs in front of each desk and the ledge along one wall that had two stools tucked under it.

"Is it legal to transact business on Sunday?" I asked as I settled in one of the chairs.

"Not if you are going to sign a contract but, even then, I can date the contract for the next day. Perhaps there is something else I can help you with?"

I presented my credentials, signed some papers—dated the following day—and, after we had conducted that part of the business, Mr. MacAdam opened the safe and retrieved some money. I counted it and placed it in my handbag. I couldn't conceive of a bank opening its doors on a Sunday in London. I inquired about accommodations from the efficient and obliging Mr. MacAdam.

"Mrs. Duffy has a commodious flat free at the moment. She was angry with the three men who rented it from her and had the constable turn them out. I know she has cleaned and refurbished it. She is just up the street. Inquire at the bakery. She is the proprietor while her husband is in the Cariboo."

"It will be open?"

"Well, no. But she will likely be home."

I thanked him and, grabbing Jane's arm, almost ran to Mrs. Duffy's establishment.

The shop was closed, but I could see her through the window cleaning her counter. She was a short woman, a little plump, and from my observation of her activity, energetic. She caught sight of us and invited us in.

"From England, are you? Looking for husbands?"

I shook my head. Jane nodded. Mrs. Duffy laughed.

"I will require a room," I said. "I am going to start a business."

"Oh, then. I'll be happy to show you what I have."

It was four rooms: two bedrooms, a kitchen, a dining room, and a sitting room. The toilet was outside, and there was one water pump for cold water in the kitchen. It would do very well. There was also a bed with a straw mattress, a table and two chairs, a horsehair sofa, and most importantly, a bookcase. There were no curtains or linens.

"Wonderful," I said. "What is the rent?"

"It's fifteen dollars a calendar month."

I almost hugged her, but I was sure that would annoy her.

"Thank you. I would be very happy to take this." It was in the middle of town, right on Government Street. I would be close to all commerce. Mrs. Duffy could advise me on a business to start, as she was in business herself.

I passed her fifteen dollars for the first month's rent and received the keys to the outer door of my flat.

"I will have my trunks delivered," I said. I was not sure how to do that, but Mr. Marshall could advise me. Mrs. Duffy took care of it.

"I'll get Alfred to fetch them. He's good at that. You need to give him two dollars."

"That would be fine. Thank you."

"I'll send him to you today. When will you arrive here?"

"Tomorrow."

"I'll have a new mattress in there for you."

I smiled at her. "I'd be most grateful." Straw was definitely uncomfortable bedding.

The whole transaction took about twenty minutes.

"Could you direct us to a restaurant?" I asked her as we were leaving.

She stood back. "There in't a restaurant open in Victoria, love, except maybe Mrs. McDonald's Restaurant and Oyster Saloon. Hungry, are you?"

I looked at Jane. "Sorry," I said and turned back to Mrs. Duffy. "We have been eating very poor food on the *Tynemouth*, and we were going to treat ourselves to a meal that had vegetables in it."

"Ahh. Come to my kitchen. I'll feed you. It's just soup and bread, but I make it all fresh so you'll get your vegetables."

We followed her down the stairs to her living quarters behind the shop. She gestured to the table and four chairs set around it. We removed our bonnets, gloves, and pelisses and sat at her table. Lunch was wonderful. I paid her a dollar for it, and then we quickly donned our outer garments again and hurried back to the barracks. We wanted to be back before Mrs. Robb sent the constables out looking for us.

I spotted the crocodile line heading down the street as we neared the barracks.

"We're going to get caught," Jane said.

"Probably." I couldn't work up any concern. I was mentally furnishing my new abode with the linens I had in my trunk, the books, the china, and crockery. I was euphoric: I had a flat in the heart of Victoria. I had my credentials established at the bank. I was starting my new life.

Mrs. Robb stamped up to the side of my bed when she arrived.

"I saw you. You were not sick! That was sly. You are under my care and you cannot go out of the compound without my permission. You went out!"

"I did, indeed," I said. "I had business matters to attend to." Before she could sputter another objection, I spoke. "Miss Saunders and I will be leaving you tomorrow. I have engaged a room, and we will settle there."

She blinked, then rallied. "Miss Saunders can't leave until she has a place." She lifted her head as if she had won a battle.

"She has a place. I will hire her." I could keep her with me until she found work.

"You are single, and, therefore, you are not suitable. No. Besides, a Mrs. Chambers has inquired for a housemaid, and I have promised her she can have Miss Saunders."

I expected Warden Robb just that moment had decided that Jane would go there to spite me.

I glanced at Jane and raised my eyebrows. She nodded.

"Very well," I said. "I will relinquish my claim on Miss Saunders and allow her to take up the position with Mrs. Chambers." Not that I could do anything about it, and Jane would need work soon. I just itched to come over the grand lady with Mrs. Robb. She brought out the worst of the gentry hauteur in me.

Mrs. Robb left us, strutting as if she'd bested me.

"Jane, if you don't like the position at Mrs. Chambers's house, just come to me. I'll make room for you while you look for something else."

"You will?"

"Yes, of course."

"I'll be a housemaid. Won't you be too grand for me?"

I thought about it. In England our friendship would be impossible, but things were different here. "This is the colonies. I have every intention of bending the rules, starting with you. We *will* stay friends, won't we?" I was suddenly afraid Jane would not want to know me.

She grinned. "We will."

That was a relief. I was going to need a friend. I was sure of that.

THE RELIABLE ALFRED, SEVENTEEN IF he was a day, came with his horse and cart and conveyed both me and my trunks to my new home. I looked around me. In this collection of huts, shacks, solid houses, dirt, and dust, I was going to make my fortune.

*seven*

# Life in Victoria

MY FIRST TASK was to examine my accounts. I had enough money to live for three months and establish a business. After that, I must show a profit. I had shelter at Mrs. Duffy's establishment and some furniture. I needed to eat. I had never cooked and didn't plan to learn now. I arranged with Mrs. Duffy to have an evening meal with her for a small sum. I would manage to live on sandwiches, fruit, and tea the rest of the day. Once I had that sorted, I roamed the streets of Victoria looking for the household goods I had neglected to bring: a kettle, a long fork for toasting bread, a butter dish, a dish pan, and a chamber pot.

Mrs. Duffy had pointed me in the direction of Wharf Street, which was close to the water and the warehouse of Caire & Grancini, where, she assured me, I'd find everything I wanted.

Seagulls screamed at the sky. Horses clopped past me. Wagons rumbled by carrying kegs that rattled as they shifted around It was reassuringly busy. The seaweed smell from the harbour was particularly strong. The tide must be out. I picked my way through the mud to the huge building where I found spades, rope, pullies, barrels, supplies for miners, as well as the usual household necessities. I paid with the cash I had, but I was determined to order cheques from the bank. I arranged to have my purchases delivered and hurried home to receive them.

Once I had settled the new acquisitions in my flat, I ventured out again to look for food. Mrs. Duffy told me to seek out the Chinese pedlar who sold vegetables and fruit from his large wicker baskets. I found him at the corner of Government and Yates. He spoke some English and, as I knew no Chinese, we managed with his English and sign language to enact an exchange of a few cents for a dozen red apples, several carrots, and a cabbage. I had trouble getting him to understand my need for eggs. It was clear he didn't sell them, but I wanted to know who did. I finally resorted to miming laying an egg. (I used to be quite competent at charades in my mother's drawing room. She'd be horrified to find me performing in the street, but I wanted those eggs.) My Chinese pedlar found the process highly diverting, and we were both laughing when he finally understood and directed me down the street. I found a dairy near the edge of town and procured some milk, eggs, and butter. I had a cold larder in my kitchen, where, at this time of year, the night air kept produce cool. I just had to remember to close the grates in the day to keep the warmer air out.

The basket I'd bought at Caire & Grancini was full and a heavy load for me to carry back to my flat. It was satisfying to unload all my purchases and find that my new accommodation was comfortable and comforting.

I would arrange for my laundry to be done by Sam Chong's, which, according to Mrs. Duffy, did good work.

The curtains and furniture would do for now. My table would act as a desk. The bookshelves loaded with my books invited me to hours of entertainment and learning. I just had to devise a plan to sustain all this.

I talked it over with Mrs. Duffy.

"You might as well call me Betsy," she said as we sat together at her kitchen table.

"Florence," I said. Class distinction didn't seem to be important here in Victoria, although I expected the aristocrats here would insist on it. I was middle-class, not even gentry any more. I would adapt.

First, I asked her about a home for my Rose du Roi. "Do you have a place for it?" It was currently managing to live in a pot on the table in my flat.

"The very place," Betsy said and dashed out the back door. I followed her to the small garden at the rear of the house.

"Right here," she said. "The soil is good. It's sheltered, and it gets full sun."

I agreed it was the perfect spot and promised to settle it in there later that day. We returned to our meal and our conversation.

"Betsy, what business is needed in this town?"

"Lots," she said as she dished out the savoury lamb stew into bowls. Her own bread accompanied it. I was grateful.

She sat down and picked up her spoon. "Lots of businesses are needed: a milliner, a seamstress, another doctor, another chemist, a greengrocer, someplace to buy gifts and paper, a school for the older children, a music store, a knife sharpener, another blacksmith, another livery stable, a milk delivery service . . ." She paused and thought. "And a hairdresser."

I stared at her. "That's quite a list."

She blew on her stew to cool it. "We have so many new people arriving all the time who need quite a lot."

I thought over her list of needs later when I was back upstairs in my flat. I didn't want to be a teacher again. It kept me away from all but my pupils, which made it a lonely occupation. I didn't have the skills to fulfil many of the opportunities Betsy had listed, but I could sew a fine seam, so perhaps I could take that work to start. What attracted me most was a stationery store. I could envision selling papers, pens, pencils, art supplies, and books—many, many books. I could read some of them before I sold them. That business would take more capital than I had at the moment, but I could look for a suitable premises and start planning.

In the first week, I found work with the family of Dr. Helmcken, Hudson's Bay Company surgeon, who lived close by at 638 Douglas Street. I worked mostly for Mrs. Helmcken, who supervised her family's wardrobes. Mrs. Duffy had recommended me to them and they seemed happy to welcome me. The Helmckens had had four sons and three daughters, but three had died and only Amy, Dolly, Jimmy, and Harry survived. I thought of my mother's lost babies. It was all too common. Still, there was enough work to keep me steadily employed. The girls were pleasant and well-mannered, although they all treated me as a servant. It was amusing at times, but grew irksome. Their house was small for such an important family and certainly smaller than the house where I'd grown up in London. The Helmckens practised the kind of social classification that occurred in England in their own twisted way. I was the seamstress in the Helmcken household, a servant. I would not be invited to parties even though in England Dr. Helmcken and his family would not be invited as guests to my mother's house, as they would not be considered to have high enough social rank. I did not like where Victoria's social division placed me.

The positive side of my social position was that I could wander around Victoria without restrictions. I found a Chinese restaurant where I discovered the joys of lightly cooked fresh vegetables and deep-fried fish. It was a treat I savoured at least once a week.

The work at the Helmckens' wasn't arduous. The doctor was rarely around, but I heard from the children how he had single-handedly saved everyone from smallpox in the spring when that savage disease had swept into the city.

"He even vaccinated the Indians," Dolly said, as if Indians were somehow not part of society.

Governor Douglas was not unsympathetic to the problems faced by the aboriginal people, who were being pushed off their land and victimized, but Joseph Trutch, the upcoming politician set to take over from Douglas, was vicious in his contempt for them. His attitude spread among the gentry, those with property and money, until it was almost a norm. I expected Trutch was afraid of the Indians as they were numerous and often armed.

They had their own rules and traditions which he didn't know and which were, therefore, suspect. The population was about four thousand colonists and about five thousand Indians. There were also many more miners and emigrants who stayed only a few days in Victoria and moved farther north and thus were not counted in the census. The two societies, white and native, rarely mixed, but smallpox was a common enemy and vaccination prevented deaths in everyone.

"But he didn't vaccinate all of them," Amy said. "Daddy doesn't think they should get everything we do as they aren't really part of us and shouldn't really be here."

I said nothing. I was a servant, after all, but I marvelled at the way in which they could accept contradictions. As far as I knew from Betsy, Mrs. Helmcken's mother, the wife of Governor James Douglas, was the daughter of a French man and a Cree woman. That meant these girls were also part Indian. Did they just pretend they weren't?

Betsy later told me that in spite of all the good Dr. Helmcken did in the city, he had let down the Indian population badly.

"Scandalous it was," Betsy said. "He kept Governor Douglas from establishing a smallpox hospital and carrying out a better vaccination system. The whites got most of the vaccine. We had lots of vaccine, but Dr. Helmcken just didn't see the need to protect the Indians. Thousands died. Scandalous," she repeated.

I worked for Dr. Helmcken, but I didn't trust him. He paid me on time—I charged a goodly amount—and I appreciated that, but I didn't like his politics. By November, I had earned enough money to add to my stake from the Female Middle Class Emigration Society and look for a store premises. I was grateful to the society for giving me the money, so I didn't have to be anyone's servant for long, or rely on my work hours for mere sustenance. I wanted a business and profit.

"On Government Street," Betsy advised. "It's the best shopping district, and it's only going to get busier."

I found just what I needed at the St. Nicholas Building nearby on the east side of Government Street. It had a flat above that came with the store premises. It was a of solid brick construction, looked out over James Bay, and was both central and accessible. The broad wooden sidewalks of Government Street encouraged pedestrian traffic as women could walk without getting mud on their hems. I could get shoppers who came down Government Street to shop at Zeiner's pharmacy, Giomore's clothier, Mrs. Duffy's bakery, or stop for tea at the Colonial Hotel. The Weiler Brothers' department store was a star attraction. The clothier and outfitters W. & J. Wilson was well-established and had a good clientele. Another Wilson, Thomas, was a draper who also attracted the shoppers. Thomas Harris, our mayor, had his meat market on Government Street. William Searby, the chemist, did as well. I was particularly interested in the Literary Institute that held its meetings above the chemist's. I hoped they would collect newspapers. I was desperate to read a newspaper that wasn't three months old. I wanted to know how the civil war in the United States was going. Who would win that? And what was happening in my old world of Russia? Or even London for that matter. I'd had a letter from Thomas, two in fact, but he told me about his family and the theatre world, not politics. We could be on an alien planet here in Victoria for all we heard about the world.

I decided to stay with Betsy and rent out the flat above the store for more than I paid Betsy. I gave three months' rent for the store and flat to the bank, who were acting for the owner. Then I hired a carpenter to build shelves and a counter. I bought a second-hand till from a friend of Betsy's and an old safe to store money and ledgers.

Once those were installed, I bought paint from Caire & Grancini and painted the store a pale yellow and the shelves a dark brown. It looked inviting. I rented the flat above to a young newspaper man, Hilary Payne, whom I'd met at the Literary Institute meetings. He picked up news like a crow picked up shiny articles and was generous in passing on what he knew. He had a separate entrance and stairs, so he came and went without bothering me, but I did enjoy it when he visited me in the store. So far, he'd paid his rent on time. It took six weeks to get everything ready and supplies ordered and delivered, but I was ready to sell products by December. It amazed me how helpful everyone was and how quickly I was ready for business.

I had received an order from San Francisco, so had new fountain pens, ink in blue, black, and green, pencils, erasers, Charles Dickens's latest—*Great Expectations*—more novels, a few science books, and some bibles. Surprisingly, the bibles sold first. Victoria was full of rough men, even violent men, but the bibles sold. I ordered more. I started a library at my store, although another woman proprietor had also started one. The subscriptions added a little to my coffers. I sold tickets for the theatre. That meant I got a free ticket for myself and took in as many concerts, plays, and lectures as I could manage.

If the moon was interested in the world as it drifted over it, it would see Victoria as a pinprick at the south end of Vancouver Island, hugging the coast of the large mainland of British Columbia. In a world of exotic locales such as Turkey, Egypt, Russia, and Africa, the moon could be forgiven for ignoring such a small place. But Victoria was busy and lively that fall. Those concerts included some of the most sought-after entertainers. Charles and Ellen Kean were here in December. Their performance was riveting. I wrote to Thomas about them. He had been unsuccessful in hiring them for his theatres and I knew he'd be interested to know they had performed in Victoria. There was always something to do and something to observe.

I noticed an upper floor flat across the street from me was occupied by two young women. From the steady stream of men who entered their stairway entrance, I assumed they were running a brothel or, at least, a two-woman enterprise. They looked prosperous and occasionally came to my store for ribbons and greeting cards.

"Violet," the blond one told me. "I live across the street."

"Florence," I said. "Welcome."

"Thanks."

"Are you doing quite well financially?" I asked. It was a question I'd never ask in London, but somehow it seemed socially acceptable here. But then, I didn't have any rules about what was socially acceptable with a prostitute in London or Victoria.

"It's a fair cop," Violet said. "Me and Maisie will have enough soon to retire. We're going to start a fish shop. Me and Maisie are from the seaside, you know. We know about fish. You do when you're from Brighton. Started guttin' them when just a nipper with me mam."

"How will you start selling fish?"

"We'll get the Indians to fish for us. Pay them and resell. It'll be fresh. We know how to keep fish fresh. Then we can take more time off, relax a bit. Maybe get ourselves a family. Maybe."

"It's possible in this country?" I asked.

"You got it. Most things are possible here. You just have to have a hard heart for a while."

I didn't quite understand that, but I nodded.

At first, I had only neighbours for customers, but soon the monied upper class, the workers, and the miners arrived to buy paper, pens, art supplies, toys, and gifts. The sailors of the British Navy in Esquimalt were numerous, and they and their officers frequented my store and seemed to buy more books than anyone else. My biggest problem was getting goods from San Francisco in time to fill my shelves. Selling from those shelves was effortless. People wanted the accoutrements of gracious living now; they didn't want to wait months to have them shipped from California or Britain. I simply had to keep ahead of them. I marked everything up, of course. Everything in my store was double the price I paid for it. My bank account grew.

I sold some needles, thread, and wool, but no yard goods. I didn't have room on my shelves for reams of cotton or wool. One morning, a young Salish woman came in the store. She hung back by the door until I smiled and gestured at her to come in further. She said hello in English, and I said, "*Kla how ya tillicum?*" in the patois used for trade. I had learned a few words from the miners, who always seemed ready to educate me. Beyond those few words, I had no understanding of the Salish language. She needed needles, but didn't have money. She offered me some beadwork. I suggested she bring me fish, and I would sell her beadwork as it was worth much more than the needles. We worked this out in charades, which left us both laughing.

I gave her a packet of needles. She left but returned before closing with a beautiful salmon.

Betsy was ecstatic. "I can cook that, and we can eat it for a week."

We had baked salmon, salmon cakes, salmon casserole, and salmon sandwiches. It was delicious. I had never tasted fish so delicate and flaky.

The young woman returned the next week. I had sold her beaded moccasins to a miner who said they would be wonderfully warm when he returned to the Cariboo. I took a ten-percent commission and gave her the rest of the money. She put the coins into a small deerskin purse she had hung around her neck and tucked into her dress.

This time she had another young woman with her. They both had golden brown skin, dark brown eyes, and dark hair, but they looked quite different. The first woman had clear skin and was a beauty; the second had smallpox scars on her forehead and cheeks. She had survived but was scarred. I felt a sudden spurt of anger against those who kept the vaccine from her.

I struck my chest. "Florence," I said, then pointed to the young woman I'd met the previous week.

She stared at me for a moment. "Kai," she said, or something like that. I repeated it. She corrected me. Her name sounded more like Kay. I called her Kay, and she beamed. I pointed to her friend.

"Tanta," she said.

I repeated "Tanta" and must have gotten fairly close, as her friend nodded and smiled.

Kay mimed that Tanta needed a packet of needles. I passed over the needles. When they left, I put "one packet of needles" against Tanta's name in my ledger.

That evening Tanta arrived alone with a sack full of clams.

That week we had fried, breaded clams, clam chowder, and clam casserole. I liked the chowder better than the casserole.

I noticed Kay and Tanta only came into my store if there were no other customers. They knew they were welcomed by me, but they were no doubt aware of the prejudice of others.

Hilary Payne often dropped into the store just before closing to gossip. He had a newspaperman's nose for any tidbit of information carelessly dropped.

"Douglas made treaties with the Indians on Vancouver Island, so we have peace. Trutch wants to tear up those treaties and subjugate the Indians out of existence. His way will cause problems."

"You mean he is going to ignore the law that says the Indian people are entitled to their land?"

"He is," Hilary said. "And he'll get away with it because the businessmen in this town see profit to be made out of that land."

I shouldn't have been surprised. I knew British law was applied unequally. Women had far fewer rights than men. As a single woman, I had more rights than a married woman, but still, I was not equal before the law. The notion that British men were destined to be in charge of the universe, including women, Indians, the Chinese, and anyone who was not them was pervasive. I was frustrated to find it becoming established here.

I settled into life in Victoria. Hilary, Betsy, and I attended the Anglican church on Sundays. The music was good but not excellent. I missed the choice of concerts at the churches in London and the plays and musicals in Soho, although I was grateful we had some here. My brother wrote occasionally to tell me what his theatres were producing. I envied him the experiences. The theatre in Victoria, at the corner of Government and View Streets near my shop, was named, unimaginatively, the Victoria Theatre, housed in a former Hudson's Bay warehouse. It had been purchased by Judge Matthew Begbie. I hadn't met him yet, but he must have had a passionate interest in the theatre to spend that much money on it. He'd renovated the warehouse into a passably good theatre and supported the concerts and plays which took place there. I paid a subscription to attend. Apparently, the theatre had a problem with drunken men interrupting the show, so had employed officers to keep order. I'd wondered at the presence of guards when I'd first attended.

The Victoria Philharmonic was an amateur society, but we who were starved for good music were tolerant and enjoyed the concerts. Plays were put on by the Amateur Dramatic Association of Victoria. We saw the occasional Shakespeare, but usually the fare was political satire. I appreciated it, as did most people in the city. The audience usually contained the elite, such as the governor, Judge Begbie, and, of course, the ever-present British Navy.

"I miss my mother," I told Hilary and Betsy one evening as we walked home from a particularly biting satire on the quarrels in the legislature. "She was a playwright, and we used to have practices at our house when I was young."

"Can you act?" Hilary asked.

"I can, although I haven't done it for years."

"You sound as though you miss that too," Betsy said.

"I hadn't realized how much." I thought about the excitement of writing and producing a play. I liked that even more than acting. I missed Jane as she was an enthusiastic singer and could have added to our entertainment, but she was still working for Mrs. Chambers and only got a half-day relief from her work. She told me in one of her quick visits that she was stepping out with a Mr. Nesbitt, so she might be free of the drudgery of a servant soon.

"I don't suppose you can join the actors," Betsy said. "For one thing, they are all men. And for another, becoming an actress would condemn you to a lower social class and might affect your business."

Sadly, that was true.

*eight*

# Establishing Myself in Victoria

THE STREETS OF Victora were nothing like the streets of London. Everything in London was stone or brick. Everything in Victoria was wood. A match could flatten this city in an afternoon. The buildings were wood. The pavements weren't pavement but wood, and wide enough that women with their yards of skirts could pass each other. I had reduced my skirts to a modest additional six inches circumference. It was cumbersome to work in my store with extraneous yardage of an extra twelve inches around me. I was unfashionable and hung up my crinoline cage to be taken out only for formal occasions. It felt wonderful to have shucked off that hoop and the weight of the extra skirt. I did get some stares as I walked to work, but once in my shop, the customers seemed oblivious to my slimmer look. I'd seen more scandalous garments on women. One woman—I think she was a woman from the goldfields—walked through town in trousers. That intrigued me. Was that acceptable in Barkerville? Would I be able to reduce my heavy weight of skirts when I finally made it north? I was sure I could sew myself a pair of trousers; I wasn't sure I'd have the courage to wear them. But I bought fabric in a tough worsted wool and made myself a pair that looked like a straight skirt until I moved, then it was clear the skirt was divided. I thought they looked elegant, but I hadn't worn them out of my flat yet.

For the first month, my shelves were not full and I only paid my expenses. After the second month, I had a small profit, and after the third, I had a very good profit. The gold was flowing into Victoria from the Cariboo goldfields, and people had money to spend. Betsy and I talked about it. Some evenings Hilary Payne forewent his usual pub habitat and joined us. He had information about the gold strikes in Barkerville.

"People are picking up gold right beside the town," he said.

"Fortunes are being made, but not by my Abel," Betsy said. "He's always staking a claim *beside* someone who strikes it rich. It's never Abel who finds the gold."

"What else can he do besides mine for gold?" Hilary asked.

"He's a good carpenter. He should come back to Victoria and build houses and ships. He could make a steady living."

"But he's got the gold bug," I said.

"He does at that. It's strong."

I knew it was strong. I had it myself. Not the lure of the gold itself, although I wanted to understand how it was mined and how to make money from it, but the possibilities in a smaller place like Barkerville where social class was less controlling and a woman could expand her business. I paid attention to the way in which I made profit in my business. Toys did well, as did newspapers and books. I studied Henry Newbury's book on gold and listened to the miners who conversed with one another as they examined the books on my shelves. I tried to learn as much as I could. My stationery shop was giving me the steady income Betsy admired, but it wasn't giving me the excitement and challenge I wanted.

I read The *Daily British Colonist* and was highly entertained by some of the articles and advertisements. "Fresh Oysters Directly from Sooke. Wanted a Young Man to Open the Oysters." I imagined a pile of oysters patiently waiting for a worker. A determined woman advertised, "Caution: All persons are hereby cautioned from purchasing a part of the Real Estate of Mr. Edward Green, recently purchased of Mr. James Thorne, the said Mr. Green having no right to title or dispose of it without my consent or signature, the same being subject to my right of dower—Elizabeth Thorne."

I sensed a quarrel in there of huge import. I didn't know Elizabeth Thorne, but I wanted to.

The report that interested me the most was on the Cariboo goldfields. "There are about sixty claims on Williams Creek which have paid well during the last season." My feet itched when I read that. I was encouraged by information further down in the article. "Cameron holds three claims of 100 feet each: one by purchase, one by pre-emption, and one for his wife who was allowed to hold it by Judge Begbie. There are other instances of females holding claims in the Cariboo."

Then, there was the promise of more riches. "Jack of Clubs. This creek is very highly spoken of by the miners, and if it turns out as expected, will give, next year, employment to five thousand men." I needed to be there by next year. I didn't let Hilary or Betsy know the intensity of my drive to get to the Cariboo.

"Judge Begbie goes up to Barkerville to adjudicate trials," Hilary said. "He says there are thousands of men there, digging up the streams and sluicing from the creeks." It must have been a difficult task to control the men, many from the United States south of us, who'd flowed through Victoria since 1858 on their way to goldfields of the Fraser Canyon and north.

I'd met Judge Matthew Begbie. He was the Chief Justice of Vancouver Island and the Colony of British Columbia and travelled extensively. He was a friend of the Helmckens and the Douglases and, when he was in Victoria, a strong supporter of the theatre.

"I understand you sing opera," I said to him when we met at one of the Literary Institute meetings.

"I do."

"What's your favourite role to sing?"

"Oh, Figaro, certainly."

"Rossini's *The Barber of Seville*. I have seen it." It had come to the Soho district when I lived there and Thomas had obtained tickets for us.

"Most amusing," he said.

Judge Begbie was a strong supporter of drama of any kind and was pushing for the development of a regular theatre. It was a struggle to create an active arts community when so many people were transient, just passing through Victoria to the goldfields or to settlements beyond Vancouver Island. I wanted to be part of the burgeoning theatre world, but I was too busy to be much help. Commerce was important to me, and I concentrated on improving my share of it.

"The banks are getting rich taking in the gold; outfitters are getting rich selling picks and shovels," Hilary said.

"I've had a lot of bread going out the door," Betsy agreed.

"They come into my shop for paper and pens to write letters home, mostly to sweethearts, or what I expect they hope will be sweethearts," I contributed. I'd heard many a miner's story of a lost love. A lonely young man of about twenty-one asked me to write to a Susan Tregath in Cornwall, asking her to come out to marry him if he sent her the fare.

"Can you afford first class?" I asked him.

"How much?"

I told him. He thought about it.

"It would be a good investment, wouldn't it?"

"Very good," I agreed.

He signed the letter and we sent it off. I hoped Susan could read.

"The lack of women here is a problem," Hilary said.

"Men are desperate," I agreed. I did feel sorry for some of them. Some women were desperate as well. I thought of some of the young girls on the *Tynemouth* who had grabbed the chance to leave the workhouse or servanthood and take their chances on a miner in the colonies.

Hilary was curious. "Do they propose marriage to you—or worse?"

I didn't think an affair would be necessarily worse than marriage, but I didn't want to shock Hilary. "A marriage proposal a week," I assured him. "None of them the least bit tempting."

The last one was Michael Horner. He was about thirty, well-dressed and well-spoken.

"I did well in Yale, where the gold was easy to get. I saved it and bought a house here in Victoria. You would live the life of a gentlewoman, and I would provide."

It sounded profoundly boring, but I didn't want to injure his sensitivities. "This is an excellent proposal, Michael, but I am determined to get to the goldfields myself and do not wish to remain in Victoria." I was going to suggest he introduce himself to a few women acquaintances of mine, but decided his love life was not my responsibility. Not all proposals I received were as delicate or refined. Some were crude and some were crude but honest.

"Come on, gel. You aren't getting any younger. I'm na' so bad." That was Jake Anderson from Glasgow. I had grinned at him.

"Ah, Jake. Find someone else."

He'd shrugged and accepted the refusal easily. He probably proposed to a woman a week.

"Really?" Betsy said surprised. "That many proposals?"

"Really. Even at my great age. I feel sorry for them, but not so sorry I'd marry those who have asked."

They nodded, agreeing that at the great age of forty, I was past being interested in marrying. It was true. That didn't mean I was uninterested in men. I found the occupations of men interesting; they had so many more opportunities than women. More men seemed to have educated themselves and so could discuss more subjects than most women. That was attractive, even seductive. I found their physical bodies immensely compelling, and I was curious about what love-making would be like. I'd imagined it with several men, but I hadn't yet found a man that had enough attraction for me to risk my reputation and pregnancy. Social rules did constrain one. My dreams were often exciting.

I put my mind back on the conversation. Hilary, Betsy, and I talked about the civil war between the American states.

"President Lincoln's Emancipation Proclamation at the beginning of this year angered the southern states, especially the plantation owners. I get the *Daily Republic* and the *Daily Herald* from San Francisco. Of course, they are a month or so late with the news," Hilary informed us.

"But at least you get the news. Can you put those papers in the Literary Institute reading room when you are finished with them?" I asked. "I feel so cut off from current affairs. I might as well be in a distant desert." I hoped Victoria would get a library soon.

"I don't miss it at all," Betsy said. "I have enough to deal with right here."

"I can see that," I said agreeably, "but I like to know what's going on."

"The slave owners protest they will go bankrupt if the slaves demand payment for work." Hilary offered the southern reasoning.

I thought there were ways to work around that. "When Britain outlawed slavery in 1834, slave owners were compensated by the government quite handsomely, so they *made* money when they freed their slaves. Simon Fraser had 237 slaves for which he claimed compensation. Yes, he and the rest of the aristocracy lost their free labour, but they were compensated financially by the government."

Hilary shook his head. "That policy is a cautionary tale. Britain is still paying off that debt. The north did offer compensation, but it was well below the value of the slaves, so the south isn't impressed."

"Tell me about the gold in California." I directed the conversation where I was most interested.

"Not a lot of opportunity left there. Mines are well-established. Not many pickings left."

I'd heard that from some of the conversations at the Literary Institute. Because the society was made up mostly of men, the conversation often turned to business.

"They'll be some mines that will pay for many years around San Francisco, but the easy pickings are gone. Men will move north, following the rush of '58."

"Still, lots in the Cariboo, though," another had said.

I repeated that conversation to Hilary and Betsy.

Betsy snorted. "Dreams! It's all dreams."

"Hey, no, Betsy. I'm sorry your Abel hasn't been lucky, but there is lots of gold flowing into this city from Barkerville," Hilary protested.

"And Horsefly River, Keithley Creek, and The Forks," I murmured, remembering the settlements the members of the Literary Institute had listed. I found the names of the goldfields fascinating.

Betsy saw the fields as a get-rich-quick delusion. I saw it as a chance for a new life. We were both right. She was right in that luck played a part in success; but careful business practices and an intelligent assessment of opportunities played a part as well. The biggest detriment to accessing the goldfields of the Cariboo for me was actually getting there.

I sold maps to miners travelling to the Cariboo and had many a conversation about the different routes. Some were mere walking trails and some were pack trails. There was a wagon trail part of the way.

"Now, you take the Port Arthur route," said Jimmy Pearson, a seasoned veteran of two years in the goldfields. "That's the best. Take the steamer to Port Arthur up the Fraser River and Harrison Lake, where you jump on the Dietz and Nelson Stage. That stage takes you in wagons and paddle steamers from the end of Harrison Lake to Lillooet, where the Fraser and Thompson rivers meet nearby. There you get Barnard's Express."

"Is it a safe route?" I was thinking of rock slides and Indian attacks, both hazards I'd heard about from miners. Barnard's Express used only a light stagecoach—not secure protection against any kind of attack.

"The first fifteen miles or so north of Lillooet is a bit dodgy, snaking along the cliffs above the river the way it does. It's easier after that, if a tad rough, to Soda Creek. From there, it's a breeze on the paddle steamer up to Quesnelmouth. Then it's a long horseback or mule trek to Barkerville."

It would take time, endurance, and money to take that trip. The cost of hiring horses, a guide, and pack mules for my goods was, at the moment, prohibitive. I would watch and wait for my chance to leave Victoria, putting away every dollar that came my way. The Royal Engineers had started on a new Cariboo Wagon Road up the Fraser Canyon from Yale, but that would not open this year, and perhaps not even next. I wasn't going to wait for a better road. A better road would bring more miners. I didn't want too many miners staking claims before I got there.

There had been an Indian uprising in the vast plateau west of Barkerville.

"Understandable," Judge Begbie had said. "Settlers are taking land that the Crown hasn't negotiated treaties for. It's land grabbing as far as the Chilcotin people are concerned."

I was confident I could deal with miners, bankers, business people, and the usual spread of personalities a society collected, but I wasn't equipped to deal with quarrels between settlers and the original people of the land. Where would I fit into that society?

*Wherever you can,* I told myself.

I didn't know how the local tribes around Barkerville felt about the influx of miners into their lands. Perhaps the same way the Chilcotin people did. I had avoided guns so far in my life and didn't want to start using them now. I had been part of a diplomat's household. I'd seen how talking often worked much better than force. I asked Judge Begbie to teach me a few words of the local dialect. He travelled in that area and was an accomplished linguist. I thought language would be a more useful skill than marksmanship. I already spoke French, German, and some Russian. I should be able to manage another language. He was agreeable but had little time, so I had only one hurried lesson after a Literary Institute meeting.

I BANKED MY PROFITS FROM my stationery business and my rental property. I watched and planned. I took advice from the miners who came to my shop.

"You can't take big steamer trunks, you know, missus," an older, dapper-looking, prosperous miner told me. "At least, you can take them on the stage coach and the paddle steamer, but you can't take them from Quesnelmouth to Barkerville. The mules can't handle that. You need pack bags. You can get them at Caire & Grancini."

I dutifully bought the awkward canvas packs, but hoped I could get someone to bring my trunks the last section of the trip so I wouldn't have to try to cram everything into those bags. Slowly over six months, I started acquiring what I thought I would need.

JUDGE BEGBIE GAVE ME GOOD advice, and I talked to anyone else at the Literary Institute meetings who had experience in the Cariboo. I spent time in the coffee houses and listened to the stories of mines, riches, feuds, and even murders. Barkerville was a rough place, but it was an opportunity for me. I worked hard at my shop and by May 1864, I had enough money with the sale of my inventory to leave for the Cariboo.

*nine*

# Up the Fraser River

In spite of the dire warnings I'd received about limiting my baggage, I packed all my books, household goods, and clothes into trunks. I had considered the wild nature of the country I would be living in and purchased a pair of boys' work boots from Caire & Grancini. I would likely do a great deal of walking and much of it in mud; I had no intention of breaking an ankle. The clerk at the store sold me some dubbin to waterproof them. I was going into the mountains. It would rain there.

"You need to break them in," the clerk told me. "You sit on the edge of the bathtub wearing the boots and immerse them in the water. When they are soaked, wear them around until they dry on your feet. It takes quite a while. Then put the dubbin on."

I did that and wore those boots in my flat, clumping around the small rooms feeling awkward, like a clown with unwieldly feet, until they dried to the shape of my feet. I hoped the clerk was right and they would be comfortable. I needed to avoid blisters. Blisters could become infected, and infection could be deadly.

I'd studied the routes. I compared the lake route via Port Arthur with the Yale route, a continuous trip from New Westminster to Yale then a difficult road to Lillooet, which was not yet officially open. Barnard's Express stagecoach company was offering an inaugural trip on the unofficial route for those adventurous enough to attempt it. It would be faster than the lake route, but more dangerous. Next year, the Cariboo Wagon Road from Yale would be complete and declared officially safe. I wasn't going to wait. The new road from Yale snaked up the Fraser River along the edge of a sheer canyon. Indians had had a pack trail along that route for years, but it had been narrow, not even wide enough for a mule. The Royal Engineers, with workers from the local Indian bands, from the towns and cities, and from China, were blasting through rock and widening the road. I would be one of the first passengers; I couldn't resist it. I bought tickets for Captain Irving's boat *Reliance* for the trip up the Fraser to Yale and Barnard's Express, the BX, from Yale to Barkerville.

My Rose du Roi had grown to waist height and was full of buds. I couldn't bear to disturb it, so I snipped off three short stalks, wrapped them in wet cheesecloth, and placed them in a tin of sawdust. I tucked them carefully into one of my trunks. Once I had all my household goods packed, I added more trunks. The steamship companies—there were several of them owned by Captains Flemming, Millard, Irving, and Moore—were vying with each other to attract the most freight. With such competition, passenger fares were low—and freight costs were extremely low. This couldn't last or they'd lose money, but it was advantageous for me at this time. I'd heard miners talk in my shop about how they longed for sweets and soap, so I bought those. I bought spirits, which I knew I could sell quickly—whiskey and brandy—as well as staples such as flour and oatmeal, and packed seven trunks of commodities. The crew of the *Reliance* accepted my trunks without any difficulty. They were used to large quantities of freight destined for the Cariboo.

Early in May I was ready. Betsy came to see me off at the dock in Victoria Harbour. I confess I more excited at being on an adventure than I was sorrowful at leaving Victoria. I wished she was coming with me, but she wanted nothing to do with the wilderness.

"I'll never see you again," Betsy moaned as we said our goodbyes. There would be miles of trees, then rivers and mountains, grasslands, and more mountains between us. She was right, I would be a long distance away and not likely to return.

"Perhaps not," I said, "but I will write."

She smiled. "You're good at that. I will look forward to your letters. You can tell me what that husband of mine is up to."

I hesitated, wondering if I should give advice. I had thought about Betsy's Abel.

"What is it?" Betsy said, correctly interpreting that I had something to say.

"If he returns to you," I said, "perhaps you could involve him in something that allows him to make a lot of money."

"Such as?" She was suspicious.

"Building houses and selling them. He's a carpenter, isn't he? There are going to be more and more people coming from Britain and even refugees from the war in the States. Some of them will have the money for a house. Watch the papers and see what people are asking to rent or buy. He could make a lot of money building houses and selling them. And it would keep him busy."

She looked thoughtful.

"Perhaps," was all she said.

We hugged. Betsy was warm, plump, and loving. I would miss her. I thanked her for her wonderful food and good care of me and gave her a pearl necklace that had been my mother's. That wasn't as generous as it appeared because I had three of them. My mother had loved her jewellery.

Hilary had given me some letters of introduction to a businessman he knew in Barkerville, a Mr. Stevenson, and had asked me for a report on life there.

"What's your rate for the report?" I asked him. I was not sure how I would sustain myself after I'd sold my wares, and any extra cash might be welcome.

He smiled and told me. I nodded. I would write for that. I would probably write for free, but I preferred to be paid.

I stood at the rail and watched Victoria recede from my sight until it looked like a dream land—vague, distant, and disappearing. I had been happy there, but it had been not proved to be stimulating or exciting, and society was constrained by the rules of class imported from England. In Victoria, I had been relegated to middle class, and not even upper middle class. I was acknowledged as a shop owner, but not invited to soirees or the gatherings of the Helmckens, Douglases, or Judge Begbie. They were friendly when we met or they came to my shop, but I wasn't part of the intellectual conversations except at the Literary Institute, where intellectual conversation took place between all who attended. I didn't know if it would be different in Barkerville. Even if it wasn't, and I couldn't find a society where I felt comfortable, I needed more stimulus to make me feel alive: new people, new ideas, new challenges, a new landscape, and some adventure. I had been used to travelling when I lived in Russia, and even when I was a child I used to travel to Shrewsbury in the beautiful county of Shropshire with my grandfather to visit his family there. So, two years in Victoria with little chance of exploring other areas had felt oppressive. It was partly my fault as I had not wanted to spend money renting a horse and trap and there were no handy railroads such as I was used to in England and the Continent. I remembered the pleasure I took in recounting my travels and my observations of life in foreign lands that were published in *Household Words*. Mr. Dickens particularly liked my observations of Russian life. I wanted more of that stimulation from new experiences and further learning about people and places.

I'd boarded the paddlewheeler for the first leg of my journey with almost giddy excitement. The *Reliance* steamed through the groups of islands off the coast, through Plumper Pass and into the Gulf of Georgia. Here, the blue Coast Mountains on the mainland were a backdrop to the calm blue ocean before us. I was on my way. After two and a half hours, we entered the wide and decidedly muddy Fraser River.

I could barely contain my excitement. So much planning had gone into this move. I'd studied the steamship companies to see who had the highest accident rate: steamships blew up with alarming regularity and many a death was recorded in the *British Colonist*. I'd checked which company had the cheapest rates and which was the fastest.

We travelled up the wide Fraser River to New Westminster. The *Reliance* was a sternwheeler and seemed to make good time against the current. My stateroom was small but comfortable. Since I was the only woman travelling on this boat, I had it to myself—which I had counted on. There was no cabin steward or stewardess, so I had to look after my own daily chores.

"Fresh water in the galley, ma'am," the young cook told me. "I'm Peter." I placed Peter at about twenty, slim, my height, so not tall for a man. He was from Lancaster via Victoria and was working for a stake to take him to the Cariboo.

"Two trips should do it," he told me. "Then I can pay my way to the goldfields. I hope there will still be gold there when I finally get there."

"It looks to be a rich strike," I reassured him. I'd almost memorized Henry Newbury's book on gold. According to the descriptions in the book and those in the *Colonist* of Barkerville and Richfield, the gold should last for some years yet. We were gambling, though; we both knew that.

The voyage was smooth, with little of the rocking and lurching that the *Tynemouth* had routinely inflicted on passengers. Of course, the river, even with its oncoming current, could not compare with the rough waves of the Atlantic Ocean. I sat on deck and watched the trees and low bushes of the Fraser Valley slide by. Occasionally, I saw an Indian village and a few women at the water's edge.

There were several passengers on board who interested me. Mr. Steele and Mr. Stevenson had both struck it rich last year in Richfield, close to Barkerville. They were reputed to have taken out sixty thousand dollars in one day. Hardly credible. I wanted to know what they would advise me to invest in, once I had some money. However, they kept to themselves, eating together and chatting with the other men, and respectfully left me alone. It did not seem appropriate at this time to bring out Hilary's letter of recommendation to Mr. Stevenson. It was frustrating, but I could see no way of breaking the social barrier without diminishing the respect my air and manners had dictated. Quite maddening.

After two hours, we docked in New Westminster. We were spending the night there, loading up with coal and allowing the crew to rest. I'd written Minnie Gillan Cox my approximate time of arrival, and she was at the wharf to meet me. Much had happened in the two years since we'd arrived on the *Tynemouth*. Minnie's governess employment hadn't lasted long, as she married John Cox, a Royal Engineer, in August of last year. She was now very pregnant.

I wasn't prepared for the upsurge of affection I felt. "Minnie, dear heart. You're blooming!" And she was. Her face held a radiance I'd never seen before on her.

"I'm happy," she said simply.

Mistress of her own house was obviously much better than being a governess in someone else's.

I invited her to the dining room and gave her tea. She was intrigued with the *Reliance* and all the ways it differed from the *Tynemouth*.

"You're travelling without Mrs. Robb," she teased me. "How ever do you manage?"

"Very well," I said and laughed. It was good to have those days on the *Tynemouth* behind us. We had worked together then and tried to help each other. We had shared a night of terror in the storm. We had dealt with worry and scarcity of food and constant dirt. I realized I had formed a bond with Minnie that would last forever—but I wouldn't want her life. Married with the prospect of a baby every year. No. No, thank you.

"Where are you going?" she asked as she sipped her tea and nibbled on the biscuits.

"To Barkerville and the goldfields."

"That's hundreds of miles from here and through the mountains!" Clearly, that appalled her.

"It's exciting." My life was indeed very different from hers.

"You know they haven't finished the wagon road. John says there is still quite a lot to do."

"I know." I was gambling that enough of the road had been finished so the stagecoach would get through. Frank Barnard had travelled that route many times by mule. He would be unlikely to risk his horses on a road which was impassable.

Minnie sighed. "You always liked the new and the dangerous."

"I suppose I always have."

"Write me and let me have a little of that excitement."

"But you don't crave excitement." That was a statement. I knew she didn't. A voyage on the *Tynemouth* was a once-in-a-lifetime event for her, and it had taken great courage for her to make it. Why would she want to hear about my adventures?

"I wouldn't want to actually *be* in Barkerville, but I wouldn't mind a little distraction, and you write so well it's a pleasure to read your letters."

I gave her a letter from Jane, who was busy cooking and baking in her own house and in the bakery she owned with her husband. She'd married Sam Nesbitt last April and already had a little girl. She and Minnie could write to each other and exchange child-rearing tips and worries. I checked myself. Was that a disparaging thought? Did I feel superior? I thought about it. I didn't think I felt superior, just different. I wanted different things from life than Jane and Minnie did. I came from a different background, with a different education. It was as though Jane and Minnie thought about their lives within the confines of a certain number of rooms in their minds. I had more experiences, more ideas from my reading and interaction with writers, so many more rooms to explore. It was likely a result of my early education and experiences. But then, Jane had learned to cook and Minnie had learned to be happy with her married life. Both skills were useful to them. I appreciated them, and their friendship, but I did not want to be them.

We left New Westminster early, before the tide turned, as the river, even this far inland, was affected by the tides. To the north were the Coast Mountains, at least ten thousand feet in height and covered in conifers. I could not see the end of the Fraser River Valley south; it was so wide. It would be another seven hours to Yale if we didn't get stuck on a gravel bar or hit a rockslide on the way. I was on the deck when we passed Fort Langley, an impressive stockaded fort. I wondered who the huge defensive log fence was designed to repel. The many Indian tribes along the Fraser seemed to be busy with their own concerns. There were no wars this far south on the Fraser. Perhaps the stockade was to keep the obstreperous miners in when they travelled up the river in 1858. Twenty-five thousand of them came through that year, according to Hilary. They did cause trouble, but that was farther up at Yale, where they assaulted an Indian woman and were killed by her tribe in retaliation. The fear of further retaliation caused the miners to form vigilante groups and, because they were mostly Americans—some of them thugs from San Francisco—they had caused Governor Douglas alarm over their intentions to annex the Fraser River goldfields for the United States. Mr. Douglas and Judge Begbie sorted that out, so Judge Begbie told me. There had been another small war west of the Cariboo in the Chilcotin country in April. I hoped the Indians near Barkerville were different people and peaceful. I also hoped no greedy settlers tried to take their land in that area. Britain and British troops were in charge now. Yale should be a place of law and order—but I had no guarantee of that. Possibly the swift justice from the woman's relatives in Yale played a part in ensuring peace.

The valley narrowed as we travelled up the river. The mountains both sides came closer with every mile.

I spent some time in the engine room. No one seemed to mind where I went on this boat. A stoker named Angus was watching the dials on the steam engine.

"What's the highest pressure reading it can safely go?" I shouted over the roar of the fire.

"One eighty and then she'll blow," Angus said. He had a Liverpool accent.

I checked the gauge. One sixty. There was soot everywhere. Angus was covered in it as he'd been shovelling the coal. He was a short man, about forty, stocky, and obviously strong as he tirelessly fed that engine. He must have some relief, but I didn't see anyone. I watched the hypnotic circling of the stern paddlewheel from where I was standing. The paddles made a slapping sound as they hit the water, propelling us forward paddle by paddle, powered by the steam which itself was powered by coal. Up and around, up and around, paddle following paddle. It was mesmerising. I blinked.

I returned to the deck and shook the soot from my clothes.

Just before Yale, the river seemed to be closed in by monstrous mountains on either side. We steamed through shallow water, where I was sure we would ground on a gravel bar.

"River's high after the snow melt," a man, a Mr. Orr, said.

I was grateful for the information.

We arrived at Yale in the early evening. There was much activity as some of the passengers were at their destination and the rest of us had to make arrangements for further travel. The BX office shed was open, and it seemed the few shops had accommodated our schedule by remaining open. The crew were busy unloading all our goods. I explored the settlement and stretched my legs. There was a certain beauty here: stark rock mountain beside us, tree-covered mountains on the other side of the river and directly north of us. The dirt street was wide and for some of the way a boardwalk provided a little relief from the dust. There were men on the streets, mostly workers, both white and Indian. I'd heard the Indians here were excellent packers. Yale had some amenities, including a grocery shop, where I purchased some fresh lettuce and radishes. I spent some time arranging the payment for my trunks to the freight haulers. I had reserved the tickets but now had to pay for them. The BX service operated the next section of the trip. I haggled with the clerk about the price and finally got a slight reduction. I paid. They promised to get my goods to Barkerville without losing any. I had bought insurance against loss before I left Victoria. I was not going to be left destitute as I had been in Saint Petersburg.

"How many are travelling by coach?" I asked him.

"Nine of you," the young man said. He must have been about sixteen, not quite grown into his hands and feet as they seemed to cause him some awkwardness. "Three on the roof," he continued, "and six of you inside. Should be fine."

I'd seen the stagecoach beside the office. Although it was the first trip it had made on this route, it looked as though it had been well-used in its previous life.

"Is it clean inside?" I asked. "Do you need help in cleaning it?"

"I'll clean it after I close up here."

"I'd appreciate it," I said, passing him a dollar. I wanted to at least start out in a clean conveyance.

We spent the night on board the *Reliance* and had our last meal about eight that night. Only the passengers continuing on stayed aboard, so the nine of us spent a convivial evening. I said my good-byes to the cook and the stoker and retired to my room.

At two in the morning, I was up, preparing to depart. I managed the stockings with the knee garters to hold them in place, the short chemise, the drawers, the corset, the over-bodice of striped blue-and-white cotton, and my new split skirt. I packed my crinoline, collapsed and fitted into one ring, into my suitcase. The stage would be full, and I couldn't take up more than my share of room. I added a heavy pair of boys' woollen socks and my work boots to my ensemble. I was unconventionally dressed, but still respectable. I could barely catch a glimpse of my face in the tiny mirror, but my hair, prone to flying out of its chignon, was likely untidy with dark strands escaping around my face.

It was the best I could do. I rolled a light woollen shawl into my handbag then loaded it with boiled eggs and bread from the kitchen as well as a few slices of ham and some pickles. Peter handed me some rather dried-out apples, but I accepted them as a gift. I managed a quick cup of tea and was at the BX stagecoach shed promptly at 3 AM Someone had lit lanterns and hung them outside the doors of the express office, so I found my way easily enough. I was happy to see wagons full of freight, including my trunks, heading up the road before me. At least, if there was any danger, the wagons would encounter it first. I, as the only woman, was offered the river-side seat in the stagecoach.

"You will get the best view from there," Mr. Orr said. He was travelling inside with me along with Mr. Stevenson and Mr. Steele. Perhaps I might get some mining information after all.

I was happy to see the coach hung over the wheels on flat wooden springs. That would help smooth our ride. The wooden wheels with metal rims—two smaller ones in the front and two large ones at the rear—looked to be sturdy. The coach was painted a cheerful red with bright yellow trim. I smiled to myself. Someone had picked those happy colours.

Mr. Robert Stevenson was perhaps thirty, tall, well-muscled as all these miners seemed to be. He had a broad face with wide-set eyes, a small moustache, and a well-trimmed beard. His hair was thick and brushed back, or at least it started that way. He was a Scot from Glasgow, which was obvious from his accent. Mr. H. M. Steele, also a fairly young man and also a Glaswegian, was reputed to own the richest claim in Richfield. Hilary had said his claim was yielding thousands of dollars a day. Mr. Orr was another miner who was apparently successful, and also, like the others, bearded with thick hair. With luck, I might get some tips on where to invest my money—when I made some money.

The other gentlemen inside with us were a Mr. Paul Black and Mr. Sandy MacIntosh. We'd had a brief introduction as we prepared to load. Sandy MacIntosh was a man of singular appearance. He was covered in hair from his long grey locks to his exceptional beard. The men doffed their hats, murmured a good morning (it was an indecent hour for conversation), and settled back in their seats. We had a four-hundred-mile trip before us by stagecoach to Soda Creek and from Soda Creek by paddlewheeler to Quesnelmouth and by mule train to Barkerville. I expected it to take four days to reach Soda Creek, then another two days to Barkerville with a stop at a roadhouse along the way. The coach would be carrying the mail so the driver would try to make the best time possible. He would bring gold back, as much as sixty thousand dollars on a trip. It made my heart beat rapidly and my hands tremble a little to think of it. I had never had so much money. I had never had the opportunity to earn so much money. Surely, some of it would come my way.

I had worn my work boots as I expected the first section of this "uncompleted" road might require me to get out of the stagecoach and walk some part of the way

We travelled farther into the mountains, crossing the river on a suspension bridge. It creaked and swayed, but since the wagons had gone before us, I doubted it would collapse. We continued into the mountains, encountering several dark tunnels blasted from the rocks. It was unnerving to pass through solid rock like some powerful ghost, but soon the tunnels were behind us. It was light now as the sun had risen and topped the mountains with rays, increasingly illuminating the slopes until we could clearly see the river.

At first, the wagon road had been about twelve feet wide and clear, but it deteriorated as we went north and farther into the canyon. Soon we were inching along on an eight-foot-wide road that still had rock debris, holes, and even boulders, while directly below us in a deep gorge flowed the Fraser River. The riverbed was filled with large rocks that choked the rushing water and created a fearsome, wild cataract. I regretted my position in the outside seat. I would be first in that water if we slid over the side.

"Miss Wilson, I could trade seats with you, if you'd rather." Mr. Stevenson, sitting at the window on the opposite side and noticing my apprehension, started to rise.

"Please stay where you are, Mr. Stevenson. Your weight on your side of the coach may be all that is keeping us on the road." The men laughed as if I'd uttered a witticism. I was entirely in earnest. The coach seemed precarious. The wooden springs creaked and groaned with the sudden lurching. We couldn't see directly ahead, only the view on either side. At times that view was sheer rock. I took deep breaths and thought of Russell Square, Thomas, and, for some reason, Mr. Dickens. I wondered how he was managing his household now he had separated from his wife, Catherine, and installed her sister to supervise his children. Ellen, the actress he had taken up with, was beautiful, and quite nice with it. Still, he was in a mess. Those thoughts distracted me until we were past the worst of the cliffside and I breathed easier. It was magnificent country, but terrifying.

We rolled into Boston Bar. I'm sure I wasn't the only one relieved to leave that narrow canyon behind. We divided ways: the men on one side of the road and me heading for the bushes on the other. I returned to the coach, where our driver was stripping the harnesses from the beautiful horses—glossy coats, bright eyes—who did not seem to be exhausted, just a little tired. A young Indian man led two replacement horses and tied them to a log rail. Our driver pulled the lead two horses free of the harness, snapped a lead rope into their halters, and led them to another rail well away from the fresh horses.

"They'd fight?" I asked, interested in the deliberate separation.

"Likely so," the driver agreed.

The young man returned with a second pair of horses. The driver led the second tired pair to the railing with the others of their team. Then the young man and the driver quickly harnessed the new horses.

"Miss Wilson." I offered my hand when the driver was free.

"Charlie Major," he replied.

I turned to the young man. "Miss Wilson," I repeated and again offered my hand.

He looked at me, at Charlie, and back at me. "Tony," he said and gingerly shook my hand.

"Beautiful horses." I admired the new team.

"Yeah." Tony patted the one he was leading. "This is Sam."

"He's lovely," I said. "Strong."

Charlie and Tony smiled at the horses.

Charlie turned to me. "You'd better get something to eat. It's a while to Spence's Bridge." It was a reminder that he wouldn't wait for me. I left them to their work. I would have to get some sustenance. I'd eaten my eggs, ham, and bread before we'd left Yale. I saw Mr. Stevenson emerging from a log cabin.

"Is there food in there?"

"Indeed. Beer, sandwiches, and cake."

It sounded good, although tea would be best. There was one table at which three of the passengers were sitting.

"Here, Miss Wilson," one of the men said. "Have my seat." He had been riding on the roof, and I hadn't met him.

"Mikelson," he said. "Zachary Mikelson."

I smiled. "Thank you." Since he'd called me by my name, he knew who I was.

The proprietor spoke to me over the heads of the waiting men. "What do you want?"

"Tea?" I made it a question.

He snorted. It seemed tea would not be forthcoming. I rose and went to the counter. There was little choice of food. The man behind the counter offered me beer, water, and a ham sandwich. I drank the water and collected the sandwich and the last piece of vanilla cake. He wanted four dollars for that. Outrageous. I paid him, though. I doubted he would enter into any bargaining. I hoped there would be competition here soon and cheaper food.

I ate my lunch and walked back the stagecoach. The horses were restless. We climbed in, the three outside passengers clambered onto the roof, and we all settled into place. Tony held the lead horse by the halter with some difficulty. Charlie barely waited for us to close the doors before he dropped the reins to indicate "go." The horses shot out of Boston Bar, rocking the coach from side to side. I clutched the strap beside me and waited to see how long this headlong flight would last. The men laughed with the excitement of it. Soon the horses ceased their wild run and settled into a steady trot.

We spoke a little then amongst ourselves. I was eager to know about Barkerville and the men took turns telling me tales of their lives there.

"You can't work your claim in the winter," Mr. Stevenson told me. "The ground is frozen solid and your pick axe just bounces off the frozen dirt."

"But come spring," Mr. Orr informed me, "thousands of miners will return and buy up equipment if they don't bring it with them, get themselves outfitted with gear and clothes, and head to their claims."

"Do they stay on their claims all summer?" I asked, worried that no one would be in town to buy my wares.

"No, no. They come in at night to read, drink in the saloons, play music, dance with the hurdy gurdy girls, and uh . . ." He stuttered to a stop.

Mr. Stevenson took over. "We all like theatre, so any entertainment that comes to town gets a big audience."

I could easily fill in what Mr. Orr didn't say. I assumed there were prostitutes in Barkerville. Every town had them.

Their conversation switched to claims, nuggets, and water. Apparently, water and the power behind it was an important part of mining. I asked the occasional question and stored their answers in my memory to be examined later. It quickened my excitement. I could hardly wait to partake in that adventure. I hadn't needed Hilary's letter of recommendation to meet Mr. Stevenson. I was learning about the mines without it.

I hadn't planned to sleep on this trip because I might never come this way again and I didn't want to miss anything, but the combination of a 2 AM wakening, the anxiety of the canyon experience, and a full stomach set me dozing. That surprised me since the road continued to be rough and the coach continued to lurch and sway.

I woke as we were approaching Lytton at the confluence of the Fraser and the Thompson Rivers. We were still in mountains, but they were not as tall as those in the Fraser Canyon, and the vegetation was much sparser. The conifers were not densely crowded together as they had been; instead they were spread out with dry grasslands covering the hills. The town was situated on a bench, a flat terrace, over the Thompson River, a beautiful spot—and warm. The Fraser reached this point from the northeast; we went directly north, leaving the Fraser and following the Thompson. Our stop here was long enough to change the horses and allow us to briefly visit a roadhouse. Charlie wanted to get to our overnight roadhouse at Spence's Bridge where we could all rest.

THE THOMPSON RIVER WAS MORE beautiful than the Fraser. It was a sparkling blue with rocky shores but not the deep canyon we'd just driven through. We had to stop several times as workers were shovelling rocks off the road.

Charlie called down to us. "They blasted rocks last night, and they're clearing it away. Shouldn't be long."

It was only about a half hour, and we were through. The road beyond the workmen was not wide but still passable. The twilight was lengthening, and it was almost dark when we arrived at the edge of the river with Spence's Bridge hamlet on the other side.

"Cook had a ferry here when I first came up," Mr. Stevenson said.

"A cable ferry," Mr. Steele agreed. "Worked well enough, but it was slow. The bridge is better."

The bridge seemed to be almost floating on the river it was so close to the water.

"Pretty high run off," Mr. Stevenson commented once we made it to the other side.

"Might take it away," Mr. Orr said.

"Thank you for keeping that thought to yourself until we were safely over," I said.

They all smiled. They seemed to think I had nerves of steel and was just being socially entertaining. I was cranky. It had been a very long day.

ten

# The Cariboo Wagon Road

The sun was below the mountains and the shadows long in the valley when we approached the Basque Ranch on the Thompson River. I was exhausted, although I had not been physically active, only sitting, but sitting for many hours. The stage had swayed, and I never got totally comfortable. The muscles of my back and legs had to constantly adjust for the lurching and sudden changes of speed and direction. Even though I had wanted to sag into a deep sleep, I couldn't do it. I peered out the coach window.

The country was magnificent: rolling hills and what would be considered mountains at home, and a wide river valley. I felt a warm, slight breeze coming up from the river and heard birdsong close by. I couldn't see any trees in the coming darkness. If there were some, they were sparse. It was perhaps too dry in this country for them to grow.

Charlie urged the horses forward and we drew into the yard in front of the roadhouse at some speed. I grabbed the cloth handle beside me and hung on. We climbed down onto the dry, hard-packed dirt. I gripped the side of the coach, afraid I would stumble and fall if I tried to walk. I gingerly moved my legs until the jelly-like feeling disappeared.

The house was a sturdy-looking log construction, the grounds devoid of a single flower or shrub, just low sagebrush dotted over the flat bench above the river. The smell of sage was a welcome relief from the smell of overheated men in the stagecoach.

Louis Minaberriet came down the steps to meet us. "Welcome to my house," he said.

*"Merci,"* I responded to his name and his accent. He switched to French, but it was an accent difficult for me to follow. He spoke French like a Basque, from near the border of Spain. I kept my French slower than I was used to speaking it. Everyone in the diplomatic world in Russia spoke French, and I had taught it to my pupils when I was a governess, but Basque French was difficult. Mr. Minaberriet and I managed to understand one another, and I believe he was happy to use his language again. I commented in French about the trip and the conditions of travel. He was interested, as we were the first of what he hoped would be a lucrative trade from the Yale route.

He was an interesting young man, about thirty. Mr. Stevenson had told us, as we approached the ranch, that Mr. Minaberriet had come from an aristocratic family in France to Oregon or San Francisco—he wasn't sure which—then headed toward the Cariboo, but stopped here at the Thompson River, where the prospects for farming were obviously favourable. He pre-empted acreage, some of it along the river where he leased out mining spots to prospectors for a percentage of their take. He was getting rich, Mr. Stevenson said, from that percentage alone, as there was gold in the river.

I was happy to find the outhouse, which seemed almost the epitome of privacy after the lack of it on the trip. Mrs. Minaberriet, a compact, efficient woman, showed me my room—bare, small, but clean and comfortable with a bed. The men were going to sleep on the floor of the kitchen when it was cleared after supper. I smiled and thanked her. She spoke some English but no French. She was a local Indian woman and had her own language, which I didn't understand. I asked her to teach me the word for food. She did so, accompanied by an indulgent smile. I said the word over and over in my mind as she escorted me to the kitchen, where everyone was gathered around a laden table.

Charlie indicated the empty chair on his right, where it was customary for lone females to sit, right next to the driver, so he could make sure she was well-served. We ate quickly and quietly. I retired to my room with a candle immediately after supper and wrote to Thomas.

*It was a long and tiring journey, Thomas, through mountains, but, oh, what marvellous scenery. You can't imagine how varied, how overwhelming, those mountains are. They became less high as we travelled further north, but still beautiful.*

*My fellow travellers are a peculiar lot. The men riding on top of the coach are uneducated workers who seem full of good will and impressive strength. The ones riding inside the coach are educated: two successful miners and a poet, although he spoke as if he were a miner as well, but all appear to be reasonably considerate and willing to cooperate when necessary. They treat me as if I were respectable—if unconventional. After many miles of mountains, rapid rivers, and indifferent roads, we have bonded into something like Chaucer's Canterbury group. We tell each other stories of our lives without exchanging anything intimate or important as we are, after all, strangers. The men are interested in my life in Russia, and I am interested in their lives in the goldfields. Some of the men are Americans fleeing from the conflict in their country.*

*"Stupid," said Mr. MacIntyre who has been travelling on the roof. "Killing one another. Someone up high is making money somewhere."*

*I agreed with him. War always seems to benefit the wealthy.*

*They are interesting travelling companions and helpful to me. My biggest difficulty is accustoming myself to our odoriferous condition. No one washes often. The smell is a trial.*

*You needn't worry about me, though, Thomas. I am well-protected and happy to be on an adventure.*

I didn't tell him I was worried I would run out of money, that I wouldn't be able to sell my goods, that the freighters would lose or steal them. There were still more days of travel and unknown hazards to face: mudslides, rockslides, accidents, other unimagined dangers. Before I'd left Victoria, Hilary had warned me of snow. Snow. In May?

In the morning, I saw Charlie handing out some mail to Mr. Minaberriet and realized that he was both delivering and gathering mail. I gave Charlie my letter and eight cents to Mr. Minaberriet for the postage. That was three cents more than it cost to send it from Victoria, but considering how many people had to take care of it, was cheap at the price.

We ate a good breakfast cooked and served by Mrs. Minaberriet. We weren't long in gathering our luggage and were ready to go by 4 AM. It would be the longest day yet as we were hoping to make it to the Clinton Hotel by nightfall. Until we arrived at Quesnelmouth, we were going almost straight north.

The valley was just as beautiful in daylight as it had been in last night's twilight. The air was dry and fresh with a tang of coolness off the river. I made the most of it and breathed deeply while I waited to load onto the stage.

The Royal Engineers were constructing this road and had made it at least passable to this point, but they had much more to do. We followed the blue Thompson River for many miles as it raced over rocks and boulders. We finally abandoned it as we headed north when the river angled to the east. We left mountains and high hills behind us and travelled through another much wider valley, the horses moving smoothly. The country was more open now, and even warmer. I regretted my petticoats. While they acted as a cushion, they contributed to an uncomfortable warmth. The hills were almost bare of trees but covered in grass and occasional flashes of yellow. I couldn't see any, but I was sure I smelled sage.

We changed horses at Hat Creek, near Cache Creek, managed a relief stop, had a quick cup of tea and a bun, but pressed on to Clinton through much of the same topography, grass and low bush, which Mr. Orr called tumbleweed and looked like a dry ball.

"It detaches from the ground in the late summer and tumbles across the land dispersing its seeds," Mr. Orr said.

"What plant is it, or is it its own species?" I asked.

"Here it is usually Scotch thistle. But other plants do the same thing."

"Curious," I said. It was the wrong time of year to see the plants tumbling, but I'd like to see that sometime.

It was very dry here and getting warmer in the coach.

"They grow grapes here," Mr. Stevenson said. "Up there on the hillsides."

"I can well believe it," I said. That was as close as I came to complaining. It wouldn't help. We were all warm.

We approached Clinton from a small hill. True to form, Charlie encouraged the horses to pick up the pace, and we drew into the yard of the Clinton Hotel in a dramatic flurry of speed, ending in a sudden stop. I was braced for it.

When we were completely stopped, I opened my door and stepped out. It looked as though two valleys met here with sage, grasslands, and dry air. It felt wonderful. I breathed in the scent of sage and the cottonwood trees, a sweet smell. I ignored the dust.

It would be pleasant to stay overnight here, but Charlie had other ideas.

"We'll go on to 70 Mile House," he said. He looked at me. "Are you in agreement, Miss?"

All the men looked at me. I realized if I said, "No, I'm too tired," they would stay. I wanted a bath and a meal, but I couldn't hold out against the collective will to push on. Besides, I also wanted to get to Barkerville as soon as possible.

"Do we have time for a meal?" I asked Charlie.

"It's all ready."

After visiting the facilities, I returned to the hotel and met Charlie by the front door.

"We have a surprise for you," he said, and escorted me to a private sitting room, where a meal was laid out before me with a tablecloth, napkin, and beautiful china. I could have cried for the thoughtfulness of it. I gulped and fought the upsurge of emotion. It was as if I was being granted special status, privilege, and consideration I hadn't had for a very long time.

"We've an hour," Charlie said, and smiled. "We're in the bar. We'll meet you at the coach."

"Thank you," I said inadequately and sat, determined to enjoy every moment of this meal.

*eleven*

# Heading to Barkerville

I WAS SO PLEASED with my relaxed and elegant meal—I'd even had a glass of Bordeaux—that I faced the next six hours to 70 Mile House with equanimity.

The names of the different roadhouses such as 70 Mile House indicated how many miles from Lillooet they were, a settlement not far from Lytton and the confluence of the Thompson and Fraser Rivers. The Cariboo Wagon Road started at Lillooet, hence it was Mile 0.

The wine had made me sleepy, and I dozed a little. The beer must have made the men livelier as they held a long and argumentative discussion about the best ways to get more gold from the gravel beds and from the clay deposits in Richfield and Barkerville. I was intensely interested but too tired to partake. It was instructive, though, to sit still and listen to their discussion; I learned the best way to register a mining claim.

"Although it's a blessing not to have to go all the way to Williams Lake to register a claim and I'm happy to have a gold commissioner in Barkerville," Mr. Stevenson said, "Commissioner Ball is a right idiot."

"He has all the power to grant licences and not a lot of sense," Mr. Steele agreed.

"He's going to cause a fight at some point," Mr. Black offered.

I stored the name of the commissioner in my memory. He would be someone I'd want to be on good terms with.

I learned that British law gave miners the right to stake a claim on any land—private, Indigenous, or Crown—and that no one could prevent miners from working that claim.

Obviously, the British lawmakers, likely Governor Douglas, thought mining was more important than any other land use.

"He enforces those working rules, though," Mr. Steele said. "The hardest one to deal with is the one requiring us to work one day in three to keep the claim."

I blinked wide awake at that. "Do you mean," I asked, "if you leave your claim for four days, you'd lose it?"

"That's right, Miss Wilson," Mr. Stevenson answered. "That protects people from staking a huge section of a goldfield. You can only have two claims and the Gold Field Rules say you have to work them. If you have a partner, it's manageable. If you are on your own, it's onerous." Mr. Stevenson rolled his R's so "onerous" came out like the long rolls of a drum. He and Mr. Steele spoke in a musical cadence that was pleasing to listen to.

"I see. Thank you."

I retired to quiet contemplation while they continued to discuss mining: who was getting a rich return and who wasn't; who was ready to sell shares and what those shares were worth. I tried to commit the names to my memory, as I had every intention of buying shares in a mine when I had the money to do so.

It was a long six hours. We did stop to give the horses feed and water and to allow the passengers to make use of the bushes at the edge of the wagon road. I walked around the stagecoach several times, trying to keep my legs from cramping.

The light had faded to twilight when we drove into the roadhouse yard with the usual flourish. I stumbled from the coach, barely able to stand. I hardly remember that evening. I know I ate a meal, went to my room, and collapsed on my bed. The bed seemed to sway like the coach. I took a deep breath and suddenly I was asleep. Someone knocked on my door at the early hour of 4 AM. I staggered out of bed, dressed, found the outhouse, had breakfast and tea, packed my few belongs, and settled into my place in the coach.

"Morning," the men mumbled in greeting as they took their positions. I responded in the same subdued monotone. We were off. Silence, punctuated by the occasional snore, reigned for two hours. We travelled through rolling hills with grasslands and often small forests of conifers, but I confess, I was in endurance mode and concentrated on keeping my dignity and managing the swaying of the stagecoach rather than appreciating the scenery.

I was brought out of my torpor by Mr. Steele's comment: "Sunflowers. Pretty."

I gazed at the hillside full of bright yellow, daisy-like flowers. The profusion seemed extravagant in this dry country.

"Just about the only flower I can recognize," he admitted.

We had a relief stop, lunch, and a change of horses at 108 Mile House, then flew on to 150 Mile House. It was six at night and Charlie decreed an overnight stop here. After a meal, we sat in the spacious general store area of the big log building. I drank my tea and mostly listened to the men talk. Mr. Davidson, the owner, was bemoaning his overextension to Mr. Steele and Mr. Orr.

"I owe Wright money, and Tormey has a mortgage on this place I can't pay. I'll have to give it up."

"Bad luck, old chap," Mr. Orr said.

No one volunteered to lend him money. Miners, in my experience, could be generous, but perhaps he had a habit of failing businesses.

"What will happen to the place?" Mr. Stevenson asked. "It's doing good business with the miners coming through. You get them even if they go east from here to Likely and over Yank's Peak."

"I do, so Eddie Tormey will probably run it. He says he will anyhow." I had never heard of this man. Mr. Stevenson nodded and grunted a "Good." I suppose that indicated the Mr. Tormey was reliable. I felt sorry for Mr. Davidson, but businesses rose and fell depending on how they were managed.

I let my eyes roam around the room. I saw a post office in a corner of the store. I was too tired to write Thomas or my Victoria friends. I took in the shelves of pots and pans, the ropes hanging from the ceiling. The stove, cold now as it was warm enough without it, sat in the centre of the store. It was cozy, comfortable. My eyes closed. I shook myself awake and excused myself.

Again, I had a small, private room, this time with a wash basin and pitcher of water. I would try to buy some biscuits or perhaps fruit in the morning. What I really longed for on our long rides was a cup of tea.

ON OUR LAST DAY OF coach riding, we rose at a civil hour of seven and were on the road by half eight. I had my energy back and observed the passing hills and valleys with interest. We sped through Williams Lake where the gold commissioner used to be stationed, a pretty village nestled in a valley. We went up an easy grade and on to Soda Creek. It was thirty miles from 150 Mile House, a long trip at home in England, but short here, compared to the miles we'd travelled each day before this. The trees, small pine and poplar, crowded the edge of the wagon trail at some points and opened up to grasslands at others. We drove past the Indian settlement and down to the Fraser River, where our paddle steamer would arrive a little after two in the afternoon. The *Enterprise* would leave early the next morning.

It was a beautiful spot; the fast-moving Fraser River surged past the landing. Two hotels, the Colonial and the Exchange, sat side by side facing the river. They were certainly going to be convenient for our embarkation. By half three, I'd booked my place on the *Enterprise,* taken advantage of a private room to wash, changed my boots for shoes, added my petticoat and overskirt, and was settled in the dining room with a cup of tea.

Activity was all around me. The *Enterprise* had just docked and the passengers were disembarking. Most, of course, were men.

Some wore the broad-brimmed hat with oiled canvas jackets over baggy work trousers common among workers. A few wore three-piece suits with natty bowler hats. Most fit somewhere in between and dressed much like Mr. Stevenson and Mr. Steele, with more casual suits and hats with a modest brim. It seemed the state of dress in the male population reflected a kind of new democracy where men moved between classes freely and dressed according to the class they preferred. Mr. Stevenson was probably the wealthiest man here, although it was hard to tell, and perhaps that was the attraction of the democratic dress code. You couldn't tell who was wealthy and who wasn't.

As much as we British tried to duplicate our society wherever we travelled in the globe and wherever we established colonies, the local people and the immigrants from other countries changed that society somewhat. I wondered how. According to Hilary and Judge Begbie, Barkerville was much like an English village but with some of the population Chinese and some Native. Surely, they would influence the culture. I was fascinated and tried to tamp down my eagerness to be on my way. I would go aboard soon.

I watched men unload freight and load our suitcases, and I presumed mail bags, onto the *Enterprise*. The captain was J. W. Doane, who had taken command last year when the boat was first put in service, having been built nearby. It looked small but sturdy.

I said my goodbyes to Charlie Major. He had fed, watered, and rested his horses, and was picking up passengers to make the return trip. They would make their first stop at the 150 Mile House roadhouse.

"Easier on the horses and the people to make this first day a shorter run. Plenty of light."

I had noticed how the days were longer this far north.

Mr. Steele called me. I picked up my valise and followed him down the long wharf to the *Enterprise*. She was a sternwheeler with two decks and a wheelhouse above.

"Let me take that," Mr. Steele said, and relieved me of my bag.

"There is a ladies' lounge," he said, and escorted me to the upper deck and a small but comfortable cabin. I smiled my thanks and sank down onto the padded chair. Luxury indeed.

A young man popped his head in. "Tea, ma'am?"

"Lovely." I could always use another cup of tea.

He arrived with it shortly, and I had finished it when the steam whistle announced our departure.

I stood, shook my skirts into acceptable order, and headed out to explore the ship. First, I looked over the upper deck. I poked my head into a much bigger lounge. Men were gathered around a table. Cards were spread on the surface. Money was stacked in the centre. Bottles and glasses of liquor covered the table.

"Miss Wilson," Mr. Steele called. "Do you play?"

"I haven't yet learned," I said. "I will leave you to it. I want to have a walk."

He waved and resumed his game. He had invited me to join a card game where betting was in evidence. That would never have happened in London, or even Victoria—not unless I was a woman of ill repute. I doubt Mr. Steele considered me a degenerate. It meant that women in the Cariboo had more freedom than women in Victoria. I was going to have to learn a new set of rules.

The lower deck was full of men, many of them sitting on their trunks and bags, also involved in card games. They waved and a few stood and doffed their caps. A young man was standing by the railing watching the riverbank slide by.

"May I join you?" I asked as I moved up beside him.

"Ah, certainly, madam." He doffed his hat.

"I am Florence Wilson. I'm on my way to Barkerville to start a business, probably a shop."

He smiled. He was perhaps in his mid-twenties, slim, wiry, tall at about six foot two, fair haired, and pale skinned. Perhaps he was tough and could endure, but he didn't look strong.

"Michael Penroy-Smith," he said. London, educated accent. What in the world was he doing here? He wore the miner's garb of loose wool trousers, heavy shirt, and jacket. His hat was the broad-brimmed miner's hat, but it looked new. I was surprised to find myself wondering if he had enough money, enough to eat, and was wise enough to survive in the goldfields. I restrained myself.

"Beautiful country," I said, referring to what the men called the "bench land" we were passing. I saw it as a terraced strip of land.

"Good for farming," Michael said.

"I assume you are going to Barkerville?"

He nodded.

"What can you tell me about the place?"

He looked thoughtful. "I believe there are vast riches there—for a few. Some people have become very rich, but many more stay poor."

"What increases your odds of becoming very rich?" I asked. After all, he wouldn't be going if he didn't have some faith he would do well.

"Listening to the men talk about where to dig, getting there as early as possible, working hard, defending your claim, and being careful with the gold you do find." He grinned. "All that is hard to do, so I don't know if I'll be one of the lucky ones. I just want to try."

"I do as well," I said and smiled.

"Good luck, Miss Wilson."

"Good luck to you too, sir."

I left him less worried about him than I had been. He seemed sensible. But then, you had to have more than sense. You had to have luck.

WE DOCKED IN QUESNELMOUTH AT 8 PM. It was still bright daylight. I carried my own valise to the gang plank, but Mr. Stevenson relieved me of it again and carried it off the boat.

I was not impressed by Quesnelmouth. It was a pretty spot. The Quesnel River flowed into the Fraser and the town was situated between them. But the town itself was wooden building after wooden building in a line along a dirt street. It looked as if it had been constructed in a hurry and consideration was given only to utility, not beauty.

Mr. Stevenson gave me information. "We are all staying overnight at the Occidental Hotel. The pack train heads out about nine in the morning. I talked to Cataline, the mule skinner, and he said it would take time to load the freight and mail brought on the *Enterprise,* and he needed to get everything well organized. You might want to talk to him yourself. His name is really Jean Caux, but everyone calls him Cataline. He's French."

I brightened. It would be pleasant to converse in French.

He indicated the main street. "This is Front Street. That's the Bank of British Columbia, and beside it is the office of the gold commissioner, Peter O'Reilly."

I was interested in both those buildings, but did not have a need for either today. I was also interested in the general store. I asked Mr. Stevenson about it.

"Yes, it carries quite a lot, but for a price."

I would investigate. I needed to know what price miners would pay if they came to Quesnelmouth for supplies and what I could reasonably charge for the same articles in Barkerville.

"That's Cataline." Mr. Stevenson pointed.

"I'd best talk to him," I said and headed toward the man who was in charge of the mule train. He was busy, shouting at a man carrying a trunk on is shoulder.

"Careful with that."

He swivelled around and caught sight of me. "*Pardonne, madame.* I didn't see you there."

I offered my hand. "Miss Wilson."

"Cataline."

I switched to French. "I will be joining your mule train in the morning. How will I be conveyed to Barkerville?"

He smiled and studied me for a moment, replying in the same language. "No stage coach yet. Just mules. Gus Wright is coming along on the wagon trail to Cottonwood, but it's not finished. You can ride?"

"Horses?"

"Mules?"

"They have four legs. I assume they will follow the mule in front of them, and I just have to stay on?"

"That's about right." He eyed me for a moment. "I don't think you can ride in a skirt? Are you sure want to go?"

I nodded. "I have trousers."

He grabbed my hand, shook it, and changed to English. "Bless you, ma'am. You wouldn't believe the screechin' that goes on when some of those women meet the mules. *Sacre Bleu.* What do they think *I* can do about it?"

I would have loved to hear about the experiences he'd had with demanding women, but I could see his attention was needed to oversee the unloading and reloading of the freight.

He paused and turned back. "I have a small pony. Would you like that?"

"If you think it would be better."

"More comfortable, at any rate."

"Thank you. In the morning then," I said.

"Nine in front of the Occidental Hotel."

"Agreed," I said and moved off to the hotel to find my room.

Mr. Stevenson had left my valise near the counter where passengers were crowding. I joined the crowd and waited my turn. I mused on the name of the hotel. Did they want to make sure no Oriental people tried to register here?

I listened to the conversations around me. It was all about the expectation of snow tomorrow. Snow! I had only a bonnet, which would be soaked in minutes. My winter coat was in my trunk somewhere in the freight. Now I would need the general store to obtain something to wear the next day.

The clerk, an older man, handed me a key. "Second floor. To the right. Number's on the door. Supper at six. Breakfast at seven. That'll be four dollars."

I mentally calculated four dollars times about the twenty people I'd seen milling around. That gave the proprietor one hundred dollars a night. Minus expenses of about twenty dollars left him eighty dollars, a very good day's take. Gold miners were happy to take out twenty dollars a day. Perhaps my gold would be in a shop where the sale of my goods would make me as much if not more than miners could dig. Of course, both this proprietor and I planned to make our money by relieving the miners of theirs.

I made a quick stop in my room then walked over to the general store. It was up the street from the hotel and full of men buying supplies. I wandered around for a time noting the prices of liquor. I knew what I'd paid for the whiskey I was transporting. This store was marking it up two hundred precent. I could do better than that. Once I had an idea of the prices asked on goods I was transporting, I looked for a rain and snow-proof hat and a coat.

I found a hat readily enough, one of those waxed canvas broad-brimmed ones. I could fashion a tie for it so it wouldn't fall off if there was a wind. I took that and proceeded to the boys' department to search for a warm coat. I found one made of heavy felt with a wool lining. I could cut the side seams so it wouldn't ride up to my ears when I was on a horse.

I thought I could knit a short wool scarf that night.

"Any yarn?" I asked the busy clerk.

"No ma'am."

I nodded. I'd stock that if I continued to operate a store in Barkerville.

I retuned to the hotel room and, after a good dinner, retired to my room and sewed for hours. I was going to be prepared for this last leg of my trip.

*twelve*

# The Last Trek on the Cariboo Wagon Road

THE MORNING STARTED with cold but no snow. Cataline introduced me to Dolly, a small, sturdy Welsh pony.

"Nice girl," he said. I assumed he meant the horse.

"Yes, she seems quiet." I stroked her nose.

"She doesn't ground hitch."

I looked at him for an explanation.

"If you dismount, either tie her up or hold the reins. Can't just drop the reins. She'll wander off, and I'm not going to chase her."

I imagined what would happen if I did let Dolly escape. I would delay the forward movement of the whole mule train or Cataline would let Dolly go free while I walked. I'd keep a tight hold of her when I dismounted.

At least twenty mules stretched out in a line before me. There were also two wagons. I hoped my trunks were in a wagon for I couldn't imagine how they would convey trunks on mules. Probably unload the trunks and pack the goods into the mule packs, but no one had asked me to do that. I had heard Cataline was scrupulously honest, so all my goods would likely arrive even if they ended up on a mule's back.

I mounted Dolly. She sat docilely in line waiting for the mule in front of her to start moving. My split skirt allowed me to ride astride, which was much more comfortable than side-saddle. I tied my shawl on the back of the saddle. There were two rawhide thongs there for the purpose of adding some possessions to travel with me.

The air was crisp and fresh. I breathed in the excitement of the country. A new country. A new city. A new chance. I was on the last section of my journey. One more overnight at the Cottonwood Roadhouse, then the next day—Barkerville. Questions crowded my brain: Would I be able to make enough on the sale of my goods to sustain myself? Would my goods make it to Barkerville, or would I arrive and find I had only the meagre cash I had with me? Would I find a place to stay? I resolutely banished those worries. There was nothing I could do about them today. Would I manage to stay on Dolly?

I heard a shout from behind me and the line began to move. I saw Mr. Stevenson, Mr. Orr, and Mr. Steele on mules about halfway down the line then lost sight of them when the line curved around a corner. I concentrated on the rhythm of Dolly's gait. She was short, so her steps were also short, but we weren't moving fast, just at a walk. I could probably rock with her gait fairly comfortably.

I looked around me, determined to remember enough about the sight to write to Thomas about it later. We were ascending the river bank and onto a flat trail. The wagons were having no difficulty on this part of the trail, but I'd heard the engineers had not yet reached the Cottonwood Ranch, so I expected we would be picking our way through the landscape on rough terrain later. I could see nothing but trees, some kind of fir or pine, as we wound over the plateau. The land did rise and fall a little, but there was nothing steep enough to slow the steady walk of the train. We stopped briefly, and I saw several men in front of me dismount and stand at the side of the trail. My bladder did feel a little uncomfortable, but I would have to pull my trousers down to relieve myself, and I was not going to expose my backside to the view of the men in the line behind me. I stayed on Dolly. As we moved on, I thought hard. I could not last all day without relieving myself. At the next stop, I dismounted, untied my shawl from the back of the saddle, tied it around my waist, and took my trousers down. I managed to empty my bladder without getting my trousers wet, and I still had hold of Dolly. A major accomplishment.

"You are an opportunist, are you, Dolly?" I murmured to her. "If I drop these reins, you'll be off." I thought about it. I was an opportunist myself. I tried to seize each opportunity to further my interests. I didn't think I would disregard everyone around me, though. "That's where we differ, Dolly." A fanciful woman would interpret the look she gave me as cynical.

It had been getting gradually colder. My heavy coat was warm enough and my leather gloves protection for my hands. My ears were cold, though, because my hat sat fashionably back on my head and didn't cover them. I managed to untie the shawl and drape it over my head and around my neck. I was glad I had done so because it started to snow. Dolly put down her head and kept moving. I put my head down, and tried to endure without complaint. I got colder and colder. I wasn't sure I could feel my feet anymore.

About three hours into the trip and after an hour of snow, Cataline rode up beside me and offered me a blanket. I looked at it, unsure of what I should do with it.

"You put it over your head and the saddle." He flung it over me, and I fumbled with it, trying to get it in place. He leaned over and adjusted it over my head and around me, so it flowed out, covering my back and the back of the saddle while it met in the front. I didn't know how I could keep it closed.

Cataline pulled out a knife and stabbed a hole in each side of the blanket, then sliced a thong of rawhide from several hanging from his saddle He handed the thong to me.

"*Merci*," I said. I managed to thread the rawhide through the holes and tie the blanket together. It made a huge difference. I was still cold, and my feet were definitely the coldest part of me, but I wasn't shivering anymore. I thought about the sketches I'd seen of the Indians from the prairie lands of Canada, where the women travelled with blankets over their heads in much the same style as I was. It made perfect sense to me now.

We trailed into the yard of the Cottonwood Ranch and roadhouse at about three in the afternoon. The snow had stopped and the country was sparkling in the sunshine. I couldn't see the Cariboo Mountains, but I knew they were not far. The mountains could wait. I was cold, hungry, and ached in every joint. Dolly, while patient and steady, was, after so many hours, not a comfortable chair. I wanted a meal, a warm room, and tea, but first I had to wait until one of Cataline's helpers could take Dolly. I couldn't just get off and leave her, or I might have to walk into those mountains to Barkerville tomorrow.

My legs ached. I hoped there was a bath.

Finally, I was able to make my way to the roadhouse. The two-storey log cabin had been built just this year and was not quite finished as there were sawdust piles and boards in one corner, but it was equipped with a woodstove that was emanating warmth into the kitchen and sitting room. Our hosts, Mr. Ryder and Mr. Smith, welcomed us and offered us soup and bread. You'd think we'd been starving at the rate we gulped down that hot soup and shovelled in the bread. We all had second helpings. I didn't notice what kind of soup it was, just that it was hot.

"We have stew ready for you in about half an hour," Mr. Ryder said. I'd caught a glimpse of someone in the kitchen, but now looked more closely and saw it was a young Chinese man. I was reassured to see him, as any Chinese food I'd had in Victoria had been delicious. I expected I could count on him to keep stew from being the bland English paste it sometimes was. Not that I was fussy about my food today. Any food, preferably hot, would likely do.

Mr. Ryder showed me to my room: a narrow bed with two blankets, a pitcher of water, and the accompanying bowl. "Outhouse at the back," he said. No bath.

"Thank you." It was almost freezing in the bedroom. I asked for an additional blanket. "I'd like one that is heavy."

"I'll see what I can do."

The blanket I'd used on the ride from Quesnelmouth was sopping. I took it to the sitting room and draped it near the stove to dry thoroughly, then proceded to the outhouse. By the time I returned I was again chilled. I sat close to the stove while I waited for stew. I thought my feet would never return to normal, but eventually they did. I'd changed into a new pair of wool stockings which helped with the thaw. I could feel my legs stiffening and an ache developing in my lower back. I need to move, but not quicky, just enough to keep my muscles from stiffening completely.

When Cataline came, I ignored my aches and pains and asked him to join me near the fire. I inquired after his rates for conveying freight and mentioned my plans for establishing a business in Barkerville. He referred me to the BX office in Barkerville and assured me he would bring as much freight as I wanted.

We adjourned to the dining room table. Although that day's trip had not been as long as usual, riding a horse or a mule was more tiring than riding in a stagecoach, and the men were as tired as I was. We ate quickly and quietly and retired to our rooms. Mr. Ryder had indeed found a heavy blanket for me. It looked to be an animal skin, a bear, I think. It was wonderfully warm.

I was much refreshed when we started again in the morning. My legs ached a little, but not as badly as I had feared.

I had purloined a small bit of sugar from breakfast by containing it in my handkerchief. I dumped it into my hand and fed it to Dolly. She seemed to appreciate it. The day was bright and not as cold as it had been yesterday. Perhaps spring was finally coming. I thought briefly of London and Russell Square. The bluebells would be a carpet under the leafy plane trees. Cherry trees would be blooming. Daffodils would surround the cottages. There were no flowers here.

We formed our line and headed east. It wasn't long before we were surrounded by the Cariboo Mountains, not as high as the Coast Mountains or the Alps, but they weren't small hills either. Dolly laboured on the inclines, and I braced my legs for the downhill ride. I had to pay more attention to what she was doing than I had yesterday, but I didn't have to worry about the cold as it was much warmer. I had tied the blanket on behind me, and tied the shawl on as well. I would need it for the rest breaks.

There was some snow on the trail and the hillsides, but it was melting quicky as the day wore on. The mountains were close beside me and the mule train often disappeared around one of the many curves and corners of this trail. The engineers hadn't touched this section of the trail yet, and it was narrow. The two wagons were having a difficult time with ruts, rocks, and hills. The drivers were skilled, and the horses pulling the wagons strong and impressive. Still, the wagons lurched and skidded at times. I hoped my consignment of whiskey would arrive intact, but it didn't seem likely. I had labelled the trunk with the whiskey in it CHINA. FRAGILE. I hadn't wanted to advertise it contained liquor and put temptation in the way of the freight workers. If any bottles broke, the smell would announce the contents. I couldn't control the drivers, so I decided not to worry about it.

IT WAS LATE AFTERNOON WHEN we arrived in Barkerville. The sun was still high in the sky, giving us a warm day. The threat of snow was a memory. Cataline stopped the mule train at the entrance of the town, where there was a flat field and a stream for the animals to drink from. My first reaction was huge disappointment. The population count for Barkerville for the previous year had been ten thousand people. That included Richfield and Cameronton, which were close by. I expected a city: shops, churches, theatres, and many people on the streets. I thought I'd see activity: people chatting, wagons, horses, a contented bustle of movement and commerce. I saw nothing like that. The town appeared to be a line of shacks and rough wooden buildings without a single redeeming feature of beauty, except the mountains on either side. Even those were scarred with the digging the miners had done. There were few people on the street. How would I make a living here? This was not what I expected. I was vastly disappointed. This might have been a huge mistake. How could I have thought it was my future? My salvation? I took myself to task.

*Gold, Florence. They found gold here. You will as well.* It looked as though I would *have* to find gold.

*thirteen*

# Arriving in Barkerville

THE CITY OF Barkerville huddled at the bottom of a canyon. Conifers fringed the top of the mountains, but the sides and the valley were denuded of any growth. It was as if a giant hand had dug a trench with a trowel, leaving bare earth, then flung wooden houses, sheds, and shacks along the road that ran through it.

Of course, I knew there would be some houses, stores, perhaps even a church, but I had expected a more stable, satisfied, and settled look in a city of this size. Not this bleak, raw, primitive settlement. It was far north of Victoria and a cold country. Spring here wouldn't mean bluebells, primroses, or blooming hawthorn hedges, I understood that. But this total absence of trees, bushes, or greenery of any kind was appalling.

I stared at the wooden houses nearest to me. One appeared to be a saloon, another a livery stable, then a bakery. The row of buildings, none taller than a first storey, perhaps with sleeping quarters or storage above the ground floor, stretched out on either side of a main street too narrow for two wagons to pass. Wooden sidewalks were about two to three feet above the muddy street and at various elevations. In the distance was another mountain blocking the far vista. There were trees on that mountain, but not in Barkerville. Surrounding Barkerville was a landscape of stumps and mud.

I could hear the thump of machinery at a distance and some hammering, sawing, the strike of shovels on rock, and a few calls, but it was strangely quieter than I expected. I had probably read too many reports of the wild towns of the California gold rush.

I dismounted and had to grab the saddle to stay upright. My legs seemed to be made of dough. I stood, wiggling my toes, moving slightly from side to side until I could stand unaided. My back ached, my shoulders as well. I hoped I hadn't done any permanent damage to my muscles.

I petted Dolly. "Good girl. You've been a lovely girl." She nuzzled my hand and I petted her for a few minutes, then I handed her over to one of Cataline's helpers and made my way to the Barnard's Express office, conscious of the picture I made: a middle-aged woman, dressed eccentrically, even scandalously, in men's trousers and work boots with a man's broad-brimmed hat, lurching a little on unsteady legs. I brushed the dust from my trousers, straightened, and tried to walk briskly. I met Messrs. Steele, Stevenson, and Orr at the freight office.

"Isn't Barkerville impressive?" Mr. Stevenson emphasized his enthusiasm with a broad gesture.

"Very," I agreed, although our impressions were likely at odds.

"We created this city in just two years. Before we struck gold, it was nothing but trees with a stream down the centre of the valley. Now it's carters and bakers and merchants. Many of us are living an unexpectedly wealthy life because of this city."

I smiled at his enthusiasm. "I trust I can do the same."

"Why not?" Mr. Orr interjected. "We need intelligent women here."

"She's not just intelligent, she's ambitious," Mr. Steele said. "You know she's here to make money. I say good luck."

"I'll need good luck and good information," I said. "Now, gentlemen, where is the best place for me to take a room while I am establishing my credentials at the bank and arranging for the sale of the goods I brought with me?"

They looked at each other.

"Mrs. Dunn Parker might have a room. She runs an excellent boarding house. She's a good woman and runs a respectable business. I think she'd be happy to converse with another woman."

Mr. Stevenson had been my companion for many days and seemed to have formed a good impression of me. I'd assume his recommendation a considered one.

"She's a thespian, too. You might have interests in common." Mr. Orr also had learned a bit about me. I'd told the men about my interest in the Victoria Theatre and my mother's playwriting days, when I had taken some minor roles at the Theatre Royal in London.

Mr. Orr pointed out Mrs. Dunn Parker's establishment and, after taking my leave of Cataline and Messrs. Stevenson, Orr, and Steele, I picked my way through the mud, carrying my valise. I passed a post office, a watchmaker's, a hardware store, a tinsmith's, a shoe store, a carpenter's shop, and what looked to be another saloon. My mood improved. There was some order and civility here. I hoped to escape notice at least until I'd had a bath and changed my clothes.

The boarding house was a two-storey building with a neatly swept front porch. I hoped Mrs. Dunn Parker would approve of me and allow me a room. I dusted off my clothes as best I could. Lined up on the porch were several pairs of boots of all sizes from a child's to an adult man's. That prepared me for the children who swarmed from the back kitchen to open the front door.

"A woman! Glory be!" The woman who spoke seemed to arise from a sea of children, her auburn hair in profuse ringlets around her pale face. She had lively brown eyes and a wide smile. She looked about thirty. "Madam, come in, do. Sure, you must be wantin' a room. Minnie, scoot up and make the front bedroom tidy."

A tall, thin girl of about five promptly scooted.

"Indeed. I want a room. I am Miss Florence Wilson, just come from Victoria."

"Come along in, do. We are in the kitchen, if you don't mind."

I relaxed. "If you don't mind my dirt and dishevelment."

She took my valise from me and handed it to another girl who disappeared with it, I presumed to the front bedroom. I could see now there were only three children.

We settled the terms of my room and board quickly. I paid her the first month from the cash I carried in my handbag. She was so lively and cheerful I decided that even if her cooking was dreadful, her personality would compensate. I didn't stay for tea as I needed to get clean and tidy. A man I assumed to be Mr. Parker brought a tin bathtub, and Minnie brought a kettle of hot water. Another girl, Sarah, brought a jug of cold. There were towels in the room.

I pulled my skirt from my valise, shook it out, found my clean drawers and stockings. I was happy to see my shoes again and deposited my boots near the door. I'd clean them later.

I had a small hat in the valise, much crushed, but shaken out and fluffed, it looked presentable when pinned to my hair at the back of my head.

I was bathed, clothed, bustled, and skirted into respectability. I dragged the bathtub to the landing and left it there for Mr. Parker. Then I grabbed my handbag and sailed forth. I needed to arrange with Barnard's Express to deliver my personal trunk to Mrs. Parker's house and store the trunks containing my sales material, whiskey and all. I also needed to find a store front from which to sell the goods, and I needed to do that quickly. It had been a long trip, but I was energized with plans.

"We'll keep them for three days, ma'am," the laconic clerk at Barnard's told me. "Then they have to move. We'll have more freight coming in."

"Do you know anyone who has some space I could use for a temporary store?" I asked him. "Those trunks hold items I plan to sell."

He was quiet for a moment. "Try May Sampson's saloon. She's got a bit of space near the front of the saloon you could have."

"Why would she let me do that? Wouldn't I be in competition with her? I'm selling whiskey among other things." I knew I was taking a risk telling anyone what was in my trunks, but I needed customers and that meant I needed to advertise.

He looked away and rolled his head a little, then said, "Give her five bottles for nothing and she'll be right."

I calculated how much that would cost me and decided it would be worth it.

It wasn't far to May Sampson's saloon, just up the street from Mrs. Parker's on the right-hand side with an elevated boardwalk in front of it. I had never entered a saloon in my life. This would be instructive.

It was a large room with a long bar on one side and a huge mirror behind it. A few tables and chairs were scattered around, but I expected most patrons stood or walked around with their drinks. There was room near the front for a table or two for my wares.

May Sampson was a middle-aged, matronly woman dressed in a bright red gown with a startling low decolletage. She seemed pleased to meet me.

"Now how can I help you, my dear?" she said after our mutual pleasantries were over.

I explained I wanted a space to sell my goods, so I could start a business of some sort.

"I can certainly tell you about business. Do you have any experience?"

"I ran a stationery shop in Victoria for two years, and I did the books for my brother's theatres when I lived in England."

"Oh," she almost crooned. "The theatre. Wonderful. We need people experienced in the theatre. Can you act?"

"A little."

"Lovely. We'll have to get you on the committee."

I felt suddenly as if I'd stepped into a fantasy world where friends and opportunities appeared without notice. I concentrated on what was necessary now. "Can I set up tomorrow and begin advertising and selling?

"You can come tomorrow, but don't come early. My girls need their sleep. About ten would be fine."

I agreed and hurried back to Barnard's office.

I gave the clerk instructions. "If you could deliver them tomorrow after ten, I will be there to receive them."

"Can do," he agreed. "Wouldn't want to wake the girls by coming too early."

I blinked as the meaning of "girls" penetrated. May Sampson ran a brothel as well as a saloon.

I considered if selling goods in a brothel would damage my reputation beyond redemption. I didn't ponder the morality of prostitution. I was not going to worry about what I didn't understand. I concerned myself only with the practicalities of the situation. Early in the day, I would not be interfering with the ladies' work. Men—and Barkerville was made up predominantly of men, more than ninety-eight percent according to Judge Begbie—would come to the saloon for beer, spirits, coffee, and tea. Perhaps for other reasons. I'd seen a row of books along the wall. They might even come there to read.

There were a few choices for a temporary spot to sell my goods besides May Sampson's saloon. Wake-up Jake was another saloon and looked quite small. Todd's store sold everything and wouldn't want me to compete so flagrantly. Besides, I wasn't going to offend May Sampson by backing out of our arrangement. I was going to live here. There were few women. I needed to be friendly to all of them.

I wondered what Mr. Dickens would make of this place. He thought all men should be equal and would approve of men dealing with each other from a position of equality: a lord and a blacksmith would have equal status here. I'm not sure he thought all women should be equal to men. I realized I did, though. A prostitute and a teacher might be equal members of the theatre society. It was a novel idea. I wondered what Mary Wollstonecraft would have made of Barkerville's society.

I retired to my room, where the one trunk I'd asked for had been delivered. It was a treat to be reunited with at least some of my belongings. I searched through and found the tin box with my Rose du Roi and added water. I'd pot it and put it on my dresser until I could establish a home for it. I found a ream of paper and began the time-consuming task of creating flyers announcing the sale to be held the next day at noon at May Sampson's saloon. "Spirits, sweets, soap, flour, and sundries," I wrote over and over. When I had twenty-five ready, I called Minnie and promised her a dollar if she delivered them around Barkerville.

Then, I set out to find the bank manager.

"In Richfield, darlin'," Mrs. Dunn Parker said. "There's the Bank of British Columbia and the Bank of British North America."

"The bank is not in Barkerville?"

"No, love. It's in Richfield. Not far, but you'd best get a trap from the livery and drive yourself there. You can drive?"

I nodded. "I can drive, but I don't know where I'm going."

"There's only one road. Anyone will point out the way."

"They will be open?"

"Always," she said. "They do business in shifts. There is so much money coming and going, it takes two men to manage it all."

I procured the trap and docile horse from the livery stable—no riding astride today—and headed south to Richfield. It had been established before Barkerville, but the gold was richer in Barkerville so some of the population had moved, following the gold. I'd learned that from Mr. Stevenson. I drove slowly and allowed the horse to pick her way over the many abandoned sluice boxes and pieces of lumber left on the road as the miners moved up the hills and farther along the creek. A few men were working at a distance where the stream, Williams Creek, turned on itself. I supposed the water might slow at the turn and would be a likely place for gold to accumulate. That made sense. I itched to wade into the creek with a gold pan and find out for myself.

The pony stopped outside the Bank of British North America. That seemed like an omen, as if the pony had known I needed this bank. I descended from the trap and tied the pony to the hitching post.

Richfield was much like Barkerville in that it had wooden sheds and stores built on poles. You needed to climb to the boardwalks to enter the buildings. I gave a fleeting thought to the stone houses of Woburn Place where I'd grown up. Daffodils would be blooming in the garden.

The bank was of wooden construction with wood floors and walls. The clerk was a Mr. Augustine. I presented the letters of credit Mr. MacAdam had given me and deposited my savings. I set up a chequing account and a separate savings account. Mr. Augustine gave me a book of cheques, took my signature in four places, and presented me with a savings pass book. I replenished my supply of cash and returned to Barkerville.

Mrs. Dunn Parker had held a dinner at the back of the stove for me.

"You're getting settled quickly then?" she asked.

"I am." I could ask her for information about Barkerville. I expected that with so few women here, conversations of almost any nature would include them, and that she would be well-informed. Barkerville had only about a hundred women and over five thousand men. I hadn't adjusted to attracting so much attention simply because I was a woman, but I did appreciate the need to have good relations with the women who were here. We would need one another.

I learned about the number of claims staked in Richfield and the growing number of claims in Barkerville from Mrs. Dunn Parker.

"Does Mr. Parker mine then?" I asked her.

“No, we don’t,” she said. “Samuel’s not strong. He works at the hotel, and we manage.”

It must have been galling to see so many discovering riches when you were unable to even try.

I thanked her for the sustaining meal and the company and headed for my room. I barely got into my nightdress before I sank into the bed exhausted and immediately was asleep.

*fourteen*

# Establishing My Business

IN THE MORNING, I rushed through my oatmeal, toast, and tea, and went to check with Barnard's office to ensure the trunks would be delivered. I was relieved to see they were being loaded onto a wagon when I arrived. The horses were sturdy, black, and stamping their feet with impatience, setting their harness to jingling. I, also, was impatient for ten o'clock, so wandered up and down the street, peering at shops and imprinting on my mind the various locations of the laundries, post office, and grocers. Smartly at ten, I was at May Sampson's door. She was there before me and had set out three tables to better display my wares. I was grateful and began unloading as soon as the first trunk arrived through her doors. Luckily, it contained the spirits, and I counted out five bottles of whiskey into May's hands before any customers arrived. I would make double the cost of bottles, but May would make twenty-six times the cost, selling them as individual drinks.

I set the spirits on the table directly in front of where I would be standing. I expected they would sell first. I put the books on a table farthest away from me. Men might want time to peruse a book before buying it. I had the flour, oatmeal, baking soda, salt, pepper, and cinnamon displayed and easy to reach. I turned one trunk around and used the open lid to display the sweets: humbugs, rock candy, licorice, toffee, and caramels. It was ten minutes to noon when I was finished. I stood back, smoothed the folds of my thick cotton skirt, and shook myself until my several petticoats settled around me. I wore my crinoline and looked much more fashionable than I had on the trip north. The skirt was dark blue and my bodice a lighter blue with dark blue trim. I wore shoes, not boots. I'd made the dress in Victoria, hoping to give the impression of a businesswoman. My hat was a light blue with a short veil and worn back on the head so as to be out of my way. Luckily, that was also fashionable. I was ready.

Promptly at noon, May opened the doors wide and an avalanche of men poured in. They all seemed to want books and whiskey at once and shoved dollars and gold at me. May stood by my side and helped keep the queues of eager buyers in some kind of order.

"Jake, stay in line, old sod, or we'll shift you right out of here," May called out to a young man who kept darting out of line to grab another purchase.

"Yes, ma'am," he acquiesced with a grin.

Thank goodness they were cheerful and cooperative.

By two o'clock, I had sold almost everything. May had stood behind the tables to help me accept payment because I couldn't possibly have done it alone.

"Well," May said. "That was fun." Her eyes lit, and she smiled. "I really like raking in the money, and I love it when the fellas are having a good time. You're going to be an asset, my girl. Welcome to Barkerville."

"Thank you," I said, truly appreciative. "You are amazing." She had been generous with her time and her ability to mange the crowd. I wondered if I would ever develop that skill.

"I am, rather. Want a drink to celebrate? You must have made a fistful."

I followed her, bemused and still reeling from the speed of the sales. "I did."

She led me behind the bar where she brought out a bottle of port. "I don't think you're the whiskey type."

"No. Port would be lovely."

I sipped and marvelled at the amount of money I'd made in two hours.

"What are you going to do now?" May asked.

I stared at her and slowly smiled. "I have a choice. I *love* having a choice."

"You've got to have a few thousand there." May was shorter than me, had a pleasing plumpness about her as if she was soft and accommodating, but her brown eyes were alert with intelligence, and I expected she had a will of iron.

I nodded in agreement and brought out my handbag stuffed with money and gold nuggets. One man, about my age, with a long beard, moustache, and distinct odour of unwashed body had shoved a nugget the size of a thimble at me. I hope he got his money's worth as I hadn't weighed the gold.

"Well, Florence. You did very well by the look of it. I can put all this in my safe overnight."

I took the bulging handbag and my ledger book with me into May's office, where her safe was located.

First, I counted the money. Five thousand six hundred forty-six dollars and twenty cents. That was about a thousand English pounds. I had never had so much money in my life. I could buy a house, stock a business, and own a carriage. I felt a warm glow of satisfaction, then a tingle of excitement as I envisioned my life as a wealthy woman. I shook with the overwhelming exhilaration of those dreams. I took a few deep breaths, dampened my joy, and gave my attention to the ledger book. I had listed all the supplies and the price I paid for each item as well as the price I expected to receive in the book before the sale. I'd done that before I left Victoria. No one haggled over the prices, so totalling the amount was easy. I had fourteen books left over and a pair of ladies' shoes. I excepted those items and added the columns of sales figures and subtracted my expenses. That left me with a profit of three thousand nine hundred and sixty dollars. I could make a living buying and selling goods.

"Did you make a good profit?" May repeated as she returned to check on me.

"I did. I made a wonderful profit. This is an astonishing place."

"You can run a very good business here. Is this what you want to do?" She gestured at the pile of money before me.

"I'm not sure. I needed money to start something. I don't know if I want to continue selling goods, though. I'll take it to the bank tomorrow then think about what I could do."

"It will be tight and tidy in my safe overnight. Come by in the morning and take it out. Here, I'll give you a receipt for it. How much?"

I told her. She wrote out a receipt for the full amount. She didn't check to see that amount was accurate.

"Do you want to count it with me?" That was the best way for May to ensure I had given her the correct amount.

"No. I'm sure you're honest. I'll give you a money bag. You put everything in it. I'll put it in my safe, and no one will touch it."

I stared at her. She could take some of my money. She could take all of it, but she was giving me a receipt, and I knew Judge Begbie; I would get it back. Besides, I had to trust someone, and it might as well be May.

"Do you have any idea what I should do?" She'd been a good source of information so far. She might have more ideas.

"Just a moment." She stuck her head out of the door. "Anthony! Bring us some tea." She turned her head and checked with me. "Does that suit you?"

I nodded. Tea was just what I needed.

May settled back in her chair, her tiny feet resting on a footstool. I could almost see her busy brain working. May seemed to be two people. The businesswoman sitting before me in her demure grey dress with white lace trim. Her dark brown hair was in neat chignon. May ran a brothel, to be sure, but a brothel was likely run on the same principles as any other business: Money came in as income and went out as expenses. A businessperson had to intercept that transaction to take as much money for herself as was prudent. May's advice would be useful. The other May was the evening entertainer who wore a bright red silk dress with a daring decolletage and black lace abundant around the sleeves and hem. That May let her hair hang down her back and spoke in a loud voice, sometimes shouting.

"You can continue with selling as you did today. Maybe do it once every two weeks. Do you like that work?" She was not shouting now. In fact, she had been a pillar of reliability and calmness all through the sale.

"Not particularly."

"You could set up a school."

I shuddered. "No."

She grinned. "How about a regular store like Todd's? The gold in Richfield won't last long and those folks will move up here. I hear the bank is moving soon. Barkerville will grow, and you can grow with it. Or, you could start another saloon. The miners have a never-ending need for a saloon."

I bit my lip. I could handle the liquor sales and perhaps the sale of food and tea and coffee, but I had no idea about running a brothel, nor did I want to. I was so ignorant of the sexual behaviour of men and women, I'd be sure to blunder. I didn't want to run a dancing saloon either. That could get raucous. As well, I felt it unbecoming to me. But I didn't want to offend May by blurting that out.

"Not all saloons are brothels," she said, correctly interpreting my silence. "Some of them are more like coffee houses with the addition of a bar. You could create your own style. As long as you serve liquor, the men will come."

I PONDERED HER ADVICE AND, in the end, I did as she suggested and established my own saloon, called the Regency. I bought a two-storey building close to the centre of town. It wasn't large, but it had enough room for a long polished wooden bar with the required mirror behind it and foot rail for gentlemen's boots. I had shelves built and loaded them with books. The kitchen was outfitted under the instruction of my Chinese cook, Song Wing, who wanted hot and cold running water and a reliable stove. The stove came in via Barnard's Express in parts, and I hired Sam Tompkins, a blacksmith, to assemble it. Song Wing hired his own staff, and I expected those scullery aides were relatives. Song Wing had a wife and other children in China. The government would only allow workers from China into the country, not families. It seemed an odd law. But I expected the officials were trying to keep British Columbia for white men, ignoring the Native people and preventing established communities of brown people. I blamed Trutch for that. He seemed to be a strong but peculiar influence on the laws of this colony.

I had tables scattered throughout with comfortable chairs. I hired a carpenter to make the tables and Sam Tompkins to create the wrought-iron chairs. I made cushions for the chairs, and once all were finished, I invited Sam to test them. If they could hold the weight of a six-foot-two, burly blacksmith, they would be sturdy enough for others. They held.

Barnard's Express was reliable and prompt. Cataline never lost a package. In a month, I was set up for business. Men came to buy drinks, read books, and play card games, betting on the outcome. It was lively most of the day, but busiest in the evening when the saloon was full of men talking, occasionally shouting, or intent on their card games, with several onlookers placing bets on the game. The lanterns gave a dim light, so the saloon was full of shadows and smoke from the many pipes and cigars.

"Come play a hand, Miss Wilson," Angus MacDonald called to me as he did every time he was in the saloon.

I'd made the mistake of playing with him once, and he seemed to think I would play every night. Too much attention to one man resulted in a marriage proposal or, less flattering, a request for a liaison. It overwhelmed me at first. I'd go home to Mrs. Dunn Parker's and stand in my room taking deep breaths, concentrating on being alone and calm.

The men made so many demands. They wanted particular drinks which I didn't carry. I learned to just smile and say I'd look into it. They usually accepted whatever I had in stock.

Besides Song Wing and his boys, I had four staff: two behind the bar, one as a waiter, and one to relieve the barman and act as a waiter when needed. I thought I had all the hours covered, but some of my employees had mining claims and would take off to work them when they'd promised to be in my saloon. I learned to serve at the bar and got comfortable with it.

I used the small room near the front door as a store and stocked it with speciality items, particularly stationery and art supplies, candy, handmade moccasins, and knitted articles. Those who didn't want to enter the saloon could frequent my store. I ordered from Victoria and bought locally. I found the Indian women to be particularly good traders. Of course, they had been trading among themselves and with the colonists for years, so they were good at it. I didn't make a lot of profit on their trades as they kept a keen eye on the price and would take their goods elsewhere if I didn't compete.

I had the front entrance constructed so customers entered into a foyer: one door went to my small store and the second, large, swinging double doors, was the entrance to the saloon. The Chinese and Indian people did not enter the saloon both because they wouldn't be welcome by other patrons and, in the case of the Indian people, because it was illegal for them to be where liquor was served. I had a stove and comfortable chairs in the store hoping the warmth would attract people during the winter months.

I did ask about Betsy's husband, Abel, but the few I encountered who knew of him were vague. I had no news.

Betsy finally wrote me.

*... You will be glad to know that Abel arrived home safely. It takes some getting used to ... him being gone for so long ... but we are chugging along not so badly. He's taken to gardening and working on a new house on Yates Street. I have my eye on some property near the edge of town. We could build a new house there and sell it. I don't want to move from Government Street. It's easy for me to get renters here should Abel take it into his head to wander off again ...*

I smiled to myself. Betsy would always be practical.

Occasionally, musicians visited Barkerville and my saloon became one of the venues they performed in. At those events, I arranged the room with the chairs facing the bar; the musicians performed in front of the bar. I heard Brahms, Bach, Liszt, and a marvellous performance of music from Offenbach's *Orpheus in the Underworld.* Thomas had written he had commissioned that musical to appear next spring in London. That made me feel more connected to the broader world.

I had a small office at the back of the saloon. I usually kept my door open when I was there, so people dropped in to chat. I wasn't always in the office, though, because I was negotiating the purchase of another saloon and checking on the property.

One evening while I was working on the books, a young man of about eighteen wandered in and sat down across the desk from me. He was tall, about six feet, thin and wiry, with blond hair and dark skin. His brown eyes looked at me with sorrow.

"I miss my ma," he blurted out. Then he closed his eyes as if embarrassed.

"Where is she?" I asked, prepared to listen.

He told me about his family in California, his mother, his sister, and his dog.

"I need to make money for them." He was earnest and burdened with responsibility. I had no idea how to help him. He had to make his own way. I imagined he would do so, if he could handle his homesickness.

After about ten minutes he stood. "Thanks, Miss Wilson. You're great."

"Will you be all right?"

"Sure. Thanks."

I smiled at him as he left, but, truly, I hadn't done anything.

He wasn't the only one who thought I'd make a good listener. Homesickness and loneliness were prevalent. I had occasional yearnings myself for an afternoon with Thomas and his family and the company of intellectuals in Bloomsbury. I kept up correspondence with my friends in Victoria, and occasionally wrote a report for Hilary. But I didn't want to return to Victoria or London. I hadn't expected my social life here to bloom the way it did. Aside from the weekly offers of marriage from men I barely knew, I was now a member of the Cariboo Drama Society, the Literary Society, and the businessmen's organization.

By September, the drama society was into rehearsals for a play in which I had a minor part. Sam Tompkins had offered to construct the sets for the play and Catherine Dunn Parker had offered to act and paint the sets. She had help, as we all contributed a few hours under her direction to create the pieces. Sam often came around to my saloon to take tea with me and borrow books. He read constantly and we talked about the books. Since I had chosen them all, I had some familiarity with them. He was about my age, perhaps a little younger.

Judge Begbie stopped to take tea with Sam and me one afternoon. He had been presiding over the murder trial of James Barry, who had waylaid Charles Morgan Blessing on the trail from Quesnelmouth to Barkerville, killed, and robbed him.

"What was the verdict?" I asked him.

"The jury found him guilty."

"And?" I asked.

"And I sentenced him to hang."

The judge did not elaborate on his reasons. Doubtless, he had pronounced those reasons in court and saw no need to inform me of them. I was sure he was fair, but not, I believe, merciful. Judge Begbie believed in the sanctity and superiority of British law and was so scrupulously devoted to it, he wasn't a man I could trust with any transgression I might commit.

He enjoyed what he called a "civilized tea" with me. It was a beautiful, sunny Cariboo day, with the sky so blue beyond the mountains it seemed almost unreal. The poplar trees at the top of the mountains were turning a bright, cadmium yellow, something I'd not seen before.

"I'm hearing great things about the cultural development of Barkerville all due to your efforts, Miss Wilson." Judge Begbie's voice held admiration. I looked at him sharply; I was accustomed to seeing him as an older man, but I realized he was only about three or four years older than me. Was he attracted to me? I had never considered him as an eligible bachelor, although he certainly was. He was a fine actor and singer, and interested in many subjects. There was no gossip about any wife or love interest around him. Likely, he was one of those men who was not interested in any involvement. Rare, but possible, so May told me. He didn't give off any feelings or indications of interest in women. With all the men surrounding me, I was learning under May's tutelage and my own common sense to read a man's interest.

"It's a survival skill," May told me. "You're handicapped because you live in your head too much. You think everything is going to be logical. It isn't. People, especially men, operate from their guts. They act because they feel. You have to read the feelings—before they act."

Some men were interested only because I was female; some were interested because I laughed with them; some were dangerously interested because they had a need to dominate; and some, like Sam, were interested because they enjoyed my company and genuinely liked me. May was of a great help to me because where I was tempted to laugh about a clumsy approach to wooing, she knew some of the men very well and would warn me not to be deceived by appearances of naivety. She told me who was best avoided. Some were genuinely amusing, though.

Jed Barclay came with a hat full of gold in big nuggets and plopped it down on my desk.

"I can support ye', gal. Why don't ya' take me on?"

Jed may have seen a bathtub sometime in his life, but not in his recent past. His beard had trickled down from his face as if attempting to act as a cloak. But he was genuine, and I didn't want to hurt him.

"I'm sorry, Jed," I'd said, gripping the hat from the brim on either side and hoisting it with its load up to him. "You take that gold to Victoria and find yourself a younger woman who can give you a family."

"Oh." He stared at me. "You're older than I thought?"

"Oh yes," I lied. I wasn't too old for children, but I certainly didn't want Jed's.

In England, Jed wouldn't have dreamed of approaching me. Here, it was totally reasonable from his point of view. It was a new world for me. Some nights, ensconced in my office, working on my ledgers and reading the agreement for the purchase of my second saloon, hearing the rustlings and occasional clang of a pot from the kitchen where Song Wing was shutting down his domain, I could hardly believe my good fortune.

*fifteen*

# An Unexpected Courtship

*December 1864*

*Mr. Hilary Payne,*
The British Colonist, *Victoria, Colony of British Columbia*

*Dear Hilary,*

*I trust this finds you well and busy as usual about the business of Victoria. I am most interested in the deposing of Governor Douglas. I fear Mr. Trutch will not be good for the colony. I quite understand the need to join with the eastern part of the continent and become one state of Canada. Do keep the news coming to me. I am happy that Jane and her husband, Mr. Nesbitt, are doing so well with their bakery. I miss popping up to Yates Street of a morning to chat with her. I don't have much time for visiting here, as I am busy with my saloon and investments. I am given much opportunity to buy shares of mining claims which amounts to me giving a miner money and he doing the daily work. I have a major portion of two claims that are doing well, so if you decide to leave Victoria and make your fortune here in Barkerville, I can introduce you to hard-working and intelligent miners.*

*You asked me to describe the way in which the gold is transported from Barkerville. It is ingenious and quite dependent on the honesty of everyone involved. The gold is handed over to the government assayer, who weighs it, gives the miner a receipt, then prepares the gold for transport. This is done by melting the gold into bricks. The assayer's office has a kiln out the back which a friend of mine, Mr. Tompkins, a blacksmith, built for them. Handy, I'm sure and efficient to make all those nuggets into bricks. Miners usually keep back some of their biggest nuggets—as proof of their success, I believe. The rest goes to the assayer's office. Certainly, the accounting has to be meticulous because everyone's gold is melted together so the only evidence of what you contribute to the brick is the accounting. It's my firm conviction that business success rests on meticulous accounting, as tedious as that sometimes is. The bricks are handed over to the bank, which maintains the responsibility for transport. The gold is then packed into special bags which keep the bricks from rubbing on each other and set on the mule train to Quesnelmouth and thence along Barnard's Stagecoach Express to Victoria. It's surprising no one tries to rob the mule train or the stage coach, but, in truth, that's a rare occurrence.*

*Do let me know how your romance is progressing. When appropriate I will send you and your bride a set of silver tea spoons with a gold nugget embedded on the handles.*

*Yours sincerely,*
*Florence*

IT WAS TRUE I was a busy with running my saloon and that it did, indeed, give me a comfortable income. I managed the ordering of supplies and the employment of a staff of workers. I hired the tradesmen I needed to keep the saloon running. Sam Tompkins gave me good advice on who to ask to do the plumbing and carpentry work.

"What is it this time, love?" he said from my office door.

"The cesspool in the kitchen needs draining."

"Oh, that's not so bad. Song Wing's been putting grease down there again, has he?"

"More likely his worker."

"Aye, more likely. And how's yourself? Tossed any malcontents out on their ear? Bought any more saloons? Started a school?"

I eyed him. He was smiling. "Do you think I'm a tad dictatorial?"

"Bossy, yes. Spicy, definitely," Sam said. "Just enough to be interesting. And firm. You need to be in Barkerville."

Sam was a cheerful man, full of conversation about anything at all. He'd had a roadhouse on the Old Cariboo Road near Yank's Peak before the road changed its route, and I could see how he would have been a favourite with his customers. He livened up my saloon when he visited.

"I'm bringing back your *Les Misérables*. What does that mean, *Les Misérables*?"

"The Miserable Ones."

"You read French?"

"I do."

"So, is it likely this Jean Valjean would live that fantastic life Victor Hugo gives him?"

I thought about it. "No, but . . ."

"You're going to say he took poetic license. That's just lazy."

I laughed. Sam borrowed books from me constantly, read them, then argued with me about them. He always made me laugh.

May visited me for tea and biscuits and gave me advice on how to manage the exuberance of the men in the saloon, which on a few occasions had been threatening.

"Smile and listen to them," she said. "They are basically lonely."

She also taught me a great deal about the relations between men and women—varied and, as far as I could see, unpredictable. She had a partner in business, a man called Red MacEwan—inexplicable as he had dark hair and a dark, bushy beard. It was a few months before I realized he was more than her business partner. He was always on hand to control any wayward men.

"He's handy, that's for sure," May told me. "He has a claim he works, so he put some money into my business."

No one seemed to lose respect for May in spite of the nature of her business and the nature of her liaison. In fact, from what I could overhear from my office when the door was open and men were congregated at my bar, they admired Red MacEwan for establishing himself so well. It was definitely different from England, although such liaisons occurred there too—witness Mr. Dickens and Miss Ternan and my own mother with Augustus Pugin—but while known, such arrangements were not socially accepted, more ignored or disparaged. Here in Barkerville, they were acknowledged and accepted.

"Lucky sod," was the general approbation.

May advised me on the anticipated needs of each season. She had warned me Christmas would be difficult for some, so I was to provide comfort and lots of liquor.

I had never seen such snow. I remembered a Christmas in Shropshire with Grandpa and Grandmama when we had snow—but not so much of it. Here, it piled up in huge drifts at the sides of the buildings, creating some insulation from the cold. I sent the barman out every day to shovel the snow from the boardwalk in front of my saloon. The skies dumped more every night until it reached the eaves.

"It's all going to be mud in the spring," Sam said.

The vision of mud surrounding my saloon reconciled me to the snow. Cold as the snow was, at least it was clean.

Many miners left Barkerville and returned to Victoria or San Francisco for the winter, as they couldn't work the frozen ground. Before they left I had secured a major share of two more mining claims. The government assayer operated out of the Hudson's Bay Company store. I had the advice of the assistant to the Hudson's Bay factor, a young man called Hugh Ross, who came to my saloon for books to read and for coffee. He was known to be tight-lipped and one to keep his information confidential, but I assumed he thought that I, as a woman, would not act on it.

"More coffee, Mr. Ross?"

"That'd be fine, lass. It's a pleasure to relax here."

"I imagine it gets hectic at the store, but perhaps not at this time of year."

"No, it's quieter now. Mind you, many a man is a wee bit fed up with mining, so claims are changing hands. The assayer is busy trying to prove which claims are valuable and which are not."

"I suppose the purchasers are asking for information."

"Aye, but he can't give out the information to na one but the owner of the claim, so ye can see it's a bit of a conundrum."

"I do see. For instance, if Mr. Dixon wanted to sell his claim on Lightning Creek, the assayer couldn't tell the buyer whether anything had come out of it lately."

"That's a good example, Miss Wilson, because it so happens Mr. Dixon is wantin' to sell and his claim is a good one, but the assayer can't tell interested parties that."

"No. That's hard for the seller." I had been thinking of buying that claim, but I hadn't expected Mr. Ross to give me information.

"We have some shortbread. Would you like some?"

"I would. Thanks."

I bought the claim from Mr. Dixon.

The saloon was quiet during the day, as the miners left in town for the winter generally didn't arrive until the evening. The Indians also left for the winter. They had far more comfortable homes elsewhere. I know some travelled back to Soda Creek on the Fraser River. It would stay much warmer there and spring would come earlier.

While I had fewer customers during December, I was busy. Our drama society had produced one play in the autumn, and we were well into another. I had a small part and enjoyed memorizing it. I'd persuaded Sam to help with the sets and act as a prompter. He'd had much opportunity to participate in drama before this and seemed to come alive in the company of actors. I felt that way myself, as if I was someone else who had fewer restraints and more emotions than my routine self. Or perhaps, just fewer restrictions on my emotions.

I was not tempted to spend the winter in Victoria. Barkerville was now my home, and I wanted to experience it to the fullest. The snow was not like the snow of England or the Alps where I had travelled. This snow was softer, dryer, powdery, as if the moisture had been extracted from it before it hit the ground.

My regular shoes would be useless in the snow and my work boots would slide. I admired the Indian moccasins, the beaded boots, brought to me for sale. With advice from several miners and Sam, I'd ordered myself a pair. It took a month because Luane Joe, a woman from Soda Creek, said she had to find a suitable deer carcass in her storage shed and tenderize it so it was supple enough to work with. She'd brought them to me before she left for the winter. She had executed beautiful stitching around the edges. I saw the join of sole and upper shoe was higher than in our colonist boots. That made sense. Moisture would be less likely to seep in through the higher join. She'd made them elegant with a beaded design.

"It's good luck," she'd told me, pointing to the design.

I thanked her and paid her.

"Sweets?" she questioned me.

We were in my small store, where I had many sweets for sale. "For the children?" I smiled. I knew perfectly well Luane had a sweet tooth, but we kept up the fiction I was giving a present to her children. I was sure they'd get some. I was happy to add a full bag of sweets to my payment. The moccasins were a treasure. With a pair of woollen stockings inside, they were also warm.

The barman and the waiter, George and Hans, kept my wood stove at the Regency full during the day, but I stoked it about nine at night to be sure to keep the water and supplies from freezing. I usually trudged back to Catherine Dunn Parker's after that, and let

George close the saloon at midnight. But lately, I'd been going the other direction to join Sam at his place. He kept his house warm all night, and I appreciated that. I also appreciated his friendship and the intensity about him when he looked at me, though he put a restraint on his behaviour. He would not bully me. He knew I wouldn't stand for it, but I knew he had scruples of his own and wouldn't press me.

We did talk about marriage. I was a tentative lover as I was uncomfortable as a mistress. He understood that. Yet I was also reluctant to marry, as the law would give all my property to my husband. Upon marriage all business transactions would have to be conducted by my husband and not necessarily with my approval. It was a huge disenfranchisement, and I wasn't about to let that happen to me. Sam said he'd sign an affidavit refusing to accept my property and returning it to me. I wasn't sure if that would hold up in court, and I was afraid to risk it. My financial security was vital to me. On the other hand, Sam was becoming more and more important. I dithered.

In the spring, I turned my attention to a library. While I offered free library service from my saloon, the books were not available to everyone. Women, children, the Chinese people, and the Indians were reluctant to spend much time in the saloon. I had already donated many of the books I'd brought with me from England to a Literary Society in Cameronton when I first arrived as I felt everyone should have a chance to read, but Cameronton was about a mile north of Barkerville and inconvenient. I still had a trunkload of books in Mrs. Dunn Parker's shed—some from England and some I'd acquired in Victoria, for which I had no room in my saloon—so decided to donate them to a library. As well, so many people were coming to my saloon for books—and only for books—that I needed to free up space for my customers. That necessitated a committee to find housing for a library. That meant setting up a society, which we did. I catalogued the books and set up a better system for loans, which meant I was the (unpaid) librarian. With only a little persuasion, the committee agreed to order newspapers from England and America. Although the news was months old by the time it reached us, it was exciting to hear about the changes in government, the arguments in the House of Commons, the protestations of the poor to the repeal of the Poor Relief and Loans Act, to the resolution of the narrow-gauge and broad-gauge railway tracks, and the continued mourning of Queen Victoria for Prince Albert. Sam, originally from Rhode Island via California, was anxious to follow the outcomes of the American battles, which he did with many comments about the stupidity of generals and the idiocy of their troops to take any part in the war. The war ended in the spring, to the relief of many. Sam read the reports of how the ceasefire was affecting both sides. He and I had a spirited argument about the nature of war, the inevitability of men to solve problems with violence, and the need to eradicate slavery. The last point was one we agreed on, just not on the methods of doing so.

IN JUNE OF 1865, SAM came bursting into my office as excited as I'd ever seen him.

"There's a reverend in town," he said. "A Reverend Hall. He could marry us."

I stared at Sam.

"He's leaving tomorrow. He's not coming back. We could get married and no one would know."

Perhaps this was our chance. Rev. Hall was a Presbyterian minister. I'd heard he was here, but I hadn't thought of asking him to conduct a marriage service. Sam took it all in hand. He persuaded the two men who had accompanied Rev. Hall to act as our witnesses. He asked for secrecy, spinning a story about my irate father. My father had died on the Isle of Jersey five years previously, but they weren't to know that. Since I was of the mature age of forty-two, they were not worried about any coercion or force from Sam. We were married at Sam's house so as to escape notice and kept the event to ourselves. We would not announce it. I was not going to tell the bank manager or anyone in authority, and that included Judge Begbie. To everyone but the minister and his friends who had left Barkerville and were unlikely to return, we were unmarried. Sam and I proceeded as usual, but it did make a difference to me. Sam had been right. As his wife, I was definitely a more enthusiastic lover.

I moved out of Catherine's place and into Sam's house. I persuaded Song Wing, with the inducement of an increase in his wages, to cook for us each evening. He usually cooked the meal at the saloon and sent it over with one of his boys. The laundry went to Sin Hap's laundry. Sam had that arrangement, and I added my clothes to the service.

Back in Bloomsbury, most of our servants were women. Here in Barkerville, most services were supplied by men. Any feminine touches such as flowers, fine china, and good linens were the responsibility of women.

I'd concluded the purchase of another saloon. It was set up to run much as the Regency did. I named it the Falcon. I wanted to name it the Middlesex after the county in central London where I was born and grew up, but Sam pointed out the name might be misinterpreted to mean a place where men who loved men would congregate, and that would limit my customers. I hadn't thought of that, so the Falcon it became. I transacted all my business myself as Miss Florence Wilson. Everyone assumed I was living as Sam's mistress and had the good manners not to mention it.

*sixteen*

# Life in Barkerville

Summer had brought the Indian families from Lillooet to the blueberry fields around Barkerville. They picked and dried the fruit and packed it into leather bags to transport home. They fished in the lakes and rivers and smoked the fish speared on long wooden poles and arranged over a smoking fire. A few days of smoking and the fish were dry enough to pack for travel. It was as if this area of the country was one of their agricultural fields, which they could maintain year after year without plowing or weeding. It worked well as long as white men didn't disrupt those fields, which they certainly did and had done in the hills around Barkerville. Luckily, there were many more hills beyond. From the women I bought more moccasins, bags, and beaded belts for the store. Luane Joe offered me a pair of tiny leather booties. They were charming, and I thought Catherine might be expecting again, so I bought them.

The Regency was noisy with the loud conversations of a hundred men, drinking, playing cards, and arguing with each other. Besides the noise they made, they created an unpleasant odour, a mixture of beer, whiskey, stale bodies, dirt, and that peculiar smell men emit when they are excited. I had gotten used to it, and after the first few minutes of entering the saloon, didn't notice it. I'd hired an extra guard to placate any angry men and divert quarrelsome customers to milder activities. The men, of various ages but mostly young, were generally a well-behaved bunch, but occasionally I needed a brawny man to establish order.

May Sampson had come over to visit, and we were settled in my office with tea—a wonderful, aromatic Darjeeling from India—and biscuits. I closed the door to the saloon to shut out the noise. It was August, the height of the mining season, and men were desperate to make good on their claims before the snow fell in September. It was eight at night, but both May and I were still at work. May could take a half hour away from her saloon, and I could manage that much time without supervising mine. I had a manager in the Falcon, a Mr. Neil Ferguson, who had few problems managing the workers. He had been a teacher in Scotland, and I supposed was used to assuming authority.

"Any news?" I asked May. We traded information on trends in the mining claims, who was quarreling with whom, and the shocking prices of supplies. I now had an interest in four claims, in one of which I was the major share holder. I had my eye on several more. I'd earned back my initial investment on the first three, so now all the gold that came my way was profit.

"I'm thinking of pulling out of Barkerville and going to California," May dropped that notion on me without preamble.

I felt as if I was being abandoned. But that was ridiculous. Everyone in Barkerville was either coming or going. Some stayed much longer than others. I wished May would stay, but didn't say so.

"I will miss you. What made you decide that now?" I was determined to be a good friend and support her, despite my growing feeling of dismay.

"I've got a fair amount saved and, now that the war's over, Red wants to go back to his people in California. He's asking me to go with him."

The war between the states had ended in the spring of this year. Americans who had fled the conflict would now consider going back. It was logical.

"And you?" May said. "Does Sam want to go back?"

While Sam was originally from the east coast of the United States, he was more recently from Brandy City, California. If he went anywhere, it would be California. He had wanted nothing to do with the war and cheerfully left his fellow Americans to the whole mess.

"He hasn't said so."

"I expect you'd wait until the baby arrives."

"What baby?"

She stared at me. "Your baby. You're pregnant, aren't you? I don't usually mistake the signs."

I frantically thought back to my last menses. I was often irregular and didn't keep track of my monthly visitor. I had also been very busy. I realized it had been several months since I'd bled. I counted back. I'd had a light showing in June. It must have been June as the snow had just left for good and business picked up substantially. No wonder I'd felt tired. I'd thought it was because I had to work so hard during that time. May had to be right.

I blinked, shocked. "I thought I was too old to have a baby. Forty-two. I'm forty-two." I estimated when the baby would be born. "I'll be forty-three! Who has a baby at forty-three?"

"Obviously, some women." She started to laugh. "Honestly, Florence, you are naive. Imagine being pregnant and not knowing it."

"I've never been pregnant before," I protested then felt foolish.

"That's true enough, I guess," May said. "No one would tell you the signs so you might not know."

Pictures of my mother placing yet another baby in a small coffin came back to me. Stories of women who died in childbirth flitted into my mind. A wave of despair washed over me. How could I have let this happen? "Oh, no. I do not want a baby."

"You are certainly old for a first baby, but you're healthy and strong."

"Not that strong." I reached out and grabbed May's hand. "May, what am I to do? I may not survive this."

"How pregnant are you?"

I thought. "Two months? Three months?"

"Nothing you can do about the pregnancy now that would be safer than childbirth. I expect you'll have the baby. It will be fine. How will Sam feel about it?"

That was all very well for her. She was more careful than I had been, and *she* wasn't the one facing childbirth. I gathered my wits. How would Sam feel about the baby?

I stared at her and thought over Sam's potential reaction to the news. "He will be euphoric. He will be indulgent, protective, besotted. The baby will be welcome to Sam."

AND SO IT PROVED. SAM immediately wanted me to stay in bed all day, every day.

"I am not sick, Sam. I'm pregnant. Millions of women are pregnant. It's normal. I like working, I like participating in the drama society. I want to be busy."

"All right. You let me know what I can do." He looked at me almost fiercely, his blue eyes drilling into mine. I wanted to be annoyed with him. To tell him not to be so optimistic, so eager to be a father, but I couldn't hurt him that way. And truth to tell, I felt almost overwhelmed with love for him. I knew he thought he was authoritarian and determined, but I saw him as endearing and loved him for it.

"You promise you'll tell me if I can help."

I promised.

He, of course, didn't stop talking to me about it, chattering away about all the things he was going to do with his son. I reminded him a few times he might get a daughter, but he ignored me, and I gave up. He did, however, keep quiet about the pregnancy to anyone else. I did not want it known.

I came across the booties I'd bought from Luane Joe. She must have looked at me and known.

Other than May, Sam, and Luane, no one knew I was expecting a baby. Women's gowns still had yards of material. I wondered if they would ever become less full and easier to wear. It was not difficult for me to hide the thickening of my waist with some dextrous needlework and an adjustment of style. I added a bow to the front of a gown and a high waist to another. I could conceal this baby all autumn.

THE LIBRARY WAS A GATHERING place for those of us interested in news from back home. I indulged in a fit of longing for my many aunts who would fuss about me in this condition, particularly Aunt Martha who, despite her unmarried state, had birthed an illegitimate child when she was young. I even unearthed my mother's journals and read from them, hoping she might have some words of advice about pregnancy, but she spoke mainly of her poetry, her plays, and the relationships of the actors and authors around her. I missed her, and I missed England. I yearned for the autumn colours of Russell Square: the oranges and reds of the oak and hawthorn leaves and the chrysanthemums and asters of the flower beds. Barkerville, in the Williams Creek Valley, showed bright yellow poplars at the top of the surrounding hills, which were beautiful, but I kept trying to find a splash of orange somewhere.

I missed the railways of Britain. I could climb onto a train there and be out of London to many new and interesting places within a day and in comfort. Not that I had done much travelling in England, but I could have. I could visit with Thomas and Laura and watch their family grow. I could write for Mr. Dickens.

I gave myself a mental shake. *Listen to yourself, Florence. In England you wouldn't have the money to travel anywhere. Besides, life isn't as safe as all that in England. A train crashed in Shropshire in June of this year killing thirteen. You might have been on it. And, at forty-two and pregnant, you'd be an embarrassment to your brother's family. Here, you are and will be much happier, more accepted—and wealthier.*

Still, I would have liked to see the elephant they had acquired for the London Zoo. Jumbo they called him. I wondered if the new Liberal party of Palmerston would make a difference to the poor. I would simply have to get my news from the fourteen newspapers the library now took and discuss them with other emigrants from England. I should transfer my allegiance and take more interest in the politics of the colonies. Certainly, Judge Begbie was an excellent source of news.

I had warning when he was going to arrive as his court dates were public knowledge. Sam disappeared to his blacksmith's shop when the judge came to tea. He didn't trust his tongue not to betray our secret marriage or the pregnancy. It was not a hardship for Sam to be absent as he had many projects he needed to finish. Equipment broke down and miners came in with shovels, metal boxes, and iron peaveys that needed straightening or sharpening.

I had leavened the social occasion with the attendance of Catherine Dunn Parker, who acted in our plays, and Fanny Bendixon, who was French, which gave Judge Begbie and me a chance to speak that language. Mrs. Bendixon owned a saloon and a brothel, but since she was a much-appreciated actress in our drama society, she was invited to tea. We sounded Judge Begbie out on the possibilities of the Colony of British Columbia joining Canada (highly likely), votes for women (highly unlikely), justice for Indians (dependent on the judges and the laws, which were capricious), the advancement of the railroad from the east to Port Moody (inevitable). The tea went well, served by one of Song Wing's many relatives, with biscuits supplied by Wake-up-Jake's kitchen. I still couldn't cook and had no intention of learning.

We did not speak much about our mining investments, but more about the new plays the drama society was considering and the possibility of establishing a Pickwick Club. Those clubs were gaining in popularity all over the world as Charles Dickens's novels were being devoured by enthusiastic readers. I understood Pickwick Clubs were silly. For one thing, everyone attending assumed a name from the novels. Still, they were blatantly devoted to silliness, which made them honest. They would unite us in the literature of Dickens felt quite nostalgic about my association with Mr. Dickens and that such a society would keep the picture of my mother and her work with him alive in my mind. Judge Begbie approved. He thought it would help to improve connections between the people of the town and discourage loneliness and isolation and, subsequently, the violations of law those two conditions engendered.

He departed to distribute British justice to all and sundry, and I breathed a sigh of relief. He was such a morally rigid man, who if he had known I was married to Sam, would have immediately insisted I obey the law and give up control of my finances.

After he left Barkerville, a flurry of claim-jumping occurred. If a man had a partner, he could leave for a time with the partner guarding the claim. The laws were clear on how long a miner could leave a claim before it was free for anyone to take. It was as little as three days, so men who mined alone were at a disadvantage. Whatever the law, the miners were committed to justice and grouped together to discipline anyone who took advantage of a lone miner. There were few disputes to be settled by the official courts. No one had been killed over it yet, but tempers had risen on occasion.

Sam told me about Talon Joe, an Indian man from Lillooet, who made his living as a packer and a miner. He owned a house near the Chinese end of Barkerville and had a few mining claims. He left his claims to go hunting in October, but no one jumped his claim. He handed out deer meat to several families when he returned. The law in Barkerville was much more fluid than Judge Begbie knew.

May was my only confidante about the coming baby other than Sam. Since May and Red were leaving Barkerville in October, I mined her for advice on childbirth and babies before she left. While she hadn't had any of her own, she'd been a support for several of her working girls who had birthed babies. I didn't tell her I suspected this baby would not live. My mother had lost many babies. Her mother, my grandmother, had only one living child. It was unlikely, at my age, I would produce a healthy child. I prepared myself.

I was going to miss May. She promised to write, and I admit to being tearful as they pulled away in a wagon and four-horse team. The road was quite passable all the way to Yale now, so her journey would be much easier than mine had been coming north.

I busied myself with my saloons, and my mining claims. The coming winter season would send many back to Victoria or San Francisco, so I was working to ensure we could survive the slower winter months. I worked with the drama society to produce a play for Christmas and helped with the music presentations. After Christmas, Sam suggested we go to Idaho. He wanted our baby to be born in the United States, and there was gold in Idaho.

"I don't know what this British colony is going to do: go with Britain, go with Canada, or go with America. But if he's born in the States, he can go back and forth with my citizenship or yours."

I was not anxious to leave Barkerville forever—I was doing well here—but I was eager to leave for a few months. I expected to have a stillborn baby and did not want to be an object of pity here. Also, I'd heard in the saloon there was a rich gold strike in northern Idaho.

THE PRACTICALITIES WERE A BIT daunting, but not impossible. I persuaded Neil Ferguson not only to continue to manage the Falcon but to take on the Regency as well. Trade was down during the winter, so he could go between the saloons and ensure that some money came in. I arranged with the bank to deposit the monthly running costs into a separate account, which I gave Neil signing authority over jointly with me, and also arranged to have his salary deposited into his account. I spent the last two weeks instructing him on how to keep good ledgers and how to balance the books. I promised to send my address to him when I knew what it was. I would return in April. I had too many paying interests here to be gone long. Sam agreed.

Early in January when there was a sudden break in the cold temperatures to a mild thirty-four degrees, we hired a trap and two-horse team from Barnard's Express and drove it over the much-improved road to Quesnelmouth. I almost enjoyed it. I felt well. Aside from the fact I was getting wider by the day, and I occasionally needed a nap, my health was as usual. I wore the warm moccasins Luane had made with heavy wool socks. I'd packed my work boots as well as more lady-like shoes. I wore the beaver coat I had made in the fall, with the fur on the inside and a beaver hat, with the fur outside. I had wool gloves and a wool scarf. Sam was similarly attired with a beaver short coat and beaver hat with ear flaps. He had leather gloves for driving. Idaho would also be cold.

The day was sunny and even warm. The horses, true to Barnard's reputation, strong and willing. We made the Cottonwood Ranch Roadhouse easily and partook of a hot supper. In the morning, we headed out of the mountains and along the plateau to the Fraser River at Quesnelmouth. There, we turned the horse and trap over to the Express office and booked our passage to Cache Creek. From Cache Creek we would buy a horse and wagon and travel east to Kamloops, where we planned to stock up on food for us and the horses and a few pots and pans for cooking, which I fervently hoped Sam knew how to do. We would stop at roadhouses every night, but we needed emergency supplies in case we were stopped by snow or other impediments. From Kamloops, we planned our trip through the Okanagan Valley south through Osoyoos to the trail to Idaho in the Oregon Territories.

Sam had talked to friends from California who had news of Idaho and found the best way in winter was through the valleys of the Okanagan down to the plateau into the Oregon Territories, then east to Leesburg in Idaho. We planned to take our time and wait out any bad weather in a comfortable roadhouse. While I hoped there would be doctor there or a midwife, in case I needed one, I knew there was gold.

*seventeen*

# Travelling Again

We bought a horse, Buckly, and a wagon at Cache Creek and drove to Kamloops, where we stocked up on supplies. Our wagon was covered with canvas, a similar material to a ship's sail, so we would have some protection from the snow, but Sam wanted to stay a day or two so he could use some magic at a local blacksmith's shop and add springs to make the ride more comfortable. I had managed so far, but my increased weight and awkwardness and the jolting of the wagon caused my back to ache, and Sam had promised to do something about it. He would also install a small wood stove to keep us warm if we had to stay outside overnight or if we got stranded by a blocked road. We had two heavy bear rugs which would be most comforting. I busied myself with adjusting small details that had irritated me on the drive from Cache Creek, such as the chamber pot sliding from side to side and clanging against anything it hit. That was easily done with an empty apple box, which Sam attached to the wooden side of the wagon.

The North and South Thompson Rivers met at Kamloops. Indeed, the name of the town meant "meeting of the waters" in the language of the local Indians. It had been an important village for the Indians around here as a trading centre and no doubt a social and political centre for the many bands in the hills around. In the summer, it would be beautiful with the lake, rivers, and grasslands surrounding the town, but now, everything was covered in snow and the countryside was bleak.

The Hudson's Bay Company had a post on the north side of the river in order to conduct their trade with the Indians, and with the constantly arriving settlers. Gold had brought many here and was still bringing them. Most of the travellers here were men, although I did meet some women while perusing the fabric in the dry goods store. I needed flannel and bought enough to make diapers, as well as spare needles and more thread. I was always tempted to buy another pair of scissors and this time, I succumbed. I'd hate to lose my scissors and have to cut material with a knife.

The sun was shining, although the temperature was at freezing. There was a brisk wind, which made the cold more intense. The high rolling hills on either side of the road, while beautiful, acted as a funnel; the wind was constant. I was happy to leave Kamloops and travel east, then south down the Okanagan Valley. I found this country attractive even in the winter—once we got past the fog and damp of the upper valley and into the sunshine of the lower. The wagon was much improved with the springs Sam had installed, and I was almost comfortable. The country remained similar throughout the journey south, and we were lucky with sunshine and relatively mild weather. Still, the journey was a long one and the last few miles difficult on rough roads. Sam and I had both heard rumours of a gold strike in Leesburg, and along with hundreds of others, sought our fortune in the town.

Leesburg was much like Barkerville: full of wooden, hastily constructed houses and stores and aligned along one street. Sam procured a hotel room for us with cooking facilities but with a common dining room, for which I was extravagantly grateful. I could manage boiled eggs and toast, and Sam cooked the stews and even tea cakes, but I expected we would eat in the dining room much of the time.

Once we had moved into the room and found accommodations for the horse and storage for the wagon, we explored the town and found the bank, or at least what was a temporary bank. I was not sure I trusted a bank that was secured only by canvas and rope.

We consulted the bank clerk together. Once we were settled in the two chairs available to customers, Sam asked about a bank account.

"Oh, certainly," the clerk said. A Mr. Jones, an unlikely name. He was probably wanted by some sheriff somewhere. He was a small young man of about twenty, with a thin dark moustache and clean-shaven chin. His dark eyes darted around as if checking for strangers or bandits. All in all, I was more inclined to trust Sam to keep our gold and money safe than this young man.

"We can open an account for you, sir."

"My wife would like an account as well," Sam said. As if I couldn't speak for myself.

I straightened. "I might," I said. "What can you offer me?"

"I am sorry, ma'am," he said somewhat pompously. "We don't do business with married women. They have no property rights here."

"I see," I said and rose. Sam also rose.

"We will talk it over," Sam said, "and come back when we decide what to do."

I was fuming as we picked our way through the snow, mud, and dirt of the main street. I was a woman of substance. I had several businesses which were making money for me while I was absent. What kind of culture was this where I was dismissed as incompetent and incapable *because* I was a woman? We had come here because we hoped to make a great deal of money in the goldfields, because Sam wanted the baby to be born in the United States, and frankly, because I was ready to get away from Barkerville for a time. This baby had every chance of not living long, and I didn't want all that attention on me in Barkerville. "Poor Miss Wilson. Poor little babe." I wouldn't be able to bear it. Better that happened in private. I had ignored what was going to happen and enjoyed travelling here, even the incipient danger of it was exciting, but I had hoped to gamble on mining claims. It was frustrating to be thwarted by archaic laws—not that the Colony of British Columbia's laws were any more accommodating.

I moved our clothes and effects into the hotel room, as that would be our home for now, while Sam went to check on Buckly. I familiarized myself with the few shops and dry goods stores. There was no library. It seemed a much rougher town than Barkerville.

I hadn't known half of the danger of this territory until I arrived in Leesburg. The waiter in the dining room of our hotel told me about the Indian Wars.

"The army came down on those Indians and wiped out hundreds of them."

"When was this?" I asked him.

"Not long ago. They were in their winter lodges, see. So just easy for the soldiers to kill them."

"Them? Women? Children?"

"Uh. I guess so." He looked thoughtful for a moment. It might have been the first time he'd thought about what that "war" might have looked like.

There had been many incidents of resistance by the local Indians to the thousands of white settlers grabbing their land without negotiation or discussion. The settlers thought that since the Indians didn't have the white system of land ownership, they had no vested interest in the land, that it was therefore "free." The local tribes who had used the land according to their ways didn't agree and had grievances that led to many skirmishes. I learned that the Snake River irregular war had been going on for years, and it was only three years before that the US Army had committed the massacre at Bear River on the Nez Perce Indians. The idea that Sam and I were intruders in a contested land made for uneasy living.

I was able to get enough information through listening to conversations in the dining room, reading the local paper, and talking to the bank clerk to instruct Sam on which claims to buy shares in—always a gamble, but we managed to make a little money by selling them to newcomers. Still, Sam made most of the money working in a blacksmith's shop. He picked up current information there as well, because he would talk to and, more importantly, listen to almost anyone.

I occupied myself by cutting out diapers from the flannel sheet and hemming the edges to keep them from fraying. The baby seemed active. I started to hope it might live. After all, I had lived and so had Thomas. Not all Mother's babies had died. By now, I'd abandoned my corsets and spent most of my day in a comfortable shift, covered by my heavy fur coat when I went outside and a concealing wool pelisse when I waddled around in the hotel. The last month of my pregnancy was decidedly uncomfortable. I found it hard to sleep and spent many a night resenting that Sam *could* sleep. I found myself off balance occasionally. I had always been able to move quickly, and now I had to be more careful and plan my sitting and rising with care. I desperately missed the conversation of May, Song Wing, and the people I'd seen every day in Barkerville. Living in this hotel room felt like a prison, and this baby felt like my jailor. I was both fearful of the coming birthing process and almost desperate for it to finally occur.

Sam had located a midwife from the local Nez Perce tribe.

"Do you think she will resent me for being white?" She might, after all, want revenge for the loss of relatives at Bear River.

"She has a reputation for being helpful and reliable. She also will be paid in gold when the baby is born. *And* I will stay with you."

I was overcome. I had never heard of a man being with his wife when she was delivering a baby. His presence did reassure me. I knew Sam would protect me. I chastised myself for being ridiculous and weak, but there it was. I was ridiculous and weak.

Ella, as she was called, didn't speak many words of English, although she did understand most of what I said. I didn't speak any words of her language. We made do with nods, shakes of the head, and smiles. She came equipped with a basket of moss, and several items she never showed me. I gave her tea, and she admired the layette I'd managed to accumulate for the baby, including the little moccasins which she fingered for some time, studying the beadwork.

Sam had made a cradle, and I had sewn the blankets and quilt for it. It sat at one side of the bed ready for the child. I wondered at times what kind of child Sam and I would produce. I was too old for this at forty-three. If I died in this endeavour, Sam, at thirty-seven, would look after the child.

Sam had gone for Ella when I first started having pains. May had told me that a first baby took some time to come, perhaps a day, so I had some tea and biscuits in the room, and Sam had agreed to fetch soup and whatever I fancied from the dining room. But surprisingly, after the first pains, the labour progressed rapidly, and it was a quick eight hours—but certainly long enough—before I struggled to push out the baby. Ella encouraged me with signs and smiles. The pains got worse and Ella began to sing, a slow haunting tune, almost a wail. It distracted me, and I found by concentrating on her song, I could endure the pains better. Sam held my hand, and I crushed it when the vise tightened on my abdomen.

"Oh God. Oh God." The grip of my muscles was excruciating.

"I'm here, Florence. You're doing wonderfully. Just wonderfully."

A new pain came, and I suddenly resented his ineffective patter.

"Bloody hell!" I screamed at him. "This is all your fault!"

Then suddenly my body had an overwhelming need to push, and the baby slid out. The relief was enormous.

Ella was busy below and in what seemed seconds she passed me a little naked body. I held it and saw it was a girl.

Ella placed a blanket over the little one, wet, slimy, and all, and cuddled her on my belly. She guided the baby to my nipple and the child began to nurse. It was a most peculiar sensation. I felt a flush of heat and a tingling all over. Surprised, I met Ella's eyes. She laughed. Then I managed a weak laugh with her. I felt another tightening of my abdomen.

"Not a twin?" I darted a quick glance at Sam.

He looked. "No, the afterbirth."

"Oh, certainly. Good."

I was tired. Sam was exhausted as well, but after I had nursed the baby and held her for some time, I passed her to him, and he managed to cradle her in his arms. When I had held her, she looked too big to have come from my body. When Sam held her, she looked tiny in his huge hands.

"What will we call her?" he said staring at the tiny little girl.

"Alice," I said. I'd picked out the name months before, but hadn't told him, as he had been sure I was carrying a boy. He didn't seem disappointed.

"Alice Nellie," I said definitely.

"Alice Nellie Tompkins." He smiled at the baby. "She's a miracle."

"I agree."

"How are you?" He turned to me, his gaze sharp.

"Sore," I said, "but alive, and I expect to stay that way."

He handed Alice back to Ella, who took her to the table where she had a wash stand set up. Once Alice was bathed and swaddled in a clean blanket, Sam carefully placed her in the cradle and returned to kneel by my bed. He kissed me on the forehead. "You are wonderful."

"True," I agreed. "But I'm never doing that again."

"No," he said fervently. "I never want you to do that again. Once is enough."

I mentally reviewed what May had told me about preventing a birth. She was an expert in that. I'd write her for more advice when I got back to Barkerville.

Ella had left me a drink of willow bark, which she had told me in gestures to drink before I slept. It took the edge off the discomfort, and I fell asleep and only woke when Alice cried. It was dark. Sam had been sleeping on the big chair by the window.

He got to his feet to help me to the commode, which I needed badly, then brought Alice to me. I unwound the swaddling blanket Ella had put on her to discovered there was moss instead of a diaper between her legs. The moss had absorbed the urine and, surprisingly, didn't smell.

"Is there any more moss?" I asked Sam. He looked and found Ella had left a basket of it. I replaced the moss and discarded the used clump into a wastebasket. "You can dump it out on any field nearby," I said. "It certainly will save washing." I thought of the hours I'd spent hemming diapers. Well, I would need them, as I didn't have enough moss to last very long and would be unlikely to find any in this snow-bound country. Ella must have gathered it in the summer, dried it, and had it ready for winter babies.

Alice had her meal, then I was ready for mine. It was the middle of the night, but I was hungry.

"What can you give me to eat?" I demanded of Sam.

"They've got soup waiting for you in the dining room. Everyone in the hotel is excited about Alice and doing all they can. There aren't many babies here, and the men are celebrating Alice's birth."

"Why aren't you down there with them?" I knew I sounded querulous, but I was tired and hungry.

"First you need to eat, then I'll celebrate."

I approved of his priorities and made short work of the ham, eggs, soup, bread, and cake he provided.

"Thank the boys in the kitchen," I said sleepily.

He left with the dirty dishes and, I assumed, stayed celebrating in the bar. He rolled in at about six in the morning.

ALICE AND I ESTABLISHED A regular schedule where she ate and slept, and I did my activities around her. I had many visitors and kept a teapot and biscuit tin ready from ten in the morning until six at night. So many strangers came that Sam organized a presentation ceremony in the bar where I appeared with Alice and men lined up to hold her for a few minutes. It was touching, and Alice didn't seem to mind. There were few families here in Leesburg, so very few children. I expected the men were missing their own children.

They all left her a present of some kind, so I was kept busy trying to sort out what was useful and what wasn't. I appreciated the kindness, although the community still made me anxious, even more so now I had Alice to worry about. The law here seemed to be one of might not justice, and the threat of another Indian war was ever present. I couldn't work as a businesswoman here, and I felt the lack of women friends. As well, I was British and an outsider. Even though we had made quite a bit of money, I was uneasy. And as kind as some people were to us, I knew I did not belong here.

*eighteen*

# The Lure of the Cariboo

IN MAY, WE harnessed Buckly to the wagon and drove all the way to Barkerville. We stopped at night at the roadhouses, where the proprietors and guests made much of Alice. Everyone wanted to hold her and, since she was at the smiles and gurgles stage, she was vastly entertaining to them. Except to feed her and change her, I had a relaxing time on those overnight stays.

We left the Cottonwood Roadhouse just when spring was tentatively emerging in the Cariboo Mountains. Snow glistened on the mountain tops but, halfway down, the faint green of the poplars promised coming warmth. It was still cold, though, and I buttoned Alice into her bunting bag and tucked a quilt around her as we headed home.

The town looked the same: the streets muddy with the elevated boardwalks, the sheds and buildings lining both sides. The hills on each side were still bare and stark, the aftermath of the earlier search for gold. I wondered how long it would take before a tree managed to grow near town.

I was relieved to see both the Falcon and the Regency were as I had left them and Sam's house undamaged. I had had visions of squatters moving in. It would be tempting for some miners who couldn't work in the freezing cold to move into an empty house where they could keep warm. Such was Sam's reputation, though, that no one did.

I was barely in the house when Fanny Bendixon arrived. She bustled in through the front door like a huge barge in a flurry of bright red and yellow skirts, a fox fur jacket, and a profusion of French flowing from her lips. It was wonderful to speak French again.

"Florence, my dear, I have missed you!" She bussed me on both cheeks, then peered at the bundle in my arms.

"Who is this?"

"This is Alice Tompkins," I said with no more explanation than that.

She raised her eyebrows. "You clever girl, you. She is adorable, no?" Fanny moved the blanket from around Alice's face and smiled at her. Alice smiled back. Fanny had a volatile temper and could erupt with little provocation, but she was known to be tolerant and kind to children.

"*Mon Dieu*. What a lovely girl. We will all spoil her."

I was afraid that might be true.

"I have brought you some eclairs from the bakery and some what you call biscuits." She placed a package on the table in the hall.

Fanny's exuberance was refreshing and her opinions always worth hearing. "Come in." I led her to the drawing room, where I unbuttoned Alice from her bag and wrapped her in a blanket.

Sam came in with a bundle of wood in his arms, greeted Fanny, and went straight to the fireplace. "We need heat first thing."

I nodded. "You'll have to wait for your tea, Fanny."

"It is of no matter. Tell me about your travels. What was the Oregon Territory like?"

"They call it the Idaho Territory now. It was much rougher than here. More brash, somehow. They seemed to think Sam was important and I was not. The bank wouldn't allow me to do business."

"Ah," she said. "The advantages of being single or a widow here."

"Louis died?" I asked.

She shrugged. "He left for California. He might be dead."

He probably wasn't, but it served her well to pretend he was. I hadn't told Fanny I was married. She was not discreet.

"Tell me about the drama society. What are they planning?" I was eager to get back into my life here. I hadn't yet taken a major role, but I usually took some part.

Fanny was a great asset to our theatre productions. She had a wonderful sense of the dramatic, which instilled energy into any play she was part of. She had to have someone read her parts to her as her grasp of written English was rudimentary, but she had a capacious memory, so she was a quick study. Once she had memorized her role, she lifted our productions to an almost professional level.

We chatted while Sam got the fire going. The house warmed gradually and soon we had taken off our wraps, and I freed Alice from her blanket and held her. Fanny demanded some time with Alice, so I retired to the kitchen where I met Sam lighting the stove.

"Is she still here?" Sam found Fanny a little overwhelming.

"She is and will probably stay for tea."

"That woman can talk!"

"And all in French," I commiserated. Sam didn't speak French.

"I tell you what. I'll unload the wagon and stack everything in the hall. Then, I'll take Buckly to the livery and make arrangements to house him. I'll groom him and settle him for the night."

I nodded.

"Then," Sam said. "I'll go to the Regency and have a drink with whoever I find there."

"All right." Sam had missed his friends and all the gossip the men provided. "And I'll rustle up Song Wing to give us some supper."

I smiled at him. "That sounds wonderful."

He kissed me then hugged me close. "It's great to be home."

"It is," I agreed.

I PICKED UP MY ROUTINE of business. Neil had done well with his management of the saloons, as evidenced by the ledgers and my bank balance, but he was anxious to work his claim. That made it necessary for me to return to work with some accommodation for Alice. I stayed home in the morning and took Alice with me in the afternoon, working in my office at the Regency for the most part, but taking her with me for an hour to check the books at the Falcon. Sam had constructed a cradle for Alice in each saloon, so she could nap. She seemed to be able to sleep wherever I put her. I was addressed as "Miss Wilson" and everyone, while giving Alice a great deal of attention, ignored what they considered her illegitimacy. Sam worked all day at the smithy and joined me for supper at the Regency about seven most evenings. Then he took Alice home with him while I supervised the early evening crowd. Miners were starting to come back to their claims after a winter in Victoria, so business in my saloons picked up. I kept my ears open for news of which claims were paying and which were starting to peter out. I sold the ones I suspected were nearing the end of their production and bought the up-and-coming ones.

"Pure gamble," Sam said, "but it often pays."

Sam, for all his chatter at work, managed to pick up a great deal of important information on the claims.

Fanny closed one saloon and opened another in June, and again included a brothel. She said it was lucrative and within her ability to manage. It was outside mine, as I didn't have her knowledge of people or the appetites and activities of men. She told me once of her past life as the mistress of a criminal boss in California.

"I was thin then and very beautiful," she said. "And much admired." After a time, she had become interested in religion and changed her habits, acquiring virtue. She left the criminal, eliciting retaliatory violence, which had been severe, but she survived. She married Louis. They'd built a hotel in Victoria which had not prospered. After that, they had come here. Fanny had let her virtue ease somewhat, as virtue did not pay well.

I knew brothels made money, but I didn't have Fanny's experience, and I didn't want it. I didn't even have sufficient knowledge of birth control. Fanny spent one whole afternoon instructing me on how to prevent a second child. I listened.

Song Wing's son Lee worked as kitchen help and waiter in the Falcon. He was the boy Song Wing often sent on errands. I seconded him to watch Alice when I wanted to go out without her. She napped for two hours every afternoon, so I used that time to work elsewhere.

This afternoon, I had an appointment at the bank, now in Barkerville, with Mr. Augustine. Sam and I had brought back considerable gold from Leesburg, and I wanted it securely stowed. Sam had constructed a safe under the floor boards in the kitchen of our house. The safe was iron and had one of the new combination locks. When we left to go to Leesburg, I'd put my poems and my mother's plays and poems there, as well as my journals. They were still there. We had stuffed the gold we brought back into that safe, and while it was secure, I preferred to have it in the bank where I could draw against it when necessary.

Mr. Agustine's eyebrows rose when I deposited the gold on his desk.

"You did quite well in the south, Miss Wilson."

I smiled. I was satisfied with my profits. "I assume we need to have this assayed and valued next door?"

"Indeed. I will accompany you."

We moved to the assay office and had the gold weighed and valued, then transferred to the bank. I managed the business quite easily and received my receipts and passbook properly updated. I felt more myself once I had that business transacted. I realized I had felt out of place in Leesburg, never part of the community and never trusting the banks there.

There were some changes in Barkerville. My Rose du Roi, although struggling through the harsh winters, was growing now and producing some roses. I didn't believe in omens, but I noticed it with pleasure all the same.

New people had arrived. Others left disappointed or euphoric with the results of their work. Catherine and her husband Samuel were active in the drama society, so she came to give me the latest news of the new play and the plans for the season. The drama society had bought Fanny Bendixon's old Parlour Saloon, which was large enough to hold our audience. Catherine and Fanny had assigned me the role of Mrs. Busybody in the farce they were planning. I would have to write Thomas and ask him to recommend more serious plays. Shakespeare was always popular, but some more modern plays would be a challenge to produce. Everyone turned out to watch no matter what we offered; our audiences were enthusiastic and constant. We did need a larger permanent playhouse and talked about it often. There were thirteen saloons in town, which occasionally offered space for entertainments, but a theatre was our dream.

Catherine had known I was pregnant when I left Barkerville, so wasn't surprised to see Alice. She was well-accustomed to babies and took them for granted. It was a welcome relief from the almost slavish devotion of my staff. She brought her youngest, Sarah, with her when she came to the house. Sarah played with some bowls and spoons from the kitchen while we practiced our lines. The drama society were still talking about establishing a Pickwick Club, but the plans were more concrete now.

"It will be great fun," Catherine said. "It's totally absurd and just silly."

I knew the members gave each other names from the pages of Mr. Dicken's novels and tried to act in character at the meetings. I was willing to try it, at least for a while. It might get tedious, but I supposed it would depend on how much effort the members put into maintaining the frivolity of it.

"Can we start it after freeze up?" I suggested to Catherine. I was going to be heavily employed that summer. Neil Ferguson had told me he was going to go mining in the good weather, as a new creek of gold had opened up, and he had registered a claim on it. I'd missed getting in on that. I would be managing the Falcon as well as the Regency.

That summer and into the autumn, I managed the two saloons and my mining claims, looked after Alice, participated in the drama society and the literary society, and danced around Judge Begbie's visits. He never saw Alice as Sam took her with him when the judge came to visit. I assumed no one told him about her, or he had the good manners to pretend she didn't exist. In any case, I escaped his scrutiny. It was a busy, almost hectic life, and I loved it.

The whole community was doing well. Catherine had started a new and much bigger boarding house, Fanny's brothel was making her money, my ventures were doing well, and Sam was industriously smithing.

Canada had become a dominion of Britain, a kind of independence that held promise of a different future than I had envisioned. I had thought Canada and the colony of British Columbia would be British forever. The British had fought the French for the country with the Indian warriors choosing sides. After the British alliance won the territory, they fought the Americans to keep it. They now were trying to bind the country together from the Atlantic to the Pacific to the Arctic Sea. The concept of an independent country, albeit with British roots, took me by surprise. I wasn't sure I wanted to be Canadian and not British.

"Glad to get away from Britain," Sam said. "My ancestors fought to be free of them."

"They aren't precisely disengaged," I responded, not prepared to fight that war again. "Canada is still part of the great Commonwealth politically, and British Columbia is still a colony."

"Not for long," Sam said. "As soon as the railroad gets to Port Moody, we will become part of Canada. Just watch."

I wasn't sure the residents of Barkerville would accept an independent Canada. Many might see now as a time to change allegiance. There were American flags over some saloons, and American celebrations on July 4. So far, we attended each other's celebrations. Still, Americans sang "God Save the Queen" with us at the end of each concert. Good will might suffice to keep British Columbia peaceful.

In 1867 Canada became an independent country with a Governor General representing the Queen. Prime Minister Macdonald had promised the railroad from coast to coast so, if it came as Sam said, then the colony would join the Dominion of Canada. It had not yet occurred. In Barkerville, in 1867, we finally had a theatre, the Theatre Royal.

IN THE SUMMER OF 1868, Luane and her family arrived on their annual harvesting visit. I sometimes took Buckly, the wagon, and Alice and drove out to Luane's blueberry field to help with the picking. Luane's children were kind, and Alice enjoyed her time with them. Of course, she was all over blueberry juice, but it didn't hurt her. At two years and a half, she was saying a few words and making her opinions known. "No!" seemed her favourite word. Luane's children were tolerant. Luane and her husband had a summer house in town near the Chinese section, but we preferred to meet outdoors in the fields and rather than in town. Luane was teaching me some of her Lillooet language. It was quite different from the romance languages of French and Italian I'd learned and different also from Russian which I had also learned when I was a governess. There were many more nuances of pronunciation in the Lillooet language than I had first suspected, and I worked hard at training my ear to hear them. Luane found my attempts amusing. She said, "*Azuỷs*," which sounded like azoych, which meant beautiful, and I must have said, "Az," which meant to pay for something. Mistakes helped me learn and provided Luane with hours of laughter.

Meat was scarce in Barkerville the summer of 1868, so I asked Luane if she and her family could get me a deer or moose that fall. She promised to keep my request in mind. In the meantime, I purchased some dried salmon from her to tide us through. I'd heard there was a cattle drive coming from 150 Mile House, but I wasn't sure it would arrive before the snow. As well as paying for the salmon with gold, I had brought some needles and beads, which I knew Luane could use. I met some friends of Luane's from the Bowron Lakes and from Soda Creek. They had also come for the blueberries and the salmon. I expected they also came, as I did, for the congenial company.

Alice enjoyed herself, but I had to keep a bonnet on her and a long-sleeved blouse as she burned easily. Luane's children seemed to just get browner. Still, they all had a coating of blueberry juice, so for some of the time, they were all the same colour.

I drove the wagon with Alice usually sleeping in the small bed Sam had made for her. I covered her in a light banket to keep the sun off her, and she'd drift off as Buckly took us home.

I had this ideal life until September 16, 1868.

*nineteen*

# The Fire

THE MORNING OF September 16, 1868, had been cold. I noticed icicles and frost on the back porch when I hurried in from a quick dash to the outhouse. By the time I headed to the Regency with Alice at about one in the afternoon, it was warm, reminding me of the hot and dry summer we'd had. The woods around us were dry and could have used some moisture. The town was feeling the effects of a dry summer: dirt drifted along the streets on any small breeze, sparks from the cooking fires routinely ignited the shakes on the rooves. Sam said the cedar on the rooves was green and should repel any fire. It seemed highly unlikely to me that wood would repel fire, but perhaps cedar had properties I didn't know about.

I was soon immersed in my ledgers and in the difficulties of ordering enough supplies to keep my cooks happy, but not too many to overreach my finances.

At three o'clock, I woke Alice from her nap and brought her with me as I made my way to the Falcon. I stopped stock still on the boardwalk. Before me, a column of smoke rose from the shed beside May's old saloon. As I watched, flames shot through the roof. The cedar shakes burst into flame. There would be nothing to stop that fire from racing through the town. There was no water available for fighting a fire. I turned and ran to Sam's smithy. Alice bounced on my hip and clutched my shoulders.

"Mummy. Ow."

"Fire!" I yelled. Sam put down his tools and joined me on the boardwalk. He took one look at the growing flames and bellowed at me, "Head for the creek. I'll get Buckly."

I grabbed his arm. "Don't you put your life in the way of that fire!"

He grinned. "I won't."

That man! He was energized by the danger, the challenge of it, the strength of it. He liked excitement more than I did. I glanced back at the fire and saw it had engulfed two houses in the time it had taken me to run to Sam. I held Alice close and ran to the shallow creek, waded through it, and struggled up the loose dirt and stones on the other side. Alice was yelling "No! No!" all the while. There were people gathering on the hillside above the creek: Fanny, Catherine and her children, the McCallums, Mr. Taylor and his family. Many more kept coming. I saw Dr. Carrell walking around, checking on the children. We all turned our faces to the beast of a fire roaring through the town. I heard explosions. Alice must have recognized the fear around her for she was now quiet.

"Must be the coal oil tins," I heard one man say. "I hope they got the dynamite out of that shed."

"I saw them putting it down a dry shaft," another responded.

"Good thinking. Otherwise, it'd blow the whole valley to pieces and us with it."

I didn't want to think about what other dangers there were hidden in sheds and houses along the street.

The fire swept on, hissing and crackling and occasionally booming. Catherine and I peered anxiously for our husbands.

Finally, I saw Sam crossing the creek leading Buckly.

"I was afraid you'd try to bring the wagon," I said.

"I thought about it, but that fire is moving too fast. The wagon will likely be safe as it's behind the livery and away from the buildings. It depends on the wind, and the way the fire moves." He handed me a blanket he'd dipped in the creek.

"Keep that close by in case embers come our way."

"Good idea." I dropped it on the ground beside me.

"Daddy, up." Alice reached for Sam. He relieved me of her, and we sat on the gravel hillside, watching the fire together. Buckly stamped and moved restlessly but stayed with us.

The fire was moving like a raging river, engulfing everything in its path. The buildings, including my own, were disappearing before our eyes. I hoped every person had escaped. The escape route was quick, just out the back of the buildings and up the hill. But some might have tried to fight the fire. That was a worrisome thought. I mentally reviewed my friends and where they might be at this time of day. Then, there were all the miners who came to my saloons. I knew so many. I didn't want to lose one of them. By four o'clock, the whole town was blazing.

"You complained about the ugly hillsides," Sam said. "Those dirt hillsides are what's keeping the fire from spreading. If we were sitting under trees right now, they'd be in flames."

I glanced around at the bare hills, the upturned earth, the exposed gravel, remnants of the work of thousands of miners. I never thought I'd be grateful for such destruction, but the bare hills contained the fire in the town site.

The heat was intense, and we moved farther up the hill. The smoke was blowing the other way, thankfully. Buckly neighed in fright. Sam comforted him and moved him with us. Sam's house burned. I thought of my treasures: my mother's writing, my own writing, Thomas's letters, my books. I felt my heart cramp at the thought of losing those. Sam put his arm around me.

"We will rebuild, my love. Trust me."

I realized I hadn't been mourning the loss of my businesses or the house itself. We could rebuild those, but I couldn't replace my mother's writing. I'd placed my precious books in the house safe, but I didn't expect that would save them. The heat would, no doubt, penetrate the iron, turning the safe into an oven, baking everything inside to a crisp. Outside the house, my Rose du Roi would not have survived.

We watched the Bank of British North America burn. I hoped their vault truly safeguarded their accounts and their gold. Most of my money was secured in the parent bank in Victoria. I had lodged my will and my marriage lines in the Barkerville safe. I hoped I wouldn't lose them.

By five o'clock, the fire had died down, having consumed almost everything in its path and stopping at the bare hillsides, where it ran out of fuel. By six, we could go back. In what had once been a thriving community, very few buildings had survived. We picked our way cautiously through the ashes and occasional embers. It was an alien world.

I looked at the ashes of my businesses. A few longer pieces of log and boards formed small piles from which came thin trails of smoke.

"Do we need to extinguish those?" I asked Sam.

"No. There's nothing left for it to burn."

I studied the remains of my fortune. Was I particularly singled out by malevolent gods for disaster? First, my inheritance had been stolen by an unscrupulous solicitor, then I was shipwrecked and my life savings disappeared, now fate had sent a fire to wipe out my prosperity here.

*Oh, for heaven's sake, Florence. You're not that important to the universe. Everyone else here will have to rebuild. You can as well. You're not special.*

I would not think just at this moment of what I had lost. I took Alice and cuddled her warm body closer and glanced at my husband. I could be grateful for some treasures.

THE CHINESE SECTION HAD SURVIVED. There wasn't a good reason for that.

"You never can tell with fire," Sam said. "Doesn't always make sense."

Perhaps the Chinese had used different wood. Perhaps their vegetable gardens had discouraged the fire from advancing. It appeared as if they had invoked some magic spell that had protected them.

*Nonsense, Florence. There was probably water around them. You just don't know about it.*

Song Wing found us and brought us to his house for a meal. I went ahead with him, carrying Alice. Sam took Buckly to a field behind the town and tied him to a tree. He checked on the wagon.

"We still have it," he told me when he joined us.

Song Wing's son was busy at the stove when we arrived, making soup. There were no women in this house.

We borrowed blankets from Song Wing and made the wagon comfortable for the night. Sam hobbled Buckly and let him graze on the grass near the creek, which had escaped the fire.

"I hope he doesn't get out of those hobbles and is still there in the morning," Sam worried as we settled down for sleep.

"Could he?"

"Not easily, but you never know if your knots are going to hold. They should."

In the morning, Buckly was still there.

Barnard's Express had lost their office, but a wagon-load of supplies arrived from Quesnelmouth. At the lower end of town, a warehouse containing hardware like nails, hammers, shovels, and picks escaped the fire, as did Scott's Saloon. It was fortuitously sitting under the flume that brought water from a spring on the hillside. It hadn't been used as fire protection, just as a source of drinkable water. The water that had dripped from it for a year or more over the saloon had repelled the fire. Scott did a roaring business this day. The McInnes Saloon survived as well, but everything else burned. Sam said he thought over ninety buildings had been lost.

We slept that night in the wagon with the fur rugs that were still in the chests. We had some pots and pans in the wagon as well, but we had breakfast with Song Wing. The Chinese had food and blankets, which they distributed generously to whomever needed them.

After breakfast, we walked to the site of Sam's house. Sam had a shovel and dug in the ashes where the kitchen had been to find the safe in the space below. I hunkered down beside him.

Sam tried the combination. It worked. He opened the safe. I peered over his shoulder at the charred remains of my journals, my mother's literary works, and my own published books of poems. They had turned to delicate flakes of grey ash. I felt a huge sadness.

"I'm sorry, my love." Sam hugged me.

I nodded. "I thought they would burn when I saw the fire sweep through." The loss still caused me a pang of sorrow. So many memories had been contained in those books and journals. It was as if part of me had died.

"The gold is still intact," Sam said, and brought out the bags we'd stashed there. Gold only melts; it doesn't disappear. It would pay for some of the reconstruction we would have to do.

THE MEN WORKED IN TEAMS. Barnard's were onto the opportunity for trade immediately and had supplies in Barkerville within three days. Sam and his team used lumber from Barnard's and nails from the warehouse and constructed a livery. When the horses were housed, they started on the business buildings. They had a plan drawn by Chartres Brew, the gold commissioner, who directed a widening of the streets and more uniform two-foot height from the ground of all buildings and boardwalks, so the boardwalks would be more even. I saw where they were going to put the Theatre Royal and demanded the adjacent lot for my new saloon.

"What are you going to call it?" Sam asked me.

"There is only one appropriate name and that's the Phoenix."

"Rising from the ashes. Of course." The whole town should have been named the Barkerville Phoenix. The Phoenix Saloon was built in ten days along with thirty other buildings, and before the end of October we had ninety-five buildings replacing most of the one hundred and sixteen that had burned. They were better built as well—Mr. Brew insisted on it. It seemed the citizens of the town took pride in creating a better-looking and safer town. I was pleased with my new saloon. It didn't have a store in front, but it had an office for me in the back and a commodious bar. I had supplies and furniture in it by the following week. We were determined to have our life and normal activities back. There was a great spirit of endeavour among the business owners, a sense that, facing disaster, we would prevail, and we would do it together.

Some people left town, discouraged by their losses and without the money to start again. But many remained. Our drama society met again, the Pickwick Club reconvened, as did the previously formed library society. The loss of the library caused much heartache, as reading was a vital activity for so many of us. I admit to wandering out of town one day and crying over the loss of my books and the loss of the books and papers from the library. It was a waste of energy, for I discovered two miners had saved almost two-thirds of the books. That was enough for us to hope for a bigger and better library in the future. I would stop complaining.

The first delivery of newspapers from London and New York put a spark of hope through the entire town. We used a small shed to start, canvassed, and got donations large and small from almost everyone, and were soon able to restock our shelves. Everyone wanted the works of Charles Dickens on those shelves. We ordered the most popular first. The new library went up quickly and Gold Commissioner Brew donated two hundred books to those saved from the fire. Barkerville residents couldn't survive without books.

The drama society met in the library and planned the coming season. We needed a space to produce plays. We had been accustomed to producing a different performance every two weeks for most of the year. It was a challenge, but our audience of perhaps two hundred a performance would be willing to see a show twice but not more than that, so we had to keep producing. We had many talented thespians and musicians. George Grant and H. Shirly Blunt took any role they were assigned and did them well. Catherine was outstanding as Fanny in *Mad as a Hatter*. I was the maid Mary Jane in that play and enjoyed it. My best role so far had been the principal in *The Area Bell*, produced in May, but there were other plays I found exciting.

Many people who lived and worked in Barkerville were part of the Theatre Royal. Dr. Carrell was wonderful as Sir Charles Coldstream, Bart. in *Used Up*. Professor Wilson had been our musical mainstay as he supplied most of the music, but he'd left town after the fire, and we badly needed a replacement. Mr. Daniel Whelan, a violinist, stepped in and was a wonderful support, so we had much to offer the townspeople. Our former theatre held two hundred and was consistently full. We hoped to have more seating space in the new one. I loved watching theatre, but I loved acting more.

It surprised me how quickly the people who stayed in Barkerville absorbed their losses and rebuilt. No one dwelt on the ashes of their family treasures, or the amount of income they'd had to do without. They just set to and began again. And they helped each other.

I felt the same spirit in the drama society. We were determined to build a new and bigger theatre. Mr. Lipsett of Scott's Saloon donated the lot. I had heard from the gossip swirling around town that he was going to, which is why I'd bought the adjacent lot. Customers would funnel from the theatre to my saloon after the performances.

The theatre was our excitement, social hub, and creative outlet. I revelled in it. Other people in town had other talents that served the theatre. Mr. Howman was an engineer and designed a building that allowed the practical use of the lower floor for the fire trucks and all their regalia and the upper floor for our stage, dressing area, and audience space. A fire brigade was now considered a necessity. Planning for fire prevention was also on our minds. The town burning to the ground was finally sufficient motivation to awaken its citizens to the need for prevention.

In six weeks, we were a town again, not with the raw energy and haphazard construction of a few years ago, but with a more planned design and thoughtful building. Spaces between buildings, something not considered previously, gave some protection from fire spreading. Water reservoirs in barrels and cisterns might help, but the most useful acquisition was a fire truck with a hose that could take water from the creek. Not that there were any trained firemen in town. What we had were young, strong, willing men who would jump to the challenge and do their best. That was much better than the belief in luck that had guided our fire protection in the past.

The firehall-theatre was built quickly, and we rehearsed all autumn for the opening play, *Still Waters Run Deep*, for January 16, 1869. I played Mrs. Sternhold, a part that was challenging and exciting to master. Sam helped with constructing the scenery and prompting at the earlier rehearsals. Alice came with us as she could sleep anywhere, and we just put a coat down for her to fall asleep on when she was tired. Catherine's children watched her and a cadre of children played at the end of the hall while we practiced our lines. We occasionally had to adjust our rehearsal time to accommodate the fire brigade's practice. They could be noisy with their yelling instructions at each other and moving their equipment.

The theatre was much bigger than the last one, with a lofty ceiling and more seating. It held over three hundred, perhaps four-fifty if we included standing room. Such was the Barkerville residents' appreciation of our entertainment that they filled the seats.

We had some benefit dances. We held a Grand Firemen's Ball at the end of December to raise money for the fire brigade. Because we didn't pay actors and actresses to perform, we sometimes had a benefit dance where the proceeds went to the actor in recognition of their donated time. We had one for Catherine in the fall.

"You know what's much better with this theatre than the earlier one?" I asked Sam one evening.

"Bigger? More elegant? Beautiful chandeliers?"

I smiled thinking of those attributes. "No, although I grant those are an improvement. It's the public support. Before, our society worked hard to present plays and performances, but we did it apart from most of the town. Now, it seems everyone feels involved."

Sam thought about it. "I expect they had a fright when they thought they might lose all those evenings of entertainment. It would be a long, cold winter without the drama society."

I agreed. Aside from the saloons where men met to exchange news and feel connected to one another, the theatre was the place where they, and women and children, could gather.

THE NEXT FEW YEARS WERE wonderful. My saloon made money—not as much as two saloons had, but enough profit to satisfy me. I bought and sold shares in mining claims and, for a while, owned a share in eight different claims. And while they did not make the huge profits they had in the past because the miners had to go deeper and worker harder for the gold, they did well enough. Alice grew quickly and with good health. The first few months of motherhood, I'd hovered over her, expecting a disaster at any moment. But I now felt that she was much the same as other children in Barkerville and similar to Luane's children in that she ate, slept, played, and socialized normally without any signs of distress. My mother's experience of having a child die no longer haunted me.

I noticed the summer Alice was four and playing in the blueberry bushes with Luane's children that all her children had a small scar on their shoulders.

"Smallpox inoculation?" I asked her. Luane picked up the sleeve of her blouse and showed me her arm. She also had the scar. I did as well, but I hadn't had Alice vaccinated yet.

"I will get it done," I promised.

"Many died," Luane said. "Many of my family. Four sisters, three brothers. Many."

"I am sorry."

"You see to it for Alice?" she insisted.

I did see Alice was vaccinated. I had the usual scares of measles, chickenpox, and mumps, but with advice from the doctor and other mothers, I managed to cope. Alice came through those illnesses with her health intact. I had been worried that the measles would leave her deaf as it had so many others, but she was fine.

AROUND THAT TIME, WHEN SHE was about four years old, I taught her how to read and write. That was the age I and most of the children I'd known in London had learned. Alice was quick and liked to read. I wrote stories for her to encourage her reading. There was no school in Barkerville. Sam said he had gone to school to learn, but I had been taught at home and expected to teach Alice. She was quick at numbers, and I found it quite easy to teach her how to add, subtract, and later multiply and divide. It was exciting to teach her because she enjoyed it. Sam taught her how to ride Buckly and how to drive him as well. By eight years old, she was an interesting and accomplished girl. I realized Sam and I were prejudiced. I suppose she wasn't as special as I thought, but she was accomplished and had Sam's affectionate nature and social inclinations. She would talk to anyone.

We would have to think about her future education and social alliances at some point, but not yet. We enjoyed our lives with our businesses, socializing, acting, playwriting, and literary society. The new Theatre Royal was still attracting good audiences, Sam's business was thriving, my business and investments were doing well. Barkerville was still a busy centre, but I was concerned about the talk of claims where the gold had petered out. There were new discoveries, though, so perhaps the gold would last some years yet. The railroad had advanced across the country and was expected to eventually come to the west coast, so the colony had made up its mind and was now a province in Canada. I accepted that. I just didn't feel Canadian. I was happy in Barkerville, but, typically, I itched for change.

*twenty*

# The Scourge of Typhoid

WE NEEDED A bigger house. Alice was now eight years old, and I wanted her to have her own room, not just a corner of my office at home. We were doing well in Barkerville, but Stanley beckoned. It was a bustling town in the Lightning Creek area, near the Cottonwood Roadhouse and the Cariboo Plateau, and was reported to have much gold still. Sam saw opportunities for himself, as the town needed a blacksmith.

He also wanted a place where Alice could go to school, now that she was older. I had never been to school. Girls of my social order in London were educated at home. My mother was an avid follower of many discoveries, so Thomas and I had been exposed to experts in science and philosophy as well as literature. Mother thought a curiosity about anything was the impetus to a good education. But Sam had gone to school in Rhode Island, where he had been raised. He thought school and learning with other children was a necessity. There was a school in Stanley.

When I asked Song Wing about moving, he told me he wanted to move to Stanley, where he had more family. In Stanley, there were three hotels where he could find employment as a cook until I either built a saloon or took over one.

"IF YOU COULD MOVE *ANYWHERE*, Sam, not just another town in the Cariboo, but anywhere in the world, where would you go? China? South America? The Sandwich Islands?"

We were sharing the dining room table. I was going through invoices, and Sam was trying to make sense of his orders for the blacksmith shop.

He stopped and looked at me. "My favourite place in the world is the Napa Valley of California."

"Tell me about it." Except for that stop in San Francisco when I had been able to go ashore from the *Tynemouth*, I'd never travelled in California.

"It's a beautiful place, Flo. Low hills with miles of farmland. Small villages. Close enough to San Francisco you can get to the plays and concerts. Grapevines as far as you can see stretched over the hills." He paused for a moment. I waited.

"No snow," he said with some longing in his voice.

"Perhaps we could go one day."

I was concerned about the diminishing payouts on my mining investments. It seemed, like in so many mining towns, there was a limited deposit of gold, and we could be coming to the end of it. Stanley seemed to be getting good returns and, since all mining was a gamble, Sam and I thought gambling on Stanley was a better choice than gambling on Barkerville.

I thought about Sam's dream of living in the Napa Valley, but Stanley was the more practical choice. It was only thirteen miles from Barkerville, so it was possible for us to drive back to Barkerville for concerts and to partake in some social events, especially in the summer, though it would be too far in the winter, and too far in any season for me to attend rehearsals. I had one whole day when I felt nauseous while I contemplated doing without my acting life.

I managed to sell the Phoenix, not for as much as I had hoped, but at least for a reasonable amount. We bought a plot in Stanley for a good price and built a new house. It was ready to move into in the spring of 1874. We enrolled Alice with Mrs. Turnbull, the teacher, who already had twelve children under instruction. Sam was right. Alice thrived.

Sam set up his blacksmith's shop and was immediately inundated with work. As well as his excellent skills, his gregarious nature attracted customers. I used some of my profits from the sale of the Phoenix to help him get established, but I could see I would get that back within three years. I took a couple of months to set up the new house, which I enjoyed. I found a carpenter for odd jobs. Song Wing took on cooking for us as well as for the Stanley Hotel, and recommended one of his many relatives for laundry and occasional household help. Sam built a small stable at the back of our house, where Buckly lived. Alice loved that, and spent many an hour talking to Buckly and grooming him. It was summer before I started investigating the possibility of setting up my saloon. Sam brought home gossip for me about what was available and what the community would like. I had my eye on a property in the centre of town. It was large enough for a bar and had room for a small store as I'd had in the Regency. I would have just enough money to stock it and get enough custom before winter to carry it through to the more lucrative spring.

The gods must have been laughing at my plans because, one evening in late June, Sam came home and complained his head hurt. I gave him some willow bark infusion and sent him to bed. The next day he seemed better, with only a little fever and went to work, but came home at noon, saying he had a headache that was unbearable. I dosed him with willow bark infusion again, and again sent him to bed. His fever increased throughout the day and by evening I had sent Alice for the doctor.

"Typhoid," the doctor told me after he'd seen Sam. Dr. MacPherson was a short, stocky Scotsman, with a drooping moustache and large brown eyes.

"Typhoid fever?" I stared at him blankly. I could hardly believe my Sam, sturdy as a fir, strong and energetic, could be felled by a fever. "What do I do for him?"

"There isn't much you can do. You're giving him willow bark to keep the fever down?"

"I am."

"Keep that up. His fever is getting dangerous."

"What else?"

Alice was on the stairs, hanging on to the banister. I had to be careful not to sound too desperate. But typhoid? That could kill.

"Bathe his skin. That will help keep the temperature down. Try to get him to drink as much water as possible, but be sure the water is safe."

"Safe?"

"There are new reports out that typhoid is caused by something in the water. So, boil the water."

I looked over his shoulder. "Alice, go to your room. I will come in shortly and talk to you."

She hesitated but complied. I turned back to the doctor.

"Can Alice and I get it from him? Or is it just in the water?"

He looked at me, his brown eyes full of compassion. I realized he did not think Sam would survive. "It seems it is both contagious from person to person *and* in the water. Can you send the bairn to another house for a time?"

I nodded. I had to think of Alice. I would not believe Sam would die. I *couldn't* believe Sam would die. "For how long?"

"He can be infectious for as much as twelve weeks."

I was stunned. I would have to find a place for Alice. She couldn't remain in this house. I would have to quarantine Sam and make sure no one came near him except me. I would have to take the risk of getting typhoid myself.

The doctor continued. "I've given him quinine as it sometimes does some good. Call me if you need me." I paid him. Then he was gone.

I checked on Sam. He was sleeping, although restless. I returned to the kitchen and washed my hands. I called Alice to wash her hands. My mother had maintained that washing your hands kept you healthy, and I wanted to use every piece of knowledge I had about disease to help Sam.

"Your daddy is very sick," I said to her as I set her down at the table and sat opposite her.

"Is he going to die?" Her dark eyes were huge with worry.

"Most people who have this disease don't die, but it can be passed on to other people."

"Like measles?" she said. Alice had had friends who had died from measles. It was a reasonable analogy.

I nodded. "Just so."

"I should not go into his room then? No hugs?"

I smiled. "No hugs with Daddy. But hugs with me."

"You aren't going to get sick, are you, Mummy?"

"I don't feel sick," I said. "So, probably, I won't get it. Some people just never get it, even though they come near it." I tried to reassure her without lying.

"Daddy's very sick?"

"At the moment, I can't tell how sick. We will have to wait and see. But he is going to be sick for some time."

"How long?"

"I don't know." Probably for as much as three months, but that was too much for her to cope with just then. "While Daddy is ill, I want you to go to somewhere that doesn't have any illness in the house."

She looked alarmed. "Where?"

"I thought perhaps Mrs. Parker's house."

She looked relieved. "Oh, that's fine. Sarah's there, and Kate."

I sent a message with Song Wing to Catherine and told her about Sam's typhoid and the urgent need to get Alice out of the house. Song Wing returned with her permission to send Alice for as long as necessary. That was brave of Catherine. She had her own children to protect and trusted I would not send Alice if she had a fever. Alice seemed healthy.

I packed Alice's bags under her supervision, kissed her good-bye, and watched Song Wing drive her away. She was sitting beside him chattering while Buckly pulled the wagon. I watched them until I could no longer see them.

If Sam died and I died, Catherine would keep Alice. My will was in the new bank in Barkerville. Not that there was much to leave Alice at the moment because I had put out a great deal of money to set up Sam's business and organize the house. There was some, however, which would allow Catherine keep Alice without a drain on her own finances.

With that practical but depressing thought, I closed the door and went back to my ailing husband.

The next three months were dreadful. Sam got worse, and I had to call on Song Wing for help to care for him as he was too weak to get out of bed during some of those horrendous days. I insisted on Song Wing's washing his hands both before and after handling Sam. Dr. MacPherson was intrigued by what he called my "hand-washing fetish." I didn't care what he called it. I trusted my mother and her scientific friends more than any doctor. She had attended lectures by important scientists who talked about the work of Semmelweis and Pasteur. I carried on. My hands were sometimes raw, but I washed them anyway.

The fever, which had been alarming, finally left Sam and he became more comfortable. By the end of August, his body had returned to normal.

But his mind had not. He had lost the sharp intelligence that had so attracted me when I first met him, that curiosity about everything, that ability to weigh new information against what he knew, and his irrepressible sense of humour. That was gone. He could still look after his personal needs, eat, walk, and even drive Buckly with some skill, but he was like a dull boy. He was sometimes bewildered by simple problems, and frustrated that he didn't know how to solve them.

"Flo, what's this for?" He held up the poker.

I bit my lip and managed to answer. "We poke the fire with it to get air in so the wood catches more quickly."

He shook his head as if he could shake knowledge loose. "I should know that, shouldn't I?"

I nodded. He left the room and I could hear him pacing back and forth in the bedroom.

Alice was back with us and after her first joyous reunion was beside herself with grief.

"Where has Daddy gone?" she cried to me. "He's not there."

"The fever affected his brain," I told her. "It isn't working the way it used to."

"Will he come back?"

I looked at her, afraid to take away hope.

"He won't. You know he won't." She ran from me to her room, and I heard her crying for hours. After that, she never mentioned it again, and her attitude to her father changed. She now treated him like a young brother she had to look after. It was as if she was resigned to the death of her father and the introduction of a new person into the family.

I felt much the same.

My finances were in a precarious state. I would have to do something.

Now that Sam was not bringing in an income, and would never again bring in an income, I sold his tools and recouped some money. I considered what we had left. I needed to confer with friends.

Both Alice and I needed to have some relaxation away from Sam. I asked Song Wing, my greatest friend in Stanley, to stay with Sam while I drove Alice to Barkerville. We would stay overnight with Catherine, attend a play, and I would talk things over with her.

It was wonderful to meet so many of my friends and to be back in the stimulating world of the theatre. After the play, I met two gentlemen from California who were investigating the prospects of setting up a mining company in Barkerville.

"Tell me about the Napa Valley," I said. Sam had said he loved it there.

It turned out they were familiar with it and gave me a glowing report of the city and the surrounding communities. They agreed that the city of Napa was a lovely place to live. It was only fifty miles from San Francisco and had theatres and schools and a new mental hospital due to open soon.

"It's going to give employment to the people of the city, and it's palatial. I've heard it looks like an English manor house." The idea of that hospital attracted me.

I sat with Catherine in her kitchen after the play. We'd spent many hours here over the years.

"I can't look after Sam and run a business in Stanley that only operates in the summer months," I told her. "If I'm going to make a move, I need to do it soon before I run out of money. Alice will need to be in a bigger place. She's going to need schools, society, and more to interest her. There is a mental hospital in Napa city if and when Sam needs more care."

"And Sam wants to go to the Napa Valley?"

"He does, or he did when he was capable of expressing such an interest."

"You want to make his last years happy."

She knew me well. "That's it."

"Go then, my dear. You've always been ready to try something new. Try California."

I was determined to go.

While I was in Barkerville, I visited the bank and arranged to have my money sent from Victoria to Napa. I took my will and my marriage lines, which had survived the fire in the bank's safe. Then, I emptied my account in Barkerville of all the money and returned to Stanley.

I packed up the house, sold it and any unwanted household goods, and pared down our belongings to what we could bring with us. Alice was a big help as she scrambled around making sure our trunks were crammed full. Buckly was still a strong, capable horse at age thirteen, so Alice and I packed the wagon and, on a bright sunny day in September, we left for California.

*twenty-one*

# South to California

SAM LOVED TO drive the wagon, so the trip south was long but reasonably pleasant. I was relieved to see him happy, and Alice found wagon-living an adventure. I had to cook, so our diet was somewhat monotonous, but augmented with fresh fruits and vegetables we acquired along the way. I was concerned about Indian attacks, as they were much more frequent in America than they were in British Columbia, but we came through the Okanagan Valley, Idaho, and Oregon without encountering any hostile men—Indian or non-Indian. Of course, Sam's size might have deterred anyone of evil intent.

We arrived in the city of Napa in October of 1874. Our first stop was a livery stable, where Sam gave Buckly a luxurious wash and feed. I consulted with the livery stable owner, a Mr. Josh Barclay. I paid him in advance for a month's stable fee, arranged the feed for Buckly, and the storage of the wagon.

"Now, Mr. Barclay, as you can no doubt see, my husband has had an injury to the brain and is not able to make plans."

"I did notice something a little bit off," he said. "Too bad about that."

"Thank you. It is quite terrible. He was a blacksmith, you see, and he still has a love of horses."

"I see that, too."

Having established some kind of connection with Mr. Barclay, the only person I had met in Napa, I asked his advice about boarding houses. He sent me to Revere House on Second Street, which did not have enough room for us, then to Mrs. Solvig Johnson's house on Coombs Street, a central location.

WE SETTLED INTO MRS. JOHNSON'S boarding house fairly comfortably. We had three bedrooms, a sitting room, kitchen, and storeroom. I took one bedroom for Alice and me, one for Sam, and one for my sewing. I needed to create some income for us and returned to my seamstress skills. Mrs. Johnson put me in way of employment. It was irksome because I felt as if I was going backward in life to my days in Victoria, sewing for a living, always on the outside of society, not participating, and not receiving stimulation from conversations or activities.

Alice went to school at the Ladies' Seminary. There was promise of a new public school to be opened in 1876. Until then, she seemed to like the school and the girls studying with her. I worked hard to see she had the clothes of a gently raised young woman. The styles still required a great deal of material. I cut down a few gowns of mine to make dresses for Alice. That helped her, but she did not bring friends home. A boarding house was not a socially acceptable home for a student of the Ladies' Seminary. I understood that.

I brought my gold to the Bank of Napa the first week and exchanged it for American paper money, most of which I put into my account. I received my passbook. The banker, a Mr. Stern, assured me that California had married women's property rights, and I could act for myself in any business transactions. It was ironic that now I could do business legitimately, I had little business to do.

We managed to live quietly with Sam helping out at the livery stable, Alice in school, and me taking in sewing from Mrs. Johnson's many contacts. It was, quite frankly, a stifling life relieved only occasionally by a stimulating meeting of the friends of a new library being planned. I hoped I could get work as a librarian.

A year went by with the predictability of routine. Sam seemed the same, without much change and, certainly, no improvement. I wrote to the Literary Society in London asking for a pension such as my mother had, citing all my work with *Household Words*, the *London News*, and the Theatre Royal in Barkerville, but they answered with a firm rejection. In their opinion, I hadn't produced enough. I fumed. They sat there in their temples of exclusion in London and refused to acknowledge that my literary work was sufficient for an award. Charles Dickens had died 1870, and I could think of no one else who would champion my cause. My father had died before I left for Victoria, and I wouldn't ask Thomas. I gave up on a pension from England, donned my spectacles, and doggedly sewed clothes.

I enjoyed the seasons in Napa as they changed only slightly, and I found I did not miss the snow in winter. Napa did not even get frost. It was hot in the summer months. Alice and I, dressed only in shifts, stayed inside during the middle of the day, then dressed and went out in the cooler evenings. Sam didn't seem to notice the heat. In late November, the air was starting to cool, although I would compare it to high summer in Barkerville.

Sam had been spending some time in Mrs. Johnson's back garden. It was a marvel of order and production. Many of our vegetables came from her industry. Even in November, the garden still produced. No wonder Sam had wanted to live here. It was a beautiful country with a climate that was easy to enjoy. I tarried on my way back from the outhouse this early afternoon. Sam was carefully guiding a growing tendril of green plant up a stick. He looked up as I came near. I stopped to watch him and enjoy the sun on my face. Sam had the sun on his shoulders. He looked like a picture of a Greek god from my early readings as a child—tall, strong, fair, and focused. I realized that was different. He was focused on me.

"Flo," he said. "You're beautiful."

I blinked. When had he last noticed my looks? Before the typhoid. Some time ago. I smiled. He came closer. His eyes seemed more alert. He reached out a hand. "Where's Alice?"

"At school."

"Come to bed," he said and pulled me to him.

I was dazed. He hadn't shown any interest in me this way since his illness. I followed him, laughing as he rushed into our flat and shut the door. He pulled me to his room and slowly and carefully undressed me. I felt precious.

Was Sam coming back to me? Was he healing? At that moment, I didn't care about the future. I wanted the closeness we'd had before—right then.

He was tender and loving, and I was delighted. After, he fell into a sound sleep as he always did.

Alice would be home soon. I rose and dressed, smiling to myself. It had been lovely. I didn't want to tell Alice I thought her father might be getting better. I didn't want to get her hopes up. That was a wise decision.

When he came down for supper, the usual cloud was before his eyes. He grunted but didn't speak. All was as it had been.

I left the house after supper, walked down to Napa Creek, and wandered along under the oak trees. The afternoon's loving had been wonderful, but it didn't mean anything. He was gone again. I cried for what we might have had. I cried for the priceless memories. I cried for Sam.

From that day, Sam got worse. Josh Barclay came to me.

"I can't keep him at the livery anymore, Mrs. Tompkins. He started a fire in the stables. Lucky I was there."

"He was a blacksmith," I said. "He misses his forge."

"Aye, oh, but you can see . . ." his voice trailed off.

I could see Buckly's free room and board going away. Mr. Barclay had let us board Buckly at the stables without cost in return for Sam's work. No work. No free board. But a stable could not risk fire.

"Yes," I interrupted him. "I can see fire is a menace you can't tolerate. Of course, I will keep him home or attend him when he's at the livery looking after Buckly."

"I'm sorry about this, ma'am."

"It's hard for us all." This was a good time to ask a favour. "About Buckly, Mr. Barclay. I wonder if you can rent Buckly out for hire a couple of times a week and apply that to his board. Perhaps I could sell the wagon and get a democrat. That would ensure Buckly didn't have heavy loads to haul." I had driven a democrat in England many years before and it would be much easier to control than a wagon as it was small and light and designed for passengers, not freight.

He thought about it, then nodded. "I could arrange that." He did arrange it and Buckly earned his keep.

SAM WAS GETTING TO BE more unpredictable. He sang sometimes. At first, Mrs. Johnson was amused, but soon she asked me to keep him quiet. He had been going to the livery, but only when Alice or I accompanied him. He went by himself once without my knowledge and started another fire. There was no talking to Sam as now he couldn't follow what I was saying, and it frustrated him. I had dashed out to get some thread one morning and came back to find him burning some books—in the stove, at least, but the real Sam would never burn books.

Right after Christmas in 1874, I dressed him in his finest, took him to the livery, helped him harness Buckly, and drove him to the new Napa Insane Asylum.

It had opened in November. I had been there earlier and talked to the doctors, registering Sam in anticipation of this day, and touring the hospital. A farm was part of the hospital facilities where I thought Sam might be happy, caring for the animals. It was impressive, but it was an insane asylum and an unhappy place.

I could not trust Sam at home any longer and Alice needed a chance to grow and prosper. The hospital was not cheap. I had to pay monthly for Sam's care, but it seemed the only option, and I was grateful I had it.

When we arrived, Sam followed the attendant without protest. I watched his back until I could no longer see it. It was the only way I could care for him, but tears ran down my face. I untied Buckly, mounted the democrat, and drove back to the livery. I stopped halfway, under a grove of trees, and cried hard. I finally hiccupped, gasped for breath, then calmed myself.

"He's gone, Buckly," I confided. "He's gone from himself and from us. I hope they are kind to him, and that he doesn't suffer. I don't think he will, as he doesn't understand most of the time what is going on around him. If he has something to eat and a bed and some time in the sunshine and gardens, he will be as happy as it's possible for him to be. But, oh, I'll miss him so!"

I wailed to the sky. Only the crows and jays heard me.

AFTER THAT, ALICE AND I attended concerts and literary groups. We took walks and buggy rides with Buckly. Money was difficult to find and hold onto. I kept Alice, Buckly, and myself on the remnants of the sale of the saloon and the house in Stanley and on my sewing. I sewed for others, but at fifty-two, my eyesight failed often for close work. I had a magnifying glass and a pair of spectacles, which helped.

Sam died on April 7, 1876. He was only forty-eight. I mourned him, but I felt he had died to me some years before. Alice and I went to his funeral, a quiet affair on the hospital grounds.

In spite of our last few years, I had loved Sam and loved my life with him. His personality had been joyous and energetic before typhoid, and he had shown me how generous, loving, and rich life could be. He'd taught me to love an argument with an intelligent combatant and how to enjoy the company of friends. Sam was five years younger than I was. He should have lived longer. We should have been prospering in this glorious valley. I felt cheated by fate once again.

*twenty-two*

# A Change in Circumstances

ALICE AND I stayed on at Mrs. Johnson's. It was central, she had friends in the neighbourhood, and she put me in the way of clients for my seamstress business. People always needed clothes and, while I didn't make the profits I had in the past with my saloon business, I managed to pay our bills.

The city of Napa intrigued me. The mild weather resulted in lush vegetation and trees I'd never seen outside of Italy. I recognized some plants, like lavender, but not others. There were woodlands of oak trees and one unique-looking tree called madrone, which had a startling burnt-orange-coloured bark and stiff, waxy leaves. It looked like what we had called arbutus in Victoria. Alice taught me about the flora.

"There are some plants that only grow here in Napa Valley, like Napa blue curls."

When she showed them to me, I realized I'd thought they were lavender.

The new library was a boon. I borrowed books and read *The Napa Daily Reporter* as well as *The San Francisco Evening Journal* and *The New York Times*. Once a week, the library got *The London Daily News*. I read it from the start to the finish, even the classified ads. I did not get hired as the librarian. I had not been long enough in the community to have support, and the position was given to a long-standing member of the library committee. I did not let my desperation for employment show, and was gracious to the newly installed librarian. I stayed on the library committee and participated in decisions as a volunteer. It was a pleasant, if rather dull, existence.

I cherished my excursions to the library meetings, partly because I was able to spend time with intelligent conversationalists there, and partly, I must admit, because I enjoyed the company of Colonel James Hopkins. He was a member of the committee, a widower, and an interesting man. He'd had a career as an officer in the US Army and had seen action in the Mexican war. He'd told me that one of the most exciting moments of his life was when he raised the flag for the United States at Monterrey in 1846. But other than that incident, he didn't talk about his war years. He talked about books, ideas, plans, and people. He was a civil engineer and surveyor who had a house in St. Helena, north of Napa, but stayed in Napa often to oversee the construction of the water dam and pipes to the state asylum.

He was unpredictable. One day he was in Napa, the next he was exploring some distant reaches of California.

"Why go so far? Are you looking for gold?"

"Sometimes."

"Why else?"

"Itchy feet."

I had to be content with that. His travels did contribute to interesting conversations. He had also been a gold prospector in San Francisco and was fascinated by my stories of Barkerville. I was intrigued by the contrast between the gold rush of San Francisco in '49 and the Fraser River gold rush of '58. Some of the same people had been in both places. James had known Fanny Bendixon. I didn't inquire how closely he'd known her.

I enjoyed him so much I found I was looking forward to his prolonged visits. He had started to call for me before the meetings and walk with me to the library. He told me about the theatre world of San Francisco, a city I had yet to revisit, even though it was a mere fifty miles from Napa. James went to San Francisco about once a month to attend to business and to take in the new theatre productions. I told him about Thomas's theater productions in London, and about my experiences with the Theatre Royal in Barkerville.

He took Alice and me to a garden party at the home of his friends, Mr. and Mrs. Barth. Alice had a wonderful time with the young people there.

"You've upped her social status," I told him as we walked home.

He chuckled. "She's a lovely girl and deserves to go to parties and have a good time."

We had been walking together for some months before I realized others were talking about us as if we were a couple and that, in fact, James was courting me. It was a fragmented courtship as James was away often and Alice was a chaperon as well as a strong reason for my cautious reaction.

James showed me how the city of Napa had been planned. He showed me how the water system worked in the Napa Valley, how the river which started at Mount Saint Helena used to flow in a serpentine manner through the valley, supporting myriad wildlife and fish. Ranchers and farmers gradually drained the fields, banked the river, and forced it into a narrower channel. It still provided fresh water for the city, but very few fish. He talked about the way the Wappo Indians had been killed or forced from their lands, which was why I saw so few of them. They lived in a separate area of the city along with the Chinese. Napa was a much more divided society than I'd seen in Barkerville. In spite of his liberal views on the equality of men and women, and his American loyalties to the ideas of democracy, James had the British belief that white, Anglo-Saxon males were destined to occupy the higher levels of society. That seemed ingrained. He recognized the incongruity of his attitudes, though, so we had some lively disagreements.

"Your civil war was so recent you are still looking for threats to your democracy," I accused him. That war that had pitted the northern states against the southern had ended in 1865, but society, even here in Napa, held festering grudges. Southerners had an accent distinctive from northerners, so one could usually tell where a person was from by the way they spoke. Trust or mistrust ensued from a first meeting.

James had fought in the Mexican–American War but not in the Civil War. I detected a sense of vigilance in him against any organization or ideology that might threaten the state or the country. There was always someone or something to fight.

He argued with me, but he didn't always want to win. He wanted to understand my thinking and follow my arguments. That was highly seductive.

One afternoon, on a temperate day, James invited me on a picnic along the river. Alice was off with a girlfriend watching an impromptu horse race. James had arranged for the cook at his hotel to provide the food, for which I was grateful, and I brought some wine. We walked along the Napa River, talking until we came to a secluded small clearing. James dropped his rucksack, and I put down the basket of wine. As I did so I heard a hiss. I glanced down, then stared at the snake rising in front of the basket. I froze.

"James," I whispered.

"Oh, God damn it." James was beside me. He had a knife in his hand. He leaned over, picked up the snake with the knife, and threw it into the trees.

"Nasty beggers," he said.

I shuddered, reached out, and grabbed him. "I hate, absolutely *hate,* snakes!"

"There, there," he said, patting my head.

I drew back a little and laughed. "Thank you."

James stood stock still. Then he drew me close and kissed me.

I kissed him back. Lovely. I had thought I was too old for passion—but apparently not.

James looked around the clearing. I saw the intention in his eyes.

"I'm sorry, James. I'd love to, but there's Alice."

"She's not here."

"But I have to be respectable if she's going to have any opportunities." I fought the rising need that was becoming more urgent with every second. "Really, James. I am truly sorry."

"Why don't you marry me then?"

What was he saying? "Why don't I marry you?" I repeated. I straightened, fisted my hands on my hips, and stared at him "You haven't asked me, you clod head!"

"I'm asking now."

I blinked and let my hands fall by my sides "That sounds just fine."

"Good." He reached for me again. "Where were we?"

ALICE WAS EXCITED. "WE WILL live in a house. We will go to the big city. I can have friends come to tea. I can have more gowns, and you won't have to sew them all. You can hire a seamstress."

She had a lot of her mother in her. Those advantages had occurred to me, including the agreeable notion of hiring a seamstress. All those things were reasonable expectations of marriage to James.

"I wouldn't marry him if I wasn't very fond of him, Alice. Come, now. We could manage on our own." I wouldn't marry him if I hadn't felt a strong urge to do so, but I didn't offer that reason to Alice. Sam had taught me that loving was highly enjoyable.

"True, Mummy. But life will be so much more comfortable with Mr. Hopkins. Admit it. Besides, I like him."

So, James and I were wed by Judge Wallace at the home of Mr. and Mrs. Barth in the city of Napa. The Barths hosted a few friends afterwards. I had invited Mrs. Johnson and Josh Barclay, and several friends from the literary society to the wedding breakfast, although they didn't call it that here. "Reception" is what Mrs. Barth called it. James had invited many more. Alice had a new gown supplied by James and not sewn by me, and had a wonderful time. She stayed with the Barths while James and I travelled to San Francisco for a few days.

When we returned, James surprised me with a new house in Napa.

"You and Alice need a good address," he said.

Alice and I packed up our possessions and said a fond farewell to Mrs. Johnson. I would drop in for tea and keep up on all our mutual acquaintances. I had informed my clients that I would no longer be available to sew for them. That felt wonderful. I didn't object to having no say in the purchase of the new house. I was simply pleased at having my own home and was determined to make a comfortable abode out of whatever James had provided. It wasn't difficult. The house was commodious and comfortable.

I was used to being in charge of a staff of employees in Barkerville, so managed the household without difficulty. I hired a cook, Mrs. Rodrigo, and two maids, Sally and Matilda. James was impressed.

"You make everything so easy," he said. "I used to have all kinds of problems about cooking and laundry and the cleaning I had to deal with every day."

James had been married before—twice. The first time had been to a woman named Harriet Perry in 1849, who sued him for divorce after three years. She didn't have enough evidence, but James eventually did divorce her. She left him to travel east. He'd married Sarah Watts in 1866. She left him as well and died in 1872 in New York. Neither woman had had children.

"Always wanted young'uns," James told me. "Alice is a bonus."

He certainly indulged her. Alice had never had so many gowns, fans, and jewellery.

"Stop," I told him after a few months of such spoiling. "Give her experiences, not things. Take her out in the buggy. She can drive, so let her. Encourage friends around, so she develops her own social groups."

James listened and adjusted his behaviour. He did want the best for her.

"I made my will," he told me one evening. "I divided everything. You get the house and Alice gets the rest of the property." The rest consisted of eighty acres of farmland in St. Helena that James was hoping to plant in grapes and several lots in town. As a surveyor, he got to know where the property bargains were and could buy them before they went on the market. Alice would be well off when James died, and I would be comfortable. I might die first. James seemed to be a young sixty-three. He might live longer than I did.

"You're so beautiful, it's hard to believe you're forty-eight," he'd told me before we were married. I was fifty-eight, but I didn't correct him. I had always given my age as whatever I thought would be advantageous and didn't see that it was anyone else's business how old I was—not even James's. I had seen him write forty-eight on our marriage certificate. I left it as it was.

I was pleased I could contribute to our marriage in a practical way. I'd worried there wouldn't be enough for me to do, but James had many property interests, many plans for buying and selling property, which I found fascinating and about which I could offer advice. James got into the habit of asking me to review any new acquisition to assess the risk and possible profits. While it was irksome to not be in charge of the businesses, I was happy to be consulted. Still, a consultant was not the owner.

"You're used to having your own money," James said a few weeks after our marriage.

"Does it show?"

"Yes." He smiled, and I shrugged.

"It's different," I said.

"Here's what we can do." James had thought about it. "I can put a salary into your account every month. You use that in any way you want. If you have any other money, don't spend it. Invest it. That way you'll have something if I die first—and you like investing."

"I do. That will work very well." I had retained some money from our sales of the Stanley house and my saloon. Not much—it had been expensive to have Sam cared for in the hospital—but I could make it grow.

Most women lived without money of their own, but that didn't suit me. James looked after the expenses of the house and provided for Alice. He bought her a pony and trap—Buckly having died some years before at the venerable age of seventeen—and more clothes and jewellery than she could ever wear. She blossomed. He indulged me as well, but not as flamboyantly. I wouldn't have liked that. A few good pieces of jewellery were lovely and the services of a seamstress a godsend, but I didn't want an overabundance of clothes. What I really wanted, and what he was happy to provide, were trips to San Francisco.

James took us to San Francisco regularly. We kept a carriage, but we travelled to and from San Francisco by train. The rail line had opened in the 1860s and was convenient and comfortable. We usually stayed at the Brooklyn Hotel, but moved to the New Palace Hotel when it was built. It was a marvel, with bathrooms, hot water, and steam heat, which we greatly appreciated in the cool, ocean-side winter. We attended the opera, first at Tivoli Opera House, which often gave us less than stellar performances although I enjoyed the dinners there, and, latterly, at the Grand Opera House. We laughed ourselves silly at the farcical productions on offer at the many other theatres and enjoyed meeting friends and seeing events with them. I met with the literary society at a private library. It was remarkable that a city so large didn't have a public library yet when Barkerville, so tiny by comparison, found it essential. I tried several private libraries and found one where I enjoyed the stimulation of sharp minds interested in the ideas garnered from books. A visit to San Francisco was like a tonic for me. Over the years, I became warm friends with many writers in the city, in particular Grace Hibbard, who was a noted poet.

In 1883, we moved to St. Helena. James's itchy feet directed some kind of move and he had business interests there. It was a pleasant place, small, but beautiful and orderly. Alice loved living in the big house. She had left the Ladies' Seminary in Napa and did not enroll in school in St. Helena. Most girls did not attend school past fifteen, and I hadn't attended school at all. In any case, I had not been impressed with the curriculum at the Ladies' Seminary as it had seemed lightweight. There hadn't been enough philosophy, serious literature, or economics in her studies to develop her mind, but I augmented her education with books I now was able to buy. I remembered the conversation I'd had with my mother the night before she died about the necessity of me finding a husband. I had thought she was worrying unnecessarily at the time. I understood her concern much better now. Alice was seventeen when we moved to St. Helena, and soon would be looking for a husband. I didn't see much opportunity for her other than marriage. She was not interested in business. She didn't want a career of any kind. It was a humbling realization. Maria Rye, of the Female Middle Class Emigration Society, would be appalled at the lack of progress for women. California Married Women's Property Rights helped because women could manage their own legal affairs, but there were still few opportunities for women in commerce. The expectation, and it was a weighty one, was that women would manage households. That's all.

To be fair, Alice wasn't the least bit interested in commerce and was thrilled to attend parties, gossip with her friends, and travel with us when we went to the city. And I was tired of being in charge of our lives and was willing to hold onto James's coattails as he created an interesting and reliable life for us. It was also a full-time job to keep up with James. He always had some plan, some scheme, some innovative idea that he worked on like the new crop of grapes that he had started to replace the old agricultural crops.

"Onions, Florence. I used to grow onions. Imagine that. Now I can grow grapes. Acres and acres of them."

"Indeed, grapes will be more interesting. Do you think we will need to travel to France to study their agriculture?"

He laughed. "Perhaps."

James liked to fish and to walk, preferably at the same time. He traipsed all over the country. One day he fished the river and walked for twenty miles. He did that on his own. I wasn't willing to go that far.

In 1885, James suffered a temporary paralysis which scared him as neither he nor his doctor knew why it had occurred. It passed, but James required little persuading when I suggested a move to San Francisco.

"Better for Alice," he said.

That was true. Alice was now nineteen and she needed a wider choice of husband than could be found in St. Helena. But there were also more doctors in San Francisco.

JAMES WAS NEVER BORING. STIMULATING, opinionated, stubborn at times, but never boring. He was affectionate, too, and made me feel appreciated and loved. However, I did not expect it to last. Likely, there was trouble in store for me—there always was—but I enjoyed this time in my life while I could. I had loved our trips to San Francisco with its theatres, concerts, and literary soirees. When we moved there, I felt as if I had come back to my proper place in society. Somewhere inside me was Miss Florence Wilson, whom I might have to rely on in the future, but outwardly I was now Mrs. James Hopkins, who could enjoy the world of theatre as a spectator and lively conversations with my husband and our circle of friends. I was aware I was a man away from poverty, something I'd been careful to avoid my whole life. But with a wary eye on Fate, I enjoyed it.

*twenty-three*

# To San Francisco

We bought a house on Jackson Street in San Francisco, where I soon organized our comforts and James pursued a fruitless search for a government-appointed position. He was looking less for money than for interesting work. He did not like being idle. To assuage his restlessness, we moved twice: once to Leavenworth Street and then to Polk Street. I liked the house on Polk Street best and decided we would stay there. James could go on his country walks in excursions to St. Helena to satisfy his wandering ambitions.

Alice did meet an eligible man and married William Inwood in 1879. She was twenty-three and old enough to make her own choice. I wouldn't have chosen William for her, but was wise enough to keep my opinions to myself. I didn't object to his occupation—compositor at a newspaper office—but to his conversation.

In the first place, he called me "Mother Hopkins."

"Please call me Florence," I'd requested, but it hadn't made any difference.

Ah, well. I could survive that.

He was a reliable man, polite, and besotted with Alice. My only complaint about William was that he was suffocatingly boring. However, he was an agreeable man most of the time, and Alice would have little opposition in running her household. James and I hosted the wedding breakfast at our home on Polk Street, and Alice and William left for a few days journey around Napa. They returned to our house, where they would live. William did not have the money for a house. Alice would inherit quite a lot of money, but she did not yet have it, so I set off a portion of the house for them where they could retreat to be separate from James and me.

I KNEW JAMES AND I were both in the decade where death was highly likely; only a few people lived past seventy-five. My brother Thomas had died in 1879. I still heard from Jane and Minnie, but so many friends had died in their fifth or sixth decade. James and I been attending the funerals of our friends for the last five years. But when James died suddenly, with no indication he had a thing wrong with him, it was a shock.

I came in from shopping and found him on the floor of the parlour.

I screamed, then sank down beside him.

"James, dear heart, how can you leave?" It wasn't as though I hadn't expected one or both of us to die soon, just not that day.

Our maid Sally rushed in.

"Get Dr. Black," I said quietly.

She glanced at James and a look of comprehension and sadness passed over her face. I did know it was too late for the doctor, but I wanted him to come in any case.

I stayed on the floor, holding James's hand. It was still warm, but he was not breathing and his eyes were blank. His hand was moving, but it was me that was shaking as I held it. Tremors ran up my body. I moaned. I wanted to wail. I struggled to compose myself. It surprised me that I had emotions that ran so deep they could make me shake and cry. I felt as strongly as I had when I was a girl. Anger, fear, sorrow, and love swept through my body, overwhelming me.

The doctor helped me make arrangements for James's funeral. I managed it with the help of Alice, who stayed with me. The Associated Veterans of the Mexican War turned out in a great, orderly military guard for his funeral at St. Luke's. James would have loved that.

JAMES AND I HAD ALMOST ten years of happy living, and I missed him greatly. His sense of humour haunted me. I imagined his quips on my life as if he were by my side, watching all I did. James always had the *mot juste*. I was lonelier than I ever had been, haunted both by Sam, with his simple attitude to life and virile enthusiasms, and James, with his appreciation of people and ideas and his zest for living. They shared a sense of humour. Perhaps they'd stride on either side of me and *riposte,* invisible guardians and commentators on my life. The fantasy faded, and I confronted the real problems James's death had engendered.

As agreed when we married, Alice received the property, and I got the house. I would live off my own investments, and my army widow's pension. With my advice and that of her solicitor, Alice was now able to buy a house and settled on one on Homestead Street, not far from me. I advised her to carefully oversee all transactions when doing business. Neither of us thought to include William.

I told Alice I would try to find a smaller house as I realized in the months following James's death that the Polk Street house was too large for me.

"We'd love to have you, Mummy. I've missed you." I thought about moving in with Alice and William. I had missed Alice as well, but she enjoyed different interests from mine, and I wasn't sure she would want me in her house for long. However, we were both mourning James, and I could live with them for a time.

Alice and William had only been married a year. A third person in the house was not easy to accommodate, I understood that. William and I were carefully polite to each other, but I knew it couldn't last. I needed to make a change before I let my irritation show.

I discussed the situation with my San Francisco friends, concealing my frank opinion of William.

"No question, Florence," Dorothy Proctor said. She was a literary friend of Grace Hibbard and a woman of decided opinions.

"You need to have a less restricting home where you can express yourself more freely."

"Yes," Grace said. "You could start writing poetry again."

I wasn't sure I was capable of writing poetry anymore, but I could certainly write travel observations, and enjoy the writings of others.

After a few lunches together, we came up with a solution. With grateful thanks to my daughter and her husband, and goodwill on both sides, I moved in with Grace, to her home at 416 Broadway Street.

Grace was a woman of determination and vision. She had found herself in a difficult situation when she was very young. She had married and had a son when her husband died at only twenty-four. She married a doctor and moved to Denver. That didn't last and, like my mother, she had left behind a miserable situation by divorcing him. She moved to San Francisco and had been there some years when I met her. Grace was a well-known poet and a writer of short stories and even novels. She was far more prolific than I, and certainly much better recognized. I admired her and enjoyed her company. She was lively, well-connected in the literary world, and thought the two of us would get along very well.

We did.

I brought the profit from the sale of the Polk Street house and James's eight-dollar-a-month army pension with me. I had some money left from my Barkerville days, so was affluent enough to attend the opera, concerts, and events that constituted our daily activities, without being a burden on Grace. I had sufficient wardrobe thanks to my years with James. Grace was not embarrassed to be seen with me. Occasionally, I even bought a new hat.

SAN FRANCISCO SUITED ME. IT was energetic, full of life. Grace introduced me to the Alcazar Theatre, where I enjoyed the kind of plays we had produced in Barkerville. The Grand Opera House had renditions of *Carmen* with Miro Delamotta as Don José. It was as good as any I'd heard in England and Russia. There was lighter fare as well. I laughed so hard at Gilbert and Sullivan's *Pirates of Penzance* that I set Grace off and we had to stuff our handkerchiefs in our mouths to keep from distracting the audience. We attended literary soirees and library meetings. I joined the audience when Grace, who was much in demand, read her poetry, but I didn't write it myself. The poetry I'd written when I was young did not compare favourably with the mature, insightful poetry of today's world. My poetry was better left in the past. I was an enthusiastic audience member, though, and enjoyed the varied artistic offerings of the city as well as the general bustle of activity. The wild life of the gold rush had ended about forty years previously, but the wealth brought into the city at that time and the increase in population continued to enliven the whole area. Occasionally, I met an old miner who told me about gold rush days. I had stories of my own about Barkerville, so we had a lively, reminiscent natter.

"There were men who fought over claims with guns and knives," Mr. Joe Corning told me. He had prospected in California and Idaho and had many stories.

"To death?" I said.

"Yep. Sometimes. Did that happen in the Cariboo?"

"Not often. I never heard of it when I was there."

"What did they do about claim jumping?"

I thought about it. "Sometimes they took it before the judge."

"Really? To a court of law?"

"Yes."

"I'll be hornswaggled."

I wanted to keep him talking just to hear another expression like that one. "And sometimes they got together with a group of miners and decided what was right."

"Never heard of such a thing. No guns?"

I shook my head. "Not over claims." I felt his disappointment and searched in my mind for some violent attack. "We had a murder there in 1867. James Barry shot Charles Blessing," I offered.

"So, guns, after all." He seemed pleased that his notion of guns as necessary proved correct.

"In that instance, yes. But it was a robbery on the trail. Barry shot him and took his fifty dollars. No claim jumping."

"Just robbery? Not for claim jumping? If that don't beat all."

I didn't meet old prospectors in the literary society, but in the coffee saloons of Market Street, and then only rarely. Mr. Corning was a regular at Westerfelds', but I seldom managed a visit there. Most of the time I was busy attending arts and cultural events. Living with Grace in San Francisco was stimulating but had enough daily routine to satisfy my English sense of order. I felt as if I had come around in a life circle to enjoy the kind of society I'd loved when I'd lived at home at Russell Square. Finally, I lived where I was most comfortable. It seemed Fate was through with sending me disasters. I hoped so, as here in San Francisco I was content.

# Epilogue

FLORENCE WILSON TOMPKINS HOPKINS died of heart disease at the home of Alice and William Inwood in San Francisco on November 23, 1902, aged seventy-nine years, nine months, and twenty-eight days. She was a remarkable woman of great courage and resilience.

# Acknowledgements

I OWE A GREAT deal to the knowledgeable staff at the Royal British Columbia Museum, the Library Archives of Shrewsbury, Shropshire, England, Emma Harper, the Dickens Museum, London, and the few authors who have even mentioned Florence Wilson, however tangentially. I also enjoyed the video produced by Richard Wright and Amy Newman. Art Downs's book on the Cariboo Wagon Road was informative for there is where I learned that Florence had ridden the stage before the Yale to Lytton Road was officially open, which told me a great deal about her determination. Barkerville also has an actor, Danette Boucher, who portrays Florence Wilson for the many visitors to the Barkerville site. The thesis by Mica Amy Royer Jorgenson on the involvement of Indigenous Peoples in the gold rush was highly informative, as was the thesis by Douglas John MacCallum on the theatre in Barkerville. Countless others to whom I am grateful are listed as references in the chapter notes at the end of the book.

I am in debt to Jennifer Barclay who, with her usual insight, did excellent developmental editing, which helped me shape the book. Kate Kennedy and Nandini Thaker at Heritage House Publishing have been invaluable. I am also indebted to my beta readers, Jill Brandon and Janice Crook, who picked out those pesky errors that seem to haunt me. This book has taken many advisors, so, if I have forgotten you, I apologize, but I appreciated every word of advice I received.

## APPENDIX I:

## Individuals Real and Imagined

*Imaginary characters are designated by an asterisk*

Abel Duffy*
Alice Margaret Tompkins
Alfred*
Angela Burdett-Coutts
Angus (stoker)*
Angus MacDonald*
Anthony*
Augustus Pugin (Frederick's father)
Ball, Gold Commissioner
Betsy Duffy*
Buckly (horse)*
Caloon (Florence Wilson's employer in Saint Petersburg. She did have a diplomat as an employer but real name not known)
Captain Alfred Hellyer
Catherine Dunn Parker
Charles Dickens
Charles Redfern
Charlie Major
Charlotte Townsend
Colonel James Hopkins
Cornwell Baron Wilson
Dorothy Proctor*
Dr. Black*
Dr. Carrell
Dr. Chipp
Dr. Helmcken
Dr. MacPherson
Duchess of St. Albans
Edward Coleman
Elizabeth Barrett Browning
Elizbeth Buchanan
Ella*
Ellen Ternan
Fanny Bendixon
Florence Wilson
Frederick Thomas (Florence's half sibling)
Fredrick Whymper
George the sailor*
George the barman*
Governor James Douglas
Hans*
Helen*
Grace Helen Hibbard
Henry and Elizabeth Newbury
Hilary Payne*

Hilda*
Hugh Ross*
Jake Anderson*
J. W. Doane
Jane Saunders Nesbitt
Jean Caux/Cataline
Jed Barclay*
Jimmy Pearson*
Joe Corning*
Josh Barclay*
Kai*
Kate Parker
Laura Wilson
Lee Song*
Louis Minaberriet
Louisa Townsend
Luane Joe*
McCallums*
Maisie*
Margaret*
Maria Duren
Matilda*
Matthew Begbie
May Sampson*
Michael Brown
Michael Horner*
Michael Penroy-Smith
Millie Gillan Cox
Minnie Parker
Miss Parsons*
Mr. Augustine*
Mr. and Mrs. Barth
Mr. Best*
Mr. Black
Mr. Bosworth*
Mr. Dixon
Mr. Holmes
Mr. Jones*
Mr. Josh Barclay
Mr. MacAdam*
Mr. MacIntyre*
Mr. Marshall
Mr. Neil Ferguson
Mr. Orr
Mr. H. M. Steele
Mr. Robert Stevenson
Mr. Stern*
Mrs. Amelia Douglas
Mrs. Blackly*
Mrs. Chambers
Mrs. Robb
Mrs. Rodrigo*
Mrs. Turnbull*
Nicholas I
Nicholas II
Peter*
Peter O'Reilly, gold commissioner
Paul Black*
Red MacEwan*
Reverend Hall
Reverend William Scott Richard Wilson
Robert Browning
Sally*
Sam the sailor*
Sam Chong
Samuel Jones*

Samuel Tompkins
Sandy MacIntosh*
Sarah Parker
Sin Hap
Solvig Johnson*
Song Wing
Talon Joe*
Taylor*
Thomas Harries Wilson
Tony*
Violet*
William Inwood
Zachary Mickelson*

## APPENDIX II:
Reader's Guide to Research and Composition

### *One* A New Life

#### IMAGINARY CHARACTERS

Mrs. Blackly
Bessie
Miss Parsons

#### FLORENCE WILSON'S FAMILY

Shropshire Archives, Castle Gates, Shrewsbury, Shropshire SY1 2AQ UK
Email: archives@shropshire.gov.uk

At this facility I researched Florence Wilson's maternal grandparents, Richard and Margaret Harries. There were no digital records, but the archivist brought me the St. Pancreas parochial records of births, marriages, and deaths. I also found evidence of Florence's grandmother Margaret Harries's inheritance and her grandfather Richard Harries's property deals.

Ancestry.com gave me the birth and death dates of Richard Harries and the names and birth and death dates of his children.

#### RUSSELL SQUARE

Walford, Edward. "Russell Square and Bedford Square." In *Old and New London: Volume 4* (Cassell, Petter & Gilpin, 1878). Accessed July 22, 2025. british-history.ac.uk/old-new-london/vol4/pp564-572.

Consistory Court Matrimonial and Testamentary Cause Papers, London Metropolitan Archives. https://search.lma.gov.uk/

scripts/mwimain.dll/yBHG4lXGHIJKr/LMA_DESCRIPTION/REFD/DL~2FC-13/$/WEB_DETAIL?GET&FILE=[WWW_LMA]messages/208.htm.

This is where I found out how Margaret Wilson would have been able to divorce her husband without a Parliamentary decree.

Wikipedia. "Mrs. Cornwell Baron Wilson." Last modified March 16, 2025. wikipedia.org/wiki/Mrs._Cornwell_Baron_Wilson

Information on Margarct Harrics Wilson on My Hcritagc sitc, which is difficult to access:

Margaret Cornwell Baron Wilson (born Harries)
*Collection:* MyHeritage Family Trees
myheritage.com/research/collections-1/myheritage-family-trees
*Site name:* Yates Web Site
*Site manager:* David Yates
*Birth:* March 27, 1796, St. Chad, Shrewsbury, Shropshire, England.
*Death:* 1846, London, Middlesex, England.
*Parents:* Richard Harries, Margaret Harries (born Davies)
*Siblings:* Martha Harries, Elizabeth Harries, Ann Harries, Richard Harries, John Harries, Hannah Peploe (born Harries), Jemima Harries
*Partner:* Augustus Charles Pugin
*Husband:* Cornwell Baron Wilson
*Children:* Richard Wilson, Florence Margaret Wilson, Thomas Harries Wilson, Constance Wilson, Cornwell Wilson, Private Wilson, Private Wilson. Richard died at age five. Those listed as "private" died as infants.

Wikisource. "Dictionary of National Biography, 1885-1900/Wilson, Mrs. Cornwell Baron." Last modified December 28, 2020. wikisource.org/wiki/Dictionary_of_National_Biography,_1885-1900/Wilson,_Mrs._Cornwell_Baron.

Chapman, Alison (ed.) and the DVPP team. "Wilson, Margaret (née Harries) (Mrs. Cornwell Baron Wilson) (F)." Digital Victorian Periodical Poetry Project, Edition 0.98.11beta, University of Victoria. Last updated May 7, 2025. dvpp.uvic.ca/wils9.html.

#### FRIENDS

Britannica. "Elizabeth Barrett Browning." Last updated June 25, 2025. britannica.com/biography/Elizabeth-Barrett-Browning.
Elizabeth Barrett Browning's relationship with the Wilson family is speculative, but Browning was a resident of the area and would likely have been in Florence's mother's circle of friends as Florence's mother was a noted literary figure.

Barron-Wilson, Mrs. Cornwell. *Memoirs of Miss Mellon Afterwards Duchess of St. Albans*. Remington & Co., 1887. The full text is available on Google Books.

#### FLORENCE WILSON'S LITERARY HISTORY

Lohrli, Anne. "Florence Wilson." Dickens Journals Online. Accessed August 2025. djo.org.uk/indexes/authors/florence-wilson.html.

Chapman, Alison (ed.) and the DVPP team. "Wilson, Margaret (F)," Digital Victorian Periodical Poetry Project, Edition 0.98.11beta, University of Victoria. Last updated May 7, 2025. dvpp.uvic.ca/wils8.html.

Florence Wilson's articles in Charles Dickens's *Household Words* are available at djo.org.uk/indexes/articles.html?author=81&reset=1.

Florence's mother wrote for Charles Dickens's newspaper regularly and Florence herself wrote some articles for him (see Appendix III for a sample). Dickens lived near the Wilsons at 48 Doughty Street, London.

*Two* ⸙ *After Bloomsbury*

IMAGINARY CHARACTERS

Mr. Holmes. There was a solicitor, but I could not discover his name.

Mr. Best. Another solicitor

The Caloon family. Florence was a governess with a diplomat's family in Saint Petersburg, but I was unable to find out the name of the diplomat.

Hilda. Florence would have had a maid in that household, but there is no record of her name.

The maids Margaret and Ellen.

FLORENCE WILSON'S LITERARY ACCOMPLISHMENTS

Lohrli, Anne. "Florence Wilson." Dickens Journals Online. Accessed August 2025. djo.org.uk/indexes/authors/florence-wilson.html.

Wilson, Florence. *Lyrics for Leisure Hours (1842)*. Cunningham and Mortimer, 1942. I own this book.

Charles Dickens Museum. Accessed August 2025. collections.dickensmuseum.com/home. Charles Dickens started his weekly magazine, *Household Words*, in 1850. He rarely credited other authors for their work.

LOSS OF THE SS *VICTORIA*

Wikipedia. "List of shipwrecks in November 1852." Last modified July 5, 2025. wikipedia.org/wiki/List_of_shipwrecks_in_November_1852.

EMPLOYMENT WITH NEWBURY'S

Wright, Richard. "Enigma: The Florence Wilson Story" Posted September 25, 2019. Vimeo, 46:59. vimeo.com/362438320. This video includes parts of Miss Wilson's life along with a description of the author's meticulous research.

#### EMIGRATION SOCIETY

Wikipedia. "Maria Rye." Last modified June 26, 2025. wikipedia .org/wiki/Maria_Rye.

### *Three* & *The* Tynemouth

#### IMAGINARY CHARACTERS

George, sailor
Sam, sailor

#### THE VOYAGE

The SS *Tynemouth*, the bride ship, sailed from London on June 9, 1862. It broke down twice on the way, had more than one mutiny, and ran out of fuel once. It took 101 days to reach Victoria, Colony of British Columbia, on September 17, 1862.

Redfern, Charles. *Reminiscences of a Long Sea Voyage in 1862*. Royal BC Museum and Archives Catalogue number E E R24. Victoria, BC. Available only in the reading room of the museum archives.

Johnson, Peter. *Voyages of Hope: The Saga of the Bride Ships*. Heritage House Publishing, 2002.

Lay, Jackie. "02 To Columbia on the Tynemouth: The Emigration of Single Women and Girls in 1862." *In Her Own Right: Selected Essays on Women's History in BC*. Accessed July 26, 2025. cc.arcabc.ca/islandora/object/cc%3A353?search=cc%253A353.

Hammerton, A. James. *Emigrant Gentlewomen: Genteel Poverty and Female Emigration, 1830–1914*. Croom Helm, 1979, 220.

#### MARIA RYE OF THE FEMALE MIDDLE-CLASS EMIGRATION SOCIETY

Wikipedia. "Maria Rye." Last modified June 26, 2025. wikipedia .org/wiki/Maria_Rye.

WikiTree. "Tynemouth Bride Ship Passengers." Last modified September 17, 2021. wikitree.com/wiki/ Space:Tynemouth_Bride_Ship_Passengers.

Townsend, Lorna. "Gold Miners of Barkerville: 'The Dregs of Society' A Forgone Conclusion." Last modified February 28, 1999. cariboogoldrush.com/barker/lorna.htm.

Hunter, Terri. "Crinoline Cargo." Posted January 10, 2016. canadahistory.ca/explore/women/crionoline-cargo.

Griffin, Kevin. "99 days at sea: Art exhibition explores the haunting bride ship Tynemouth." *Vancouver Sun*, March 8, 2019. vancouversun.com/news/local-news/99-days-at-sea-art-exhibition-explores-the-haunting-bride-ship-tynemouth.

#### FEMALE MIDDLE-CLASS EMIGRATION SOCIETY

Wikipedia. "Maria Rye." Last modified June 26, 2025. wikipedia.org/wiki/Maria_Rye.

#### MARRIED WOMEN HAD NO PROPERTY RIGHTS IN THE COLONY OF BRITISH COLUMBIA

Clarkson, Chris. "Families and Property Rights in Canada" in *Canadian History: Post-Confederation*, edited by John Douglas Belshaw. Licensed under a Creative Commons Attribution 4.0 International License. tinyurl.com/475vmk5j.

Wikipedia. "History of British Columbia." Last modified July 13, 2025. wikipedia.org/wiki/History_of_British_Columbia. This provides a broad view of the colonists' settlement of British Columbia.

Wilson, Florence. "Only a Governess." *Household Words*, Volume XIX, Magazine No. 476, May 7, 1859, 546–549.

Wikipedia. "Charles Dickens." Last modified August 10, 2025. wikipedia.org/wiki/Charles_Dickens.

### *Four — Troubles on the Sea*

#### IMAGINARY CHARACTERS

Mr. Bosworth

#### VOYAGE

Humphreys, Danda. *On the Street Where you Live, Volume 3: Sailors, Solicitors, and Stargazers of Early Victoria.* Heritage House Publishing, 2001.

Redfern, Charles. *Reminiscences of a Long Sea Voyage in 1862.* Royal BC Museum and Archives Catalogue number E E R24. Victoria, BC. This is available only in the reading room of the museum archives. Redfern described the cabins. He wrote the article sixty years after he experienced it.

Johnson, Peter. *Voyages of Hope: The Saga of the Bride Ships.* Heritage House Publishing, 2002.

#### PORT STANLEY

Jane Cameron National Archives. "Ships Registry at Port Stanley for 1862." Accessed August 2025. tinyurl.com/4wum8ra9.

The Falkland Islands and South Atlantic. "Early Stanley." Accessed August 2025. falklands-southatlantic.com/stanley%20heritage.html. This page includes a picture of Port Stanley in 1867 and a brief early history of the settlement.

The Falkland Islands Company. "History of the Falkland Islands." Accessed August 2025. the-falkland-islands-co.com/about-us/history-of-the-falkland-islands/.

### *Five — The Falkland Islands and Up the Pacific Coast of North America*

#### IMAGINARY CHARACTERS

George, the sailor

#### SAN FRANCISCO

Wilson, Florence. "Only a Governess." *Household Words,* Volume XIX, Magazine No. 476, May 7, 1859, 546–549.

Bygonely. "What San Francisco Looked like in the 1860s through Historic Photos." Accessed August 2025. bygonely.com/san-francisco-1860s/. There are lots of ads with this article,. but the photos are interesting.

Bay Area Census. "Bay Area: Decennial Census Data." Accessed August 2025. census.bayareametro.gov/historical-data/1860-1940/bay_area. Population of San Francisco in 1862.

Pacific Coast Architecture Database. "Russ House Hotel, Financial District, San Francisco, CA." Accessed August 2025. pcad.lib.washington.edu/building/20357/.

San Francisco Public Library. "Bank of California at California and Sansome Streets, San Francisco, 1868." Accessed August 2025. calisphere.org/institution/144/collections/.

San Francisco Public Library. "East Side of Montgomery between Sacramento and California, 1867." Accessed August 2025. calisphere.org/item/fe6413a52b3f94f00a2d15b0bdb05c07/.

### *Six* *Arriving in Victoria*

IMAGINARY CHARACTERS

Mr. MacAdam
Betsy Duffy
Alfred, the delivery boy

Wright, Richard. "Enigma: The Florence Wilson Story" Posted September 25, 2019. Vimeo, 46:59. vimeo.com/362438320. This video includes parts of Miss Wilson's life along with a description of the author's meticulous research.

ListingsVictoria. "The Earliest Years" Accessed August 2025. listingsvictoria.ca/earliestyears/. In spite of the lack of attribution, this is an interesting source for learning about daily life in Victoria.

University of Victoria Humanities Computing and Media Centre. "Victoria's Victoria." Accessed August 2025. web.uvic.ca/vv/1860.html.

Palmer, Daniel. "City of Victoria turning clock back to 1862." *Victoria News*. Posted August 1, 2012. vicnews.com/news/city-of-victoria-turning-clock-back-to-1862-13175.

Green, Valerie. "1862: a year of change." *Times Colonist*. Posted July 29, 2012. timescolonist.com/archive/1862-a-year-of-change-4563394.

Digital Museums Canada (Langley Centennial Museum). "The Arrival of the Tynemouth." Accessed August 2025. communitystories.ca/v2/philip-jackman/story/the-arrival-of-the-tynemouth/.

Digital Museums Canada (Langley Centennial Museum). "Sarah Ann Lovegrove." Accessed August 2025. communitystories.ca/v2/philip-jackman/story/sarah-ann-lovegrove/.

Wikipedia. "John Sebastian Helmcken." Last modified April 21, 2025. wikipedia.org/wiki/John_Sebastian_Helmcken.

Township of Esquimalt. "The History of Esquimalt." Accessed August 2025. esquimalt.ca/culture-heritage/centennial-2012/our-history.

### *Seven — Life in Victoria*

#### IMAGINARY CHARACTERS

Violet and Maisie, neighbours and prostitutes
Hilary Payne, reporter
Kai and Tanta, Salish women traders

#### LIFE IN VICTORIA

Knowledge Network. "British Columbia: An Untold History." Accessed August 2025. bcanuntoldhistory.knowledge.ca/1860. A series of articles on life in 1860.

Green, Valerie. *Above Stairs: Social Life in Upper-Class Victoria 1843–1918*. TouchWood Editions, 2011.

Green, Valerie. "1862: A Year of Change". *Times Colonist*. Posted July 29, 2012. timescolonist.com/archive/1862-a-year-of-change-4563394.

Library and Archives Canada. "The Helmcken Children." Accessed August 2025. epe.lac-bac.gc.ca/100/205/301/ic/cdc/helmcken/people/kids.html?nodisclaimer=1.

University of Victoria Libraries. "Dr. John Sebastian Helmcken." Last updated April 10, 2025. libguides.uvic.ca/colonialplacenames/helmcken.

Peterat, Linda. "Food Security in 1860s British Columbia". BC Food History. Posted May 4, 2020. bcfoodhistory.ca/1860s-food-security-in-bc/.

Vallance, Neil. "Sharing The Land: The Formation of the Vancouver Island (or 'Douglas') Treaties of 1850-1854 in Historical, Legal and Comparative Context." PhD diss., University of Victoria, 2003.

University of Victoria Humanities Computing and Media Centre. "The Theatre Royal." Victoria's Victoria. Accessed August 2025. hcmc.uvic.ca/project/vicvic/student/theatreroyal/index.html.

Luxton, Donald and Associates. "Caire & Grancini Warehouse 1214 Wharf Street, Victoria Conservation Plan M." May 2019.

### *Eight — Establishing Myself in Victoria*

IMAGINARY CHARACTERS

Abel Duffy
Michael Horner
Jake Anderson
Jimmy Pearson

**LIFE IN VICTORIA**

*British Times Colonist*. "Miss Florence Wilson is Leaving the Colony." Monday Morning, February 29, 1864, p. 2. Accessed August 2025. tinyurl.com/euktds4v.

Wikipedia. "Cariboo Gold Rush." Last modified December 15, 2024. wikipedia.org/wiki/Cariboo_Gold_Rush.

*The Daily British Colonist Supplement*. "Additional Mining News." Vol. 8, No. 120, p. 4. October 28, 1862. Accessed August 2025. archive.org/details/dailycolonist18621028uvic. Article on mining in Barkerville.

### *Nine* *Up the Fraser River*

**IMAGINARY CHARACTERS**

Peter, cook on the paddlewheeler
Angus, stoker
Tony, horse wrangler
Zachary Mikelson, miner

**THE CARIBOO WAGON ROAD**

Downs, Art. Edited by Ken Mather. *Wagon Road North: The Saga of the Cariboo Gold Rush*. Revised and Expanded Edition. Heritage House Publishing, 2021.

Rhoden, Barbara. "In 1948, historic roadhouse at 59 Mile destroyed by fire." *The Ashcroft-Cache Creek Journal*. July 4, 2023. ashcroftcachecreekjournal.com/community/in-1948-historic-roadhouse-at-59-mile-destroyed-by-fire-5885212.

Rhoden, Barbara. "Golden Country: Lost roadhouses of the Cariboo Wagon Road." *The Ashcroft-Cache Creek Journal*. June 27, 2017. ashcroftcachecreek-journal.com/local-news/golden-country-lost-roadhouses-of-the-cariboo-wagon-road-5830050.

Yardley, Carollyne. "Barnard's Express." Cariboo Gold Rush. Last updated November 30, 1998. cariboogoldrush.com/wagonroa/barnard.htm.

BC Gold Adventures. "Stagecoaches on the Cariboo Road." Accessed August 2025. bcgoldadventures.com/stagecoaches-on-the-cariboo-road/.

Sale, Barry. "Haphazard History: BX integral part of B.C. Interior's development." *The Williams Lake Tribune*. Posted August 5, 2024. wltribune.com/local-news/haphazard-history-bx-integral-part-of-bc-interiors-development-7459747.

Barnard's Village. "History – Barnard's Express." Accessed August 2025. barnardsvillage.com/history/.

***Ten* *The Cariboo Wagon Road***

I lived in the Cariboo from 1963 to 1986 and travelled through this country many times.

THE CARIBOO WAGON ROAD

HistoricPlacesDays. "Historic Hat Creek."Accessed August 2025. historicplacesdays.ca/places/historic-hat-creek/.

Yardley, Carollyne. "Roadhouses: 70 Mile House Roadhouse." The Cariboo Gold Rush. Last updated November 30,1998. cariboogoldrush.com/wagonroa/70.htm.

Village of Clinton. "Village of Clinton Historic Walking Tour." 2022, accessed August 2025. village.clinton.bc.ca/wp-content/uploads/2022/01/Clinton_WalkingTour_2021_Online.pdf. This is the third version of the town's walking tour booklet. This version was developed in collaboration with the Village of Clinton, the Clinton Museum Society, High Bar First Nation, Whispering Pines / Clinton Indian Band, and Studio2 Design, and includes a map.

*Eleven* ❦ *Heading to Barkerville*

IMAGINARY CHARACTERS

Michael Penroy-Smith

FROM QUESNELMOUTH TO COTTONWOOD RANCH

Wikipedia. "Cataline." Last modified December 13, 2023. wikipedia.org/wiki/Cataline.

Wright, Richard Thomas. *Barkerville and the Cariboo Goldfields.* Heritage House Publishing, 2013.

Black Press Media Staff. "Haphazard History: The town of Soda Creek." *The Williams Lake Tribune.* Posted June 6, 2021. wltribune.com/community/haphazard-history-the-town-of-soda-creek-5532949.

Davies, Stephen and the Schoolnet Digital Collections Team. "Mining Claims." The Cariboo Gold Rush. Last updated November 20, 1998.cariboogoldrush.com/mining/claims.htm.

Van Kirk, Ken Mather and Dorothy Sweet. "Biography of WM. Barker" in *Dictionary of Canadian Biography, Vol XII, 1891–1900.* University of Toronto Press, 1990. You can read an excerpt at cariboogoldrush.csp.net/site/en/index.php?area=primary&source=barker.

Mills, Thomas. "Adapting to Miners' Practices: The Development of Gold Mining Law and the 1863 Mining Board." BC Studies, no. 196 (2017/18). ojs.library.ubc.ca/index.php/bcstudies/article/view/189376.

Hoogeven, A. "Sovereign Intentions: Gold Law and Mineral Staking in British Columbia." *BC Studies,* no. 198 (2018).

The People. "The People of the Cariboo Gold Rush: Thomas Elwyn." Accessed August 2025. epe.lac-bac.gc.ca/100/205/301/ic/cdc/time/galler04/frames/elwyn.htm.

Bescoby, Isabel M. "Society in Cariboo during the Gold Rush." *The Washington Historical Quarterly*, vol. 24, no. 3 (1933), 195–207. jstor.org/stable/40475520.

Yardley, Carollyne and Industrial Art Internet Group Ltd. "Roadhouses: 150-Mile House." The Cariboo Gold Rush. Last updated November 30, 1998. cariboogoldrush.com/wagonroa/150.htm.

Schoolnet Digital Collections Team. "150-Mile Roadhouse Davidson's Lake Valley Ranch and Roadhouse Lots 11, 12, 13 and 14 G.1., Cariboo." The Cariboo Gold Rush. Last updated November 30, 1998. cariboogoldrush.com/maps/150.htm.

Patenaude, Branwen C. *Trails to Gold*. Horsdal & Schubart Publishers, 1995.

***Twelve* — *The Last Trek on the Cariboo Wagon Road***

AllTrails. "Best Trails in Barkerville." Accessed August 2025. alltrails.com/canada/british-columbia/barkerville--2.

Wikipedia. "Cottonwood, British Columbia." Last modified August 6, 2025. wikipedia.org/wiki/Cottonwood,_British_Columbia.

***Thirteen* — *Arriving in Barkerville***

IMAGINARY CHARACTERS

May Sampson, saloon owner
Mr. Augustine, bank clerk in Richfield

Bescoby, Isobel. "Some Aspects of Society in the Cariboo from Its Discovery to 1871." Master's diss., UBC, 1932.

The Cariboo Gold Rush. "Richfield." Last updated December 1, 1998. cariboogoldrush.com/towns/rchfld.htm.

BC Gold Adventures. "The Gold Rush Saloons." Accessed August 2025. bcgoldadventures.com/the-gold-rush-saloons/.

Townsend, Lorna. "Gold Miners of the Barkerville: 'The Dregs of Society' A Foregone Conclusion." The Cariboo Gold Rush. Last updated February 28, 1999. cariboogoldrush.com/barker/lorna.htm.

Van Kirk, Sylvia. "Bendixon Fanny." *Dictionary of Canadian Biography, Vol. 12*. University of Toronto/Université Laval, 2003. Accessed February 5, 2025. biographi.ca/en/bio/bendixen_fanny_12E.html.

Sterne, Dianne. *Catherine Dunn-Parker-Austin*. Accessed August 2025. granitecreekbc.ca/archive/Catherine_Dunn-Parker-Austin.pdf.

Wright, Richard Thomas. *Barkerville and the Cariboo Goldfields*. Heritage House Publishing, 2013.

### *Fourteen* *Establishing My Business*

#### IMAGINARY CHARACTERS

Anthony, a barman
Song Wing, Florence's cook and friend
Angus MacDonald, miner
Jed Barclay, miner

#### FINANCE

Wikipedia. "History of Canadian Currencies." Last modified May 25, 2025. wikipedia.org/wiki/History_of_Canadian_currencies.
The British pound was worth 4.8666 Canadian dollars in 1864.

#### MURDER

Young, Ron. "Murderer Will Hang." The Cariboo Sentinel & Gold Rush Trail Journal Newspaper Archive. Accessed August 2025. barkerville.com/vol2/blssing1.htm.

#### THEATRE ROYAL

Friends of Barkerville Newsletter. "Barkerville's Theatre Royal, Part 2: 1900–1958." Issue 1, volume 23 (2023). Accessed August 2025. issuu.com/friendsofbarkerville/docs/fob_newsletter_spring_2023_final/s/23123838.

FOOD

Peterat, Linda. "Butchers of Barkerville: Food Processing and Marketing." BC Food History. Posted April 8, 2021. bcfoodhistory.ca/butchers-of-barkerville/.

### *Fifteen* ⸙ *An Unexpected Courtship*

IMAGINARY CHARACTERS

Red MacEwan, partner to May Sampson
Hugh Ross, employee of Hudson's Bay Company
Mr. Dixon, miner
Luane Joe
George and Hans, barman and waiter at the Regency

THEATRE

McCallum, Douglas John. "Barkerville Theatre in Context: a case study in our theatrical past." MA diss., UBC, 1981. Available on Google Scholar: tinyurl.com/3u63nkst.

REV. JOHN HALL

There are contradicting dates given for when John Hall came to Barkerville. One source says 1865 and one says 1864. I think it highly unlikely that Florence arrived in May of 1864 and married in June of 1864, so I went with 1865.

University of Victoria Humanities Computing and Media Department. "St Andrews Church in the Heart of Victoria." Victoria's Victoria. web.uvic.ca/vv/student/st_andrews/thechurch.php.

THE CARIBOO WAGON ROAD

BC Gold Adventures. "The Cariboo Wagon Road–Richfield to Barkerville." Accessed August 2025. bcgoldadventures.com/the-cariboo-wagon-road-richfield-to-barkerville/.

### *Sixteen ☙ Life in Barkerville*

IMAGINARY CHARACTERS

Neil Ferguson
Luane Joe
May Sampson
Talon Joe

Royer Jorgenson, Mica Amy. "It Happened to me in Barkerville": Aboriginal identity economy, and law in the Cariboo gold rush, 1862–1900." MA diss., University of Northern British Columbia, 2012.

Digital Atlas of Idaho. "Exploration and Expansion." *Digital Atlas of Idaho*. www.isu.edu/digitalatlas/geography/.

Leesburg and Grantsville, Idaho. "Intermountain Histories." https://www.intermountainhistories.org/items/show/492.

PERSONAL CONTACTS

Susan Costanzo, Department Chair, Western Washington University, Bellingham, WA 98225-9061.

Frank Oesterheld, Electronic Records Archivist, Washington State Digital Archives.

Taryn Jones, Archivist and Librarian Archives, Royal BC Museum, Victoria, BC.

### *Seventeen ☙ Travelling Again*

IMAGINARY CHARACTERS

Mr. Jones
Ella, the midwife

ALICE'S BIRTH

There are no reliable references for where Alice Nellie Tompkins was born. Some sources say Idaho and some say Oregon. Since Idaho had been part of the Territory of Oregon previously and only became the Territory of Idaho in 1863 there may have been some confusion in stating "Oregon." Idaho seemed the most likely place, particularly since the gold rush in the Leesburg area occurred in 1866 and would have given Florence the motivation to go there. There are no references to Alice's birth, so the scenes in Leesburg are speculative.

Wikipedia. "Territorial Evolution of Idaho." Last modified November 6, 2024. wikipedia.org/wiki/Territorial_evolution_of_Idaho.

Wikipedia. "Territories of the United States." Last modified July 29, 2025. wikipedia.org/wiki/Territories_of_the_United_States. (See specifically "Organized vs. unorganized territories.")

Wikipedia. "Oregon Treaty" Last modified July 25, 2025. wikipedia.org/wiki/Oregon_Treaty.

Osoyoos. "History of Osoyoos." Accessed July 2025. osoyoos.ca/community/about-osoyoos/history-osoyoos.

Wikipedia. "Kamloops." Last modified August 12, 2025. wikipedia.org/wiki/Kamloops.

Hunter, Makoto. "Leesburg and Grantsville, Idaho." Intermountain Histories. Accessed February 6, 2025. intermountainhistories.org/items/show/492.

Western Mining History. "Leesburg, Idaho." Accessed August 2025. westernmininghistory.com/towns/idaho/leesburg/.

Wikipedia. "Leesburg, Idaho." Last modified July 1, 2025. wikipedia.org/wiki/Leesburg,_Idaho.

Wikipedia. "Snake War." Last modified February 24, 2025. wikipedia.org/wiki/Snake_War.

Wikipedia. "Bear River Massacre." Last modified July 30, 2025. wikipedia.org/wiki/Bear_River_Massacre.

*Eighteen* ❧ *The Lure of the Cariboo*

IMAGINARY CHARACTERS

Lee Song
Mr. Augustine

Royer Jorgenson, Mica Amy. "It Happened to me in Barkerville": Aboriginal identity economy, and law in the Cariboo gold rush, 1862–1900." MA diss., University of Northern British Columbia, 2012.

Ashcroft Journal. "Barkerville." UBC Library Open Collections: BC Historical Newspapers. Accessed August 2025. open.library.ubc.ca/viewer/bcmining/1.0441703#p0z-2r0f.

Canada History Society. "Barkerville." Accessed August 2025. canadahistory.ca/sections/places/settlements/Barkerville.html.

In Praise of Canadian History. "Fanny Bendixon." Accessed August 2025. interestingcanadianhistory.wordpress.com/2014/07/30/canadas-saddly-forgotten-colourful-characters-madame-bendixen/.

*Nineteen* ❧ *The Fire*

IMAGINARY CHARACTERS

The McCallums
The Taylors

BARKERVILLE

McCallum, Douglas John. "Barkerville theatre in context: a case study in our theatrical past." MA diss., UBC, 1981. Accessed August 2025. open.library.ubc.ca/soa/cIRcle/collections/ubctheses/831/items/1.0095359. See Chapter Three: Theatre Royal.

Wright, Richard Thomas. *Barkerville and the Cariboo Goldfields.* Heritage House Publishing, 2013.

THE FIRE

Young, Ronald. "The Great Fire of Barkerville—1868: An account of the destruction by fire of the town of Barkerville on the 16th

Sept. 1868 by Red Dally." *Cariboo Sentinel*. Accessed August 2025. barkerville.com/vol10/bville_burns.html.

***Twenty ⸙ The Scourge of Typhoid***

IMAGINARY CHARACTERS

Mrs. Turnbull, teacher
Dr. MacPherson

STANLEY

Quesnel Museum and Archives. *Stanley Hotel Day Books*. Accessed August 2025. quesnelmuseum.ca/node/187.

Last Ditch Mining. "Stanley." Accessed August 2025. lastditchmining.ca/stanley.

Wikipedia. "Stanley, British Columbia." Last modified October 27, 2021. wikipedia.org/wiki/Stanley,_British_Columbia.

TYPHOID

Moorehead, Robert. "William Budd and Medicine." *Journal of the Royal Society of Medicine*. Vol. 95, Issue 11 (2002): 561–564. Accessed August 2025. pmc.ncbi.nlm.nih.gov/articles/PMC1279260/.

Smith, Yolanda. "Typhoid Fever History." News Medical Life Sciences. Last updated May 3, 2023. news-medical.net/health/Typhoid-Fever-History.aspx.

Fifield, W.C.B. "Typhoid Fever and Pleurisy." Boston Medical Surgical Journal, vol. 88, no. 19 (1873): 461–464. nejm.org/doi/full/10.1056/NEJM187305080881901.

Kallen, Laura. "Typhoid Mary's missing ingredient." Coalition Against Typhoid. Posted October 15, 2018. tinyurl.com/3377ajeh.

*Twenty-one* ❧ *South to California*

IMAGINARY CHARACTERS

Josh Barclay, livery stable owner
Solvig Johnson, landlady
Mr. Stern, banker

NAPA, CALIFORNIA

City of Napa. "History of Napa." Sandbag Information. Accessed August 2025. cityofnapa.org/282/History-of-Napa.

Wikipedia. "Napa, California." Last modified August 11, 2025. wikipedia.org/wiki/Napa,_California.

Wikipedia. "Napa Valley Opera House." Last updated July 20, 2025. wikipedia.org/wiki/Napa_Valley_Opera_House.

Wikipedia. "Sam Kee Laundry Building." Last modified July 26, 2025. wikipedia.org/wiki/Sam_Kee_Laundry_Building.

*Napa Valley Marketplace Magazine*. "Napa State Hospital: The Early Years." December 28, 2018.

Bruce C. Cooper Collections. *A Brief Illustrated History of The Palace Hotels*. Original text, annotations, modern and composite images by Bruce C. Cooper. Accessed August 2025. thepalacehotel.org/#souvenir.

Napa County Historical Society. *The Presence of the Past: April 15–September 25, 2021*. Exhibition catalogue. Accessed August 2025. napahistory.org/programs/past-exhibits/presence-of-the-past/.

SAN GRANCISCO

San Francisco Public Library. "History of San Fracisco Public Library." Accessed August 2025. sfpl.org/about-us/history-san-francisco-public-library.

*Twenty-two* ⸙ *A Change in Circumstances*

IMAGINARY CHARACTERS

Mrs. Rodrigo
Sally
Matilda
Dr. Black

FAMILY

I obtained James Austin Hopkins's matrimonial history from Ancestry.com in the subscription area. As well, Ancestry.com had newspaper articles about him. ancestry.ca/search/?name=James+Austin_Hopkins&event=_napa-napa-california-usa_68701&birth=1819&name_x=_1.

NAPA

Napa County, California. "Napa Library." Accessed August 2025. countyofnapa.org/614/Napa-Library#:~:text=In%201901%2C%20George%20E%20Goodman,of%20Napa%20for%2060%20years.

City of Napa. "Napa History." Accessed August 2025. cityofnapa.org/282/History-of-Napa.

*Twenty-three* ⸙ *To San Francisco*

IMAGINARY CHARACTERS

Sally
Dr. Black
Dorothy Proctor, society lady
Joe Corning, the prospector

SAN FRANCISCO

Wikipedia. "Grace Hibbard." Last modified January 18, 2024. wikipedia.org/wiki/Grace_Hibbard.

Wikipedia. "William Westerfeld." Last modified September 5, 2023. wikipedia.org/wiki/William_Westerfeld.

## APPENDIX III:

"Only a Governess" by Florence Wilson

This article originally appeared in *Household Words*, Volume XIX, Magazine No. 476, May 7, 1859, pages 546–549. The text was reproduced here was obtained from Dickens Journals Online (djo.org.uk).

If you look over the advertising columns of of the Times, you are struck with the number of people in the world wanting to earn their daily bread. It is very rare indeed to see the same advertisement twice; so that it is evident that, for obtaining employment advertising is the best medium. But do all succeed in gaining what they seek? Does the tradesman who advertises for a loan of thirty pounds for a few weeks to meet some pressing engagement, and who offers security to four times that amount find some benevolent usurer to help him out of his difficulties? Does the nobleman's family find that combination of cook and housekeeper for the sixty pounds per annum, without perquisites, which it offers? Does the careful mother find the desired young person of ladylike manners and superior education to undertake the entire charge, not only of her six children, but of their wardrobes, for a fifth of that sum. I had formerly speculated during the hour I hired the Times upon what the result of such advertisements would be.

A time came when I found my curiosity gratified. Circumstances compelled me to have re- course to the advertising sheet. I drew up a neat advertisement, and it was inserted conspicuously after "Required a Family's Washing." I suppose washing is a higher art than teaching. For, the half- dozen advertisements setting forth the advantages of a good drying-ground, and that families' washing is done in the first style at moderate charges, are always placed first on the list. Mine stated that a lady of good education and manners, would be happy to devote several hours of the day to the cultivation and improvement of others.

On the morning my advertisement appeared, I waited with feverish anxiety for the messenger who was to bring the letters from the library at which, for a consideration, the answers were to be received. The first that came I opened with a nervous trepidation. It was the printed circular of a magazine, with my own advertisement cut out and pasted therein, pointing out the great sale and circulation of that periodical both at home and abroad, and describing the benefit I should derive from using its columns to make my desires known amongst the nobility, clergy, gentry, and the public at large.

The course of the day brought other letters, almost as disappointing. One was from the friends of an invalid old gentleman, who resided almost beyond the limits of omnibus route. An appointment was made. I kept it, and was received by a formal-looking old lady, a friend of the advertiser, who had undertaken the task of looking out for a likely person. The house was large, well furnished, and everything about it bore unmistakable signs of comfort; of, indeed, affluence. The lady, notwithstanding her age, was dressed with some attention to the niceties of the toilette; her handsome black silk dress, lace collar, sleeves, and cap, being in perfect taste.

This lady made known, in stately accents, that my services would be required each evening at six o'clock to read to her friend until ten. For this the sum of six shillings a-week was offered, with other advantages. These had need, I thought, to be very great; but, on narrow investigation, they were reduced to one very slender privilege:

"If you are punctual," said my informant, "you can always

have a cup of tea. Mr. Donnert, being a great invalid, is obliged to be regular with his meals, and his hour for tea is six exactly."

I asked if the omnibus fare would be paid; for otherwise it would be quite impossible for me to accept such terms. The lady was indignant. "I never heard," she replied, "of such a preposterous idea! I thought all you ladies seeking your living by head-work, were only too happy of a walk. It must be such a relief after the confinement of the day."

"True," I observed, very quietly, "but a walk of more than four miles out and four miles home, would be too much exercise even for health; not to speak of the time that would be lost; which, to people in my circumstances, is a consideration."

This ended the interview. Scarcely condescending to speak another word, the old lady went slowly to the bell, rang it, and dismissed me with a cold "Good morning."

The writer of the next letter which led to an interview, had been neglected in her youth, and was anxious, in mature age, to repair in some degree her frequent errors against the laws of Lindley Murray. This lady admitted that she had not even availed herself, since her marriage, of the advantages her husband's position gave her to improve herself, as she might have done; but she was now really anxious to learn, and to become acquainted with literature. She had heard much talk of three writers—Shakespeare, Bulwer, and Byron—but did not know which of them was still living. She had a desire to learn French, "a few words just to introduce into conversation. It looks clever; besides I visit Bullon in the season, and a phrase or two goes a long way there, I find." Her time, she added, was much taken up with her numerous friends; but, she was so anxious to get on and to surprise her husband on his return from one of the colonies (which would happen in a few months) that she had determined to devote three hours a-day to this honourable task.

She seemed so earnest and zealous for improvement, that I flattered myself I had now found the employment I had been seeking, for something above starvation pay. But, alas! I was again doomed to disappointment. On being asked to name my terms, and replying (modestly as I thought) that half-a-guinea a-week would not be too much, I so startled the lady by this exorbitant demand, that she required time to think it over; and eventually offered me the third of what I had asked. At last an arrangement was made, by which I agreed to give a little less time for a little less money; and, four times a-week, I make a lengthy call upon Mrs. Smith. Her desire for improvement was genuine; but she had considerable difficulty in the accomplishment of her purpose. Her fear of the servants discovering her secret, constantly interrupted our lessons: "if they did," she said, "they would lose all respect for me." She was confident that cook and housemaid could both beat her in reading and writing; but it would not do to let them know that. When either of them, entered the room which they did frequently with some message, or something to be known-the confusion in which grammar and spelling-book were thrust out of sight under the table, or scrambled under a newspaper, and the flustered manner in which we began a conversation about the opera, the fashions, or some other news of the day, must have revealed to their quick sight that there was something more going on, than mistress would have liked them to know.

Another lady offered me her four children, between the ages of five and ten, to instruct in English, music, and French (if dancing and Latin could be included, it would be more desirable) five mornings in the week, from nine till one. For this one pound per month was thought sufficient remuneration. I objected that this sum was too little. The reply I got furnished one of those curious instances of perverted logic to which the framers of mean excuses are frequently driven. It was actually asserted that my task would be all the easier, and that my services ought, therefore, to be purchased at a cheaper rate, because mamma's little darlings had never before been placed under any kind of instruction. The lady proceeded, more consistently, to assure me that her children would give me "no" trouble; they being the quickest, most obedient, and loveable children I could possibly have to do with. She admitted that something less than five shillings per week was a small recompense for teaching and training four children four hours a-day five days in the week, but added that she thought she could put a little needlework in my way, to make up a better income. As my mornings only would be engaged, I could thus also turn the other hours to advantage. It would make a change from the teaching; which, she acknowledged, must be, as a constant employment, rather wearisome.

This experience differed very little in one respect, from my other experiences. Almost every lady I waited upon spoke as one conferring a great favour, and seemed to put in a latent sort of claim upon the whole of my time, even when the hours mentioned in the negotiation were few, and the remuneration very niggardly.

A widow next replied to my advertisement. She wished me to take charge of two little girls, aged respectively ten and twelve. She scarcely inquired from me my qualifications for the office of teacher; but laid greater stress on my capabilities for managing a household. She was, she said, absent from home during a great part of the year; for, when not travelling abroad, she visited her husband's relations with her maid, from whom she had expectations; and was therefore obliged to keep up appearances before them. Her desire was to find some clever and trustworthy person, who could teach her children, attend to all their wants, and manage her household while she was away. This lady had scarcely attained the middle age, and made the most by expensive and well-chosen dress of considerable personal attractions. Something struck me that I had seen her before; and, when she mentioned that each autumn I should have the privilege of taking her children with her for a little while into the country, I remembered that I had once seen this selfish woman at the South Eastern Railway-station, huddling her two children and servants into a second-class carriage, and then securing, for herself, the best first-class seat she could find.

The widow approached the subject of terms with caution, but not without tact. Everything connected with the situation was (as usual) pointed out as an advantage to me; and, when all such "advantages" had been piled up to the highest, point, and set against (so as to lessen) my claim for remuneration, the lady mentioned the amount of salary. For undertaking, not only the intellectual, but the moral training of her two little girls; for attending to their clothing; for managing the house and servants, and economising tradesmen's bills; for, in short, relieving this erratic widow of every responsibility as a mother and a mistress, I was offered the sum of ten pounds a-year and my board.

Another lady who, in the evening of her days, had been left in dreary solitude, wished to meet with a daily companion of agreeable manners and lively conversation. She must be musical, amiable, obliging, and well dressed. She must commence her duties every morning soon after nine, and remain till eight or nine in the evening. She would have to work, read, and play, and accompany the lady in her drives and visits. The appearance of this person was repellant. In her youth she might have been passable; but the cold grey eye and the stony-looking features seemed to indicate that she had never been capable of a kindly feeling. Yet I felt a kind of pity for her, thinking that hers must have always been a joyless existence. She looked as if it were impossible for a smile ever to cross her marble features. She repeated again and again that her companion's dress must always be nice and ladylike. She had always been accustomed to have all around her in the best style. She had an intense horror of common things, and common people, and could not endure them about her. The reason why she preferred a daily to a resident companion was, that she knew, generally speaking, such people had friends; and she could not be troubled with her visitors. If we came to terms, therefore, it must be understood that I must provide a lodging of my own to receive my relatives or acquaintances in-of course before breakfast, or after supper. The statuesque old dame added the discouraging statement that she had tried many companions, but that they had all left her after a few weeks. I did not wonder at this, from the frigid, unsympathising manner she showed to all about her, and therefore declined the ten shillings a- week which she thought a sufficient income for a lady to dress well upon; besides keeping some sort of a roof over her head.

Many similar letters came. The invariable reply I met with when I thought the remuneration too small to be accepted was, "That is your affair. You can do as you please about accepting or rejecting my terms; if you do not take them, there are hundreds of well-educated females who will only be too happy to do so." And this always was spoken in a kind of resentful tone, as if I had materially injured them by refusing their offers. But the argument is, alas, a just one. The circle of employment for women is too narrow, and the number of competitors too great; yet, although the market-price (the proper term, I believe, to be used on this occasion) for such talents is so very low, why cannot there be a better feeling exhibited towards the governess? She is endowed with feelings like the rest of humanity: why, then, should those feelings be so carelessly outraged as they often are, and she made to feel that she is a being quite apart from the rest of the world-a kind of Pariah? Why should she be so often spoken of contemptuously us "only a Governess?"

DUKE MORSE

MARION MCKINNON CROOK is a nurse, an educator, and the author of more than twenty-five books, including the bestselling *Always Pack a Candle*, which won the BC Historical Federation's Community History Book Award, and its follow-up *Always On Call*, a finalist for the BC Book Prizes Bill Duthie Award. In addition to her nursing degree, McKinnon Crook holds a master's in liberal studies and a PhD in education. Now a full-time writer, she also writes the British Book Tour mystery series under the name of Emma Dakin. She lives on the Sunshine Coast in BC. For more information, visit marioncrookauthor.com.